Professional Studies in Primary Education

Edited by

Hilary Cooper

SAGE

Los Angeles | London | New Delhi
Singapore | Washington DC

Professional Studies in Primary Education

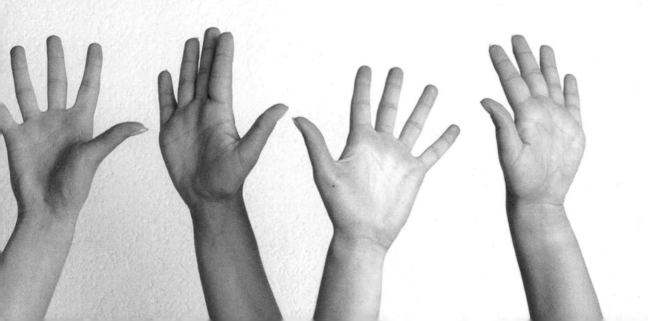

Education at SAGE

SAGE is a leading international publisher of journals, books, and electronic media for academic, educational, and professional markets.

Our education publishing includes:

- accessible and comprehensive texts for aspiring education professionals and practitioners looking to further their careers through continuing professional development

- inspirational advice and guidance for the classroom

- authoritative state of the art reference from the leading authors in the field

Find out more at: **www.sagepub.co.uk/education**

CONTENTS

About the Editor vii
About the Contributors ix
Foreword xiii
Samantha Twiselton

PART 1 INTRODUCTION TO PROFESSIONAL STUDIES **1**

1 **History of Education** **3**
 Susan Shaw

2 **Philosophy of Education and Theories of Learning** **18**
 Hilary Cooper

3 **Planning, Monitoring, Assessment and Recording** **32**
 Suzanne Lowe and Kim Harris

4 **Classroom Organisation and the Learning Environment** **57**
 Jan Ashbridge and Jo Josephidou

 5 **The Role of the Adult**   73
    Jan Ashbridge and Jo Josephidou

PART 2   INCLUSIVE DIMENSIONS OF PROFESSIONAL STUDIES   89

 6 **Reflective Practice in the Early Years: A Focus on Issues
    Related to Teaching Reception-age Children**   91
    Lin Savage and Anne Renwick

 7 **Inclusion and Special Educational Needs**   108
    Verna Kilburn and Kären Mills

 8 **Behaviour Management**   123
    Deborah Seward

 9 **Personal and Social Development**   135
    Kären Mills and Verna Kilburn

10 **Dialogical, Enquiry and Participatory Approaches to Learning**   149
    Donna Hurford and Chris Rowley

11 **Race, Culture and Ethnicity**   162
    Diane Warner and Sally Elton-Chalcraft

PART 3   FROM TRAINEE TO TEACHER   177

12 **Reflective Practice**   179
    Andrew Read

13 **Enquiry and Critical Thinking**   195
    Diane Vaukins

14 **Exploring Issues in Education**   208
    Andrew Slater

15 **Statutory Professional Responsibilities**   225
    Nerina Díaz

16 **Moving into Newly Qualified Teacher Status and Beyond**   241
    Hilary Cooper

Index   249

ABOUT THE EDITOR

Hilary Cooper is Professor of History and Pedagogy at the University of Cumbria. After many years teaching in London primary schools and undertaking her doctoral research on child development using data collected as a class teacher, she lectured in Education at Goldsmiths' College, London University. In 1993 she became Director of Professional Studies in the Department of Education at Lancaster University, then Reader, and later Professor of Education at St Martin's College, now the University of Cumbria. She has published widely.

ABOUT THE CONTRIBUTORS

Jan Ashbridge is Subject Leader and Senior Lecturer in Early Childhood Education at the University of Cumbria. She was a Foundation Stage Teacher for 12 years and also a senior advisory teacher for the Foundation Stage with Cumbria Local Education Authority. Jan has been involved in planning and delivering training sessions to students and Early Years educators across the north-west of England in all aspects of young children's learning and the skills adults need to support this. She has published a number of book chapters on this subject.

Nerina Díaz has had extensive teaching experience in primary schools throughout the world. She is presently working as a Senior Lecturer at the University of Cumbria, teaching Education Studies and tutoring students who are completing school placements. Her current research interests lie with students' perceptions of the academic requirements and assessments for Higher Education.

Sally Elton-Chalcraft taught in a range of junior, infant and middle schools, and two other ITE institutions before joining St Martin's College, now the University of Cumbria, where she is Course Leader for Religious Studies and Primary QTS. She is also Minority Ethnic Recruitment and Retention Coordinator for the University of Cumbria QTS programmes. She has researched and published in the areas of research methods, children's spirituality and multicultural education. Her publications include *It's Not Just About Black and White Miss: Children's Awareness of Race* (Trentham Books, 2009) and

Doing Classroom Research: A Step-By-Step Guide for Student Teachers (Open University Press, 2008) with A. Hansen and S. Twiselton. She lives on the edge of the Lake District with her husband, three children and two cats.

Kim Harris is Senior Lecturer in Education at the University of Worcester. Her background is in primary teaching and initial teacher education. Previously, she worked for eight years as a Senior Lecturer in Music Education at the University of Cumbria and taught as a Primary School Class Teacher in Berkshire and Cumbria working across both KS1 and 2. Her particular areas of interest are music and mathematics initial teacher education. Her research interests focus on teacher development in primary music education and the induction and professional development of academic staff in teacher education within the Higher Education sector.

Donna Hurford is a Principal Lecturer in the Faculty of Education, University of Cumbria with a specialism in Education Studies and Global Citizenship. After teaching in KS1 and KS2 classes in Lancashire schools with an ICT responsibility, Donna moved to Higher Education, initially specialising in ICT education. Since working at the university, Donna has been involved in a variety of research projects on aspects of Assessment for Learning (AfL), criticality in Global Citizenship and collaborative research. Her current research, which she hopes to develop into a PhD, is focused on student teacher responses to AfL.

Jo Josephidou is a Senior Lecturer at the University of Cumbria. She works predominantly within the early years team but also teaches inclusion modules and Modern Foreign Languages (MFL) on the primary programmes. She came to the university as a teacher fellow after many years teaching in the primary school where she was Foundation Stage leader and SENCO. Her particular interests are early years education and inclusion.

Verna Kilburn is a Senior Lecturer in Inclusion and Special Educational Needs at the University of Cumbria. Previously, she taught in primary schools in London, Newcastle and Jamaica.

Suzanne Lowe is Senior Lecturer in Education Studies and Inclusion at the University of Cumbria. Previously she has been a Primary School Class Teacher working across both KS1 and 2 for 10 years. She was a Leading Teacher of Mathematics within Cumbria for four years. Suzanne has also been involved in education in local museums and is currently actively involved in governance of a local primary school as Chair of Governors. Her particular area of interest is inclusion and her MA examined aspects of educational leadership, curriculum development and children's cognitive processes and learning.

Kären Mills is a Senior Lecturer in the Faculty of Education at the University of Cumbria. After teaching across the key stages in schools in both Lancashire and a London borough, Kären moved to Higher Education to teach on ITE courses, particularly Education and Primary Mathematics. More recently, she has contributed to the SEN specialism offered to undergraduates. Research interests include approaches to blended learning and students' perceptions of assessment, both peer and self. She is passionate about preparing ITE students to look at the holistic development of the child, as well as curriculum development and is shaping her ITE programme around this.

Andrew Read is Programme Leader for the PGCE at the University of East London with specialisms in Education and Music. After teaching in schools in Tower Hamlets, East London, Andrew moved into Higher Education, initially as an English specialist, later moving into the field of Educational Studies. Working in collaboration with Donna Hurford, Andrew has been involved in research projects on aspects of Assessment for Learning (AfL), criticality in Global Citizenship and collaborative research. His current research focuses on student perceptions of independent learning and how this impacts on pupil experience.

Anne Renwick is a Senior Lecturer at the University of Cumbria, teaching across the full range of early years programmes. She has worked in a number of primary schools in the North-east and Cumbria, teaching Nursery, Reception and Key Stage 1 children. Before joining the university, Anne was employed as a Senior Early Years Advisory teacher for Cumbria Children's Services supporting practitioners in a range of early years schools and settings. Anne has developed her own research on the subject of professional development for the children's workforce and her Master's dissertation focused on support for teachers working in children's centres.

Chris Rowley is a Senior Lecturer in environmental and geographical education at the University of Cumbria. He taught at a variety of schools before joining Charlotte Mason College of Education in 1987. He was a member of the SAPERE Committee (Society to Advance Philosophical Enquiry in Education) from 1997 to 2003. An interest in children's understanding of the environment led him to work with teachers around Morecambe Bay between 2003 and 2004 to co-produce *Thinking on the Edge* (Lewis and Rowley, 2004). In 2004, Chris was co-editor of *Geography 3–11* (Fulton) and in 2010 of *Cross-curricular Approaches to Teaching and Learning* (Sage).

Lin Savage is a Principal Lecturer at the University of Cumbria with responsibility for early years programmes. Previously, Lin had over 25 years of experience teaching early years and primary children in Cumbria and London. She was an Advanced Skills teacher and worked as an Early Years Advisory Teacher and Area SENCO for Cumbria Local Education Authority. Lin is interested in all aspects of early years education. Her Master's research focused on early years students' experience of joining the workforce. Recent research has included a consideration of the professional status of early years educators.

Deborah Seward graduated from St Martin's College and taught for many years in a range of primary schools. She completed her MA, Developing Teacher Expertise, whilst working as a Senior Lecturer in History Education for St Martin's College, Carlisle campus, before becoming the head teacher of a small primary school in North Cumbria. As a head teacher, she was particularly interested in cross-curricular teaching and the development of creative approaches to learning and teaching, successfully leading a Creative Futures project within the school. She has a wide range of experience in mentoring students and Newly Qualified Teachers and has recently returned to a Senior Lecturer role at the University of Cumbria where she works on the early years programmes as a module and cohort leader.

Susan Shaw is a Principal Lecturer in the Faculty of Education at the University of Cumbria. She spent 20 years in primary schools, with positions ranging from class teacher to head teacher before becoming a lecturer. She has an NPQH and is a Fellow of the Higher Education Academy. She is passionate about preparing ITE students to understand the holistic development of the child as well as curriculum development, and is shaping her ITE programme around this. She and her husband often spend weekends near a riverbank supporting their two children in their interest in canoe slalom.

Andrew Slater taught for many years, working both in primary and secondary schools. Whilst working in the higher education sector, he has maintained a particular interest in urban education and strategies to enhance community cohesion. His doctoral study focused upon pupil interaction. Wider interests include citizenship education and the use of story within training.

Samantha Twiselton is Executive Dean of the Faculty of Education at the University of Cumbria. Her interests and research centre on student teacher development and curriculum development and she uses this to inform the reshaping of ITE programmes at the university. She is very active in the British Educational Research Association (BERA) and Universities Council for the Education of Teachers (UCET), where she is a member of the executive committee. She was a primary classroom teacher for a number of years. She is a primary English specialist, a passionate believer in the importance of evidence-based teaching and strongly encourages all her students to see research as central to good practice. She lives in the Lake District with her husband and two children.

Diane Vaukins is a Senior Lecturer and Partnership Tutor at the University of Cumbria and the Module Leader for the three-year BA/QTS mathematics specialist course. Prior to lecturing in Higher Education she was a primary school teacher and deputy head teacher. She has a keen interest in working with schools to encourage creativity in mathematics.

Diane Warner is a senior lecturer at the University of Cumbria, working with undergraduate student teachers and also teaching on the MA in Education Programme. Her professional areas of interest and study are English education, developing English specialist knowledge, such as teaching Shakespeare in the Primary School and student perceptions and experiences within ITE. Previously she worked in an inner city school, with a high percentage of Asian Muslim children and led the gifted and talented programme across the school. Her article, 'Moving into the Unknown', about white student teachers' perceptions of teaching for racial and ethnic diversity, can be found in *Racial Equality Teaching* (2010) 29(3): 39–43. She is a member of the Teacher Education Research Network.

FOREWORD

Samantha Twiselton

Learning to teach in the primary years is a complex and potentially very confusing process. There are so many different aspects that need to be attended to. An effective Professional Studies course and its underpinning reading will provide a 'spine' that will help you (if you are a primary student teacher) to connect all these together and – crucially – to your placement learning. This book will support your developing understanding of and competence in Professional Studies and provide you with an underpinning framework for the rest of your learning. Many studies show that the most effective teachers are very good at connecting a range of different kinds of knowledge together in a way that leads to the best actions to meet the needs of their learners. This book is all about making connections and linking knowledge, understanding and values to professional practice in the classroom.

The structure of the book

The book is organised into three parts. The first five chapters introduce you to the philosophy which underpins the book: the range of professional issues about which teachers have to make judgements and decisions in interpreting statutory frameworks. It does so in the context of what we might call the foundations of Professional Studies, that is the generic professional knowledge, skills and understanding which underpin the curriculum. These chapters outline the history of state primary education in England and of educational philosophy and show how understanding of these areas helps you to make judgements about implementing the basic components of professional studies, planning, assessment and managing the learning environment.

Part 2 is concerned with different aspects of inclusion, the need to take into account children's varied individual needs and strategies for doing this, in order to provide equal educational opportunities. The third part of the book deals with strategies for critical thinking about educational issues and reminds you of the statutory requirements you will need to take into account in doing so. It concludes with a review of the increasingly sophisticated professional development you should have, after engaging with the previous chapters, which forms a good basis for your continuing professional development.

The three sections are essentially sequential, each deepening your thinking about the educational decisions and judgements required and how to engage with them. The expectation is that, having read the book sequentially and reflected on each section, either independently or preferably with others and related them to your increasing experience of practice in schools, you will have developed an informed personal, educational philosophy. However, it is also expected that you will return to previously read chapters with deeper understanding as your experience of theory and practice increases.

Recurring chapter features

Each chapter has consistent features. At the beginning of each chapter, there are statements about the learning which you should acquire through engaging with the chapter, and an introduction outlining the content of the chapter. Embedded in each chapter are activities which will help you to consider, or if possible discuss with others, the issues raised within the chapter. At the end of each chapter, there is a summary of the content which enabled you to engage with the learning objectives at the beginning of the chapter, followed by questions for discussion of the issues raised and a summary of the chapter content. Finally, there are suggestions for further reading and reasons why this may be of interest.

The website

Most chapters have website material which extends the chapter content. This may include additional material which space limitations prevented including in the book, references to further reading or to related web links, or further activities for exploring questions raised in the chapter. The companion website for the book can be found at www.uk.sagepub.com/cooper

The philosophy underpinning the book

The book will help you to make professional decisions related to teaching, planning and assessment, classroom organisation and behaviour management in a way that is responsive to individual and diverse pupils' needs. It does this by showing you how to reflect on and develop your practice and how to make links between theory and practice. It will raise your awareness of controversial issues and develop your ability to inform yourself about these from relevant literature and contemporary comment. The book promotes practice that is informed by value judgements and promotes the educational development of the whole child: social, emotional and cognitive. It aims to help you develop innovative and creative teaching and learning, drawing on children's diverse interests and localities. It does this through suggesting interesting, memorable ways of discussing and interacting. This book aims to enable you to meet current and future government requirements within a broad and deep interpretation of the concept of 'professional studies'.

The chapter authors

The authors of this book are themselves excellent role models in this respect. All involved have direct experience of and expertise in values-based, enquiry driven and evidence-based practice. They are all passionate about the importance of critically reflective practice to the role and identity of the teacher and have all themselves an excellent track record of working in this way, both in the university and in the classroom.

Part 1

INTRODUCTION TO PROFESSIONAL STUDIES

The first five chapters of this book introduce readers to the philosophy which underpins the book and establish what we might call the foundations of professional studies in primary education. The philosophy of the book aims to show that, within statutory requirements, teachers are nevertheless responsible for constantly making professional decisions and judgements in all aspects of teaching and learning, interpreted through the qualities and skills of confident professional integrity. In Part 1 you will read about the history of primary education so that you can take an objective and long term view of the present and of future changes. You will learn, through philosophical enquiry, how to ask questions about, debate and challenge educational theories, practices and policies. And you will begin to see how there are complex decisions and judgements to make and evaluate, in planning and assessment, in creating an effective learning environment and in your interactions with children and adults in school. You will begin to develop your own educational philosophy which will enable you to become a teacher who is capable of managing change with integrity.

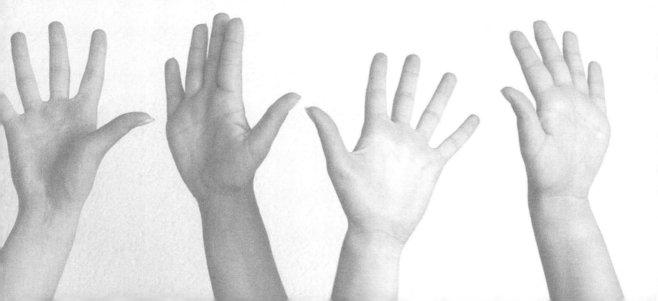

CHAPTER 1

HISTORY OF EDUCATION

Susan Shaw

By the end of this chapter, you should:

- have a knowledge of the education system from 1870 onwards

- have an understanding of changes in the philosophy, curriculum, management and accountability in primary schools

- be able to speculate about the future of education

- begin to form your own professional philosophy and values

- understand the need to respond to changes with professional integrity.

Introduction

In order to fully appreciate and understand the education system that will be in place once you qualify, it is necessary to have an insight into the influences and decisions that have taken place in the past, to form and develop this system. The norm today is for all children aged 5 years to attend primary school. However, compulsory primary education in England did not begin until 1880. Before this, there were many types of formal and informal schooling. This chapter will highlight some key dates, people and events that have contributed to the current education system and the primary curriculum.

It considers the impact of legislation on teaching and learning (for example, the curriculum and the effects of increasing centralisation, testing and league tables) and the advantages claimed for this legislation (that is, the values underpinning the National Curriculum). It shows how an informed educational philosophy helps us respond to centralised changes and considers the development of new curricula.

1870: the beginning of compulsory state education

Rationale

By 1870 England was a largely industrial rather than an agricultural society. Conditions in many of the rapidly expanding cities were often very bad. Compulsory schooling was introduced, partly to provide the labour force with the basic skills and routines necessary in an industrial society and also to attempt to prevent civil unrest, which people feared as a very real possibility.

Church and State

The Education Act of 1870, known as the 'Forster Act', laid down the requirement to establish compulsory, elementary education in England. It recognised a dual education system consisting of both voluntary denominational schools and non-denominational state schools. These were intended to supplement rather than replace schools already run by the churches, guilds and private individuals or organisations. In other countries, the church was less involved in state education but in Britain, as a result of the 1870 Act, the church has continued to play a substantial part in the education of young children.

School boards

School districts were formed throughout the country and where there was not enough educational provision for the children in a district, School Boards were formed. They set up schools which became known as Board Schools. These had to be non-denominational. The School Boards could charge a weekly fee if there were insufficient funds, but the fee was not allowed to be more than 9 pence. The School Boards had to ensure that children between the ages of 5 and 13 attended the schools in their districts and this was enforced by an Attendance Officer.

The curriculum

The curriculum in the 1870s mainly consisted of the 3 Rs (reading, writing and 'rithmetic) and religious instruction, which was an integral part of the school curriculum but was not actually compulsory. There were some additional aspects, for example drill and 'object lessons'. Object lessons involved the study of an artefact. Needlework was an extra for girls and carpentry an extra for boys. Her Majesty's Inspectors visited the schools to test children's skills in the '3 Rs' and teachers' payment was based on the children's attainment, i.e. it was 'payment by results'.

In some respects, as we shall see, primary education remains tied to its Victorian roots. The exceptionally early start for formal schooling, the generalist primary school teacher, the separation of 'infants' and 'juniors', the focus on the basics at the expense of a broader curriculum remain and have not been seriously questioned. But the Victorian Elementary School was intended to prepare the poor for their 'station' in life rather than to broaden their opportunities.

1902–1944

There were three developments in education during this period: the Balfour Act (1902) which created Local Education Authorities, the Fisher Act (1918) which raised the school leaving age from 12 to 14, and the Hadow Reports (1923–31) one of which recommended school transfer at 11, so creating the idea of the primary school.

Reflective task

Read *Children, their World, their Education*, Chapter 13 (Alexander 2010), which compares the curriculum past and present. In groups, compare the curriculum in the late 1800s with the curriculum of today. Compare similarities and differences. To what extent are the external forces which influence the content of the curriculum the same or different today? If you could put together a primary curriculum, what would your priorities be?

Post World War II: primary schools and three types of secondary school

The Butler Education Act of 1944

The tripartite system for secondary education

The education system offered primary education, secondary education and further education. The tripartite system of secondary education, implemented in the 1944 Act, offered three types of education after the age of 11: grammar schools for the most able, based on 'intelligence tests', secondary modern schools for most pupils, and secondary technical schools for those perceived to have technical or scientific ability. This was intended to increase opportunities for all.

Church schools

After the 1944 Act, the Church of England still had control of most rural schools and many urban ones. The 1944 Act put church schools into two categories: 'voluntary aided' (where the church had greater control) and 'controlled' (where the Local Education Authority had greater control), and this is still the case. This control is in regard to buildings, staffing and the religious curriculum and worship.

Local Education Authorities

Primary education and secondary education became free for all children up to the age of 15. The Local Education Authorities (LEAs) took more responsibility and there was a rise in their status. They had to ensure that there was sufficient provision for the educational needs of pupils in their geographical area. Through the provision LEAs offered, they had to make sure that pupils had an effective education which contributed to their spiritual, moral, mental and physical development, but they were not responsible for the more detailed curriculum.

The curriculum

The Act gave head teachers, in consultation with governors, control of the school curriculum and resourcing. The Act said very little about the curriculum, apart from religious education. Teachers were left to decide what to teach and how to teach it. Religious education and collective worship were to take place in all schools, and if you worked in an aided school you could be dismissed by the governors if you did not deliver religious instruction 'efficiently and suitably'. It is quite clear at this point that there was no expectation that the national government would ever have control of the curriculum.

Special Educational Needs provision

The 1944 Act included provision for Pupils with Special Educational Needs. If pupils were deemed to be unable to profit from being educated in a mainstream school, their education had to be provided in a special school. At this time, the types and degrees of disability were named and this was the case until 1981, when it was agreed that these labels were inappropriate.

Effects of the 1944 Education Act

The selection process, rather like SATs (Statutory Assessment Test), had an effect on primary education. The need to 'get children through' the eleven plus had the same effect as the need to get Level 4 or 5 at age 11. There were also large classes through the late 1940s and 1950s and a shortage of teachers. Whole-class teaching continued and the curriculum emphasised basic literacy and numeracy. 'Writers looking back at the early curriculum saw that, in fact, the tradition derived from 1870 was still dominant' (Galton et al. 1980 p. 36). It was not until the 1960s that more formal class teaching gave way to new ideas. In 1964 the Schools Council was formed and the partnership between LEAs, schools and universities led to more experiments with the curriculum.

The Plowden Report: a new philosophy of education?

There had not been a specific review of primary education since the Hadow report of 1931. The context of the time in which the Plowden Report (1967) was written was one of a liberal view of education and society. The emphasis of the Plowden Report could be encapsulated in the phrase 'at the heart of the educational process lies the child' (Plowden 1967 p. 9). Plowden advocated experiential learning, increased parental involvement, universal pre-school education and opportunities for the less privileged. It highlighted firmly the need for differentiation and supported the requirement for personalisation when saying 'individual differences between children of the same age are so great that any class … must always be treated as a body of children needing individual and different attention' (Plowden 1967 p. 25). Chapter 2 also discusses testing, and the use of IQ (Intelligence Quotient) tests in eleven-plus selection tests in the 1950s and 1960s. Plowden says that they 'should not be treated as infallible predictors. Judgements which determine careers should be deferred as long as possible'. It was the Labour government of this time that almost removed all eleven-plus tests at the end of primary schooling, but since it lost the election in 1970, it failed to quite eradicate all testing at 11. There are many aspects of the Plowden Report that most primary teachers would agree with.

> One of the main educational tasks of the primary school is to build on and strengthen children's intrinsic interest in learning and lead them to learn for themselves rather than from fear of disapproval or desire for praise. (Plowden 1967 p. 532)

The persistent acknowledgement of individual learning, flexibility in the curriculum, use of the environment, learning by discovery and the importance of the evaluation of children's progress has a certain resonance, not only with educational theory but in the philosophy of many teachers.

The Plowden Report endorsed the move away from formal class teaching to group work, projects and learning through play and creativity. Chapters of the report challenged the existing aims of primary education, classroom organisation and the curriculum and supported 'child-centred' primary schools. It was a real attempt to enlarge the concept of primary education.

Nevertheless, most schools changed very little. The HMI primary survey (DES 1978) reported that only 5 per cent of primary schools was 'exploratory' and three quarters still used 'didactic' methods.

Back to basics, market forces and increasing centralisation

Economic recession led to cut backs in educational expenditure and was partly blamed for the series of 'Black Papers' written by right-wing educationalists. The first paper was published in 1969. Specifically focusing on the 'progressive education' being developed in the primary schools, the writers challenged the figures on reading standards, accused teachers of neglecting basics and concentrating too much on informality. The years 1992 and 1998 also saw a return of the 'back to basics' theme and a desire to challenge 'progressive' ideas in education.

Her Majesty's Inspectorate 1975

In 1975 Her Majesty's Inspectors (HMI) began a survey of the primary curriculum. This included assessments of children's work at 7, 9 and 11. The report was not published until 1978. It criticised teachers' underestimation of children's abilities and noted the lack of specialist teachers. The questioning of teacher assessment, which later resulted in Standardised Attainment Tests (SATs), and the content of the curriculum are recurring themes for both Conservative and Labour governments and successive Secretaries of State for Education.

Callaghan's Ruskin Speech – Great Debate on Education 1976

Labour Prime Minister, James Callaghan, 'brought comfort to his Tory enemies … schools were convenient scapegoats, education a scarecrow …'. This was 'the impression conveyed by the Prime Minister' (Morris 1988 p. 7). He argued that not just teachers and parents but also government and industry had an important part to play in formulating the aims of education.

In his historic speech, Callaghan spoke about:

- a public debate on education; employers, trades unions and parents, teachers and administrators were to make their views known
- a curriculum which paid too little attention to the basic skills of reading, writing and arithmetic
- how teachers lacked adequate professional skills, could not discipline children or teach them good manners and did not manage to instil in them the need for hard work
- the underlying reason for all this which was that the educational system was out of touch with the fundamental needs of the country.

This Great Debate on Education seems to have been ongoing since 1976 and consecutive governments have increasingly tightened their grip on education. Whether 'progressive education' was slowed down by James Callaghan's speech or by the next 18 years of Conservative rule and education policy is debatable.

The 1979 Education Act

Margaret Thatcher was Education Secretary before becoming Prime Minister. She overturned Labour's 1976 Act and gave back to LEAs the right to select pupils for secondary education at 11. However secondary education was popular and reversal did not gain the backing expected.

A framework for the curriculum 1980

This was the first of a long series about what the curriculum should contain: *Framework for the School Curriculum* (HMI 1980a), *A View of the Curriculum* (HMI 1980b), *The School Curriculum* (DES 1981a), Circular 6/81 (DES 1981b). *The School Curriculum 1981* encouraged putting a high priority on English and mathematics:

> It is essential that the early skills in reading, writing and calculating should be effectively learned in primary schools, since deficiencies at this stage cannot easily be remedied later and children will face the world seriously handicapped. Para 35.

However, schools also had to provide a 'wide range of experience, in order to stimulate the children's interest and imagination and fully to extend pupils of all abilities' (DES 1980 p. 10). Religious Education, Topic Work, Science, Art and

Craft, Physical Education, Music and French were all mentioned in this report, alongside personal and social development. From 1981 to 1986, Sir Keith Joseph had responsibility for implementing education policies, right down to everyday practice.

The Curriculum from 5 to 16 (HMI 1985)

This was a forward-looking document talking about 'areas of learning and experience'. This concept was developed in the introduction of a National Curriculum, in the Education Reform Act 1988. The curriculum of all schools had to provide pupils with the following areas of learning and experience: aesthetic and creative, human and social, linguistic and literary, mathematical, moral, physical, scientific, spiritual and technological.

Parent power

Successive governments had tried to get parents to engage with education. The Conservative government of the 1980s saw parents as consumers and clients. The 1980 Education Act gave more power to parents. Parents were encouraged to serve on governing bodies. Growing parental choice meant that parents had the right to choose their children's schools and could appeal if they were not accepted by the school they chose. The forerunner of league tables began when exam and test results were published. The Warnock Report (1978) gave parents new rights in relation to Special Educational Needs. LEAs identified the needs of children with learning difficulties but also had to produce 'statements' for parents on how these needs would be met. Parent power was increased in the 1984 Green Paper, *Parental Influence at School* (HMI 1984), which reiterated the role and responsibilities of parents and the vital role parents have to play in the education system.

The 1986 Education Act

The 1986 (1) Education Act introduced the requirement that the LEAs had to give governors financial information on the financing of schools. The 1986 (2) Education Act took the proposals in the 1985 White Paper, *Better Schools,* arguing yet again for breadth, balance and progression in order to achieve standards in literacy and numeracy; a close throwback to comments by HMI in 1975. *Better Schools* opened with: 'The Government will: take the lead in promoting national agreement about the purposes and the content of the curriculum ...' (DES 1985 p. 1).

The Education Reform Bill 1988

The Great Education Reform Bill (generally known as Gerbil) was seen as the most important Education Act since the 1944 Act which aimed to give more power to schools. However, from the LEAs' point of view, it was taking power from them and giving it to the Secretary of State.

A National Curriculum

The Act had large implications for primary schools. The government proposed a common curriculum for pupils aged 5 to 16, a National Curriculum. This was a shift away from teachers deciding what was taught to central government having control. The curriculum was in discrete subjects and there were three core subjects (English, mathematics and science) and seven 'foundation subjects'. Prior to this, teachers wrote schemes of work they considered appropriate for their pupils.

Written by a government 'quango' of subject specialists and with a substantial content base, teachers were hardly involved in the development of the National Curriculum and felt they were deliverers of a curriculum rather than designers and pace-setters. The National Curriculum had three main aims: the school curriculum had to provide opportunities for all pupils to learn and to achieve; pupils across the country were entitled to the same broad curriculum; and the curriculum should aim to promote pupils' spiritual, moral, social and cultural development and prepare all pupils for the opportunities, responsibilities and experiences of life (DES 1988).

The *Three Wise Men Report* (DES 1992) was a government commissioned report which emphasised the need for a return to quality in primary school pedagogy. 'Whatever the mode of curriculum organisation, the breadth, balance and consistency of the curriculum experienced by pupils must be of central concern' (DES 1992 p. 23). The *Three Wise Men Report* was written by Robin Alexander, Jim Rose and Chris Woodhead, all of whom had a further impact on primary education beyond this document.

Assessment

Before the Education Reform Act, pupil progress was tracked by teacher assessments. The Act introduced compulsory national standard attainment tests (SATS) at 7, 11 and 14. The tests were based on the 1988 Black Report produced by the National Curriculum Task Group on Assessment and Testing (TGAT). The results had to be published annually in league tables. This allowed the government to compare schools directly in terms of this data.

Local Management of Schools

Local Management of Schools (LMS), flagged in the Education Act, was not introduced until 1991. It allowed the delegation of financial and managerial responsibilities to schools. Management for the budget was the responsibility of the school and budgets were taken away from LEAs. There were some centrally held resources in the LEAs, such as curriculum advisory and support services and school library services, although these increasingly diminished during the 1990s. There were mixed views amongst head teachers as to whether LMS gave greater flexibility but they certainly had greater responsibility.

Grant Maintained schools

Although grammar schools were not reintroduced, Grant Maintained (GM) schools were introduced. Schools were able to opt out of LEA control and be funded directly by central government. It was seen as a bribe to schools to encourage them to opt out, especially as they were offered additional funding. Grant Maintained schools also had more control over admissions and were allowed to select up to 10 per cent of their pupils on ability.

The Office for Standards in Education

The creation of the Office for Standards in Education (Ofsted) also resulted from the 1988 Education Act, although it wasn't actually set up until 1992, when it replaced visits to schools by Her Majesty's Inspectors with a more rigorous inspection system. When Ofsted inspected schools, a report was to be published, and the emphasis was on inspection and not support. It came across as an antagonising system and stressful for teachers as there was naming and shaming of failing schools when they were placed into 'special measures'. Chris Woodhead, one of the authors of the Three Wise Men Report, was appointed Her Majesty's Chief Inspector of Schools and Head of Ofsted in September 1994.

The National Curriculum Revised: The Dearing Report 1993

The Dearing Report made several key proposals about the National Curriculum and the changes cost an estimated £744 million. He advised that the curriculum should be slimmed down, the time given to testing should be reduced and around 20 per cent of teaching time should be freed up for use at the discretion of schools. However, the proposals were difficult to implement as government wanted literacy and numeracy to take up 50 per cent of the timetable, leaving the other eight subjects to be squashed into the remaining 50 per cent.

'Education, Education, Education' 1997

'Ask me my three main priorities for government and I tell you education, education, and education' (Blair 1996). Blair put education right at the top of the political agenda during the election of 1997. Speaking to the Labour Party conference after becoming Prime Minister in 1997, he stated: 'Our goal: to make Britain the best educated and skilled country in the world; a nation, not of a few talents, but of all the talents. And every single part of our schools system must be modernised to achieve it' (Blair 1997).

Excellence in Schools 1997

This White Paper pointed towards the importance of the basics and set a target of 80 per cent for all 11-year-olds to reach the 'required standard' of literacy and 75 per cent to reach the 'required standard' of numeracy by 2002.

It was proposed that class sizes should be less than 30 for 5–7-year-olds and this was adopted in the School Standards and Framework Act 1998. There was to be at least an hour a day spent on English and mathematics in primary schools and this set the scene for the literacy and numeracy strategies.

LEAs set targets for raising standards in individual schools. Governors had to publish school performance tables which showed the rate of progress pupils made against the targets set. Schools deemed 'failing' by Ofsted could not hide. LEAs could intervene in the schools, which were given two years to improve or they would be closed or forced to have management changes imposed.

Back to basics 1998

Yet again the 'back to basics' theme returned, and schools no longer had to teach National Curriculum programmes of study in all subjects, just in the three core subjects. This set up the background for introducing the literacy and numeracy strategies.

Literacy and numeracy strategies 1998 and 1999

Both these strategies were very prescriptive, giving both the content of what had to be taught and the delivery method. These were daily lessons which, although not statutory, were often seen as mandatory. Schools had to be very brave to break the mould and deliver their own ideas of lessons and schemes for literacy and numeracy. The National Literacy Strategy (DfEE 1998), the National Numeracy Strategy (DfEE 1999b) and National Learning Targets were introduced (DfEE 1999a). The Labour government was now seen to be telling teachers how to teach, in addition to teaching the National Curriculum, which had been seen as telling them what to teach.

National Curriculum 2000

The launch of a National Curriculum review took place in 1997. However, it was 2000 before all the changes took place. To the huge relief of teaching staff, the curriculum was slimmed down, but not without the addition of Citizenship. However, whilst testing was happening at the age of 11, creativity was not top of the list in the classrooms of Years 5 and 6. The paper, *Schools – Achieving Success* (DfES 2001), proposed allowing successful primary schools to opt out of the National Curriculum and seek to develop innovation. The Foundation Stage for children aged 3–5 years was introduced and had six Areas of Learning. This may have influenced the thinking for the development of the curriculum in the Rose Review (DCSF 2009).

Every Child Matters 2003

In 2003, the government published its Green Paper *Every Child Matters* (ECM) (DfES 2003a) following the death of Victoria Climbié. The ECM agenda had five clear outcomes which schools needed to consider in the development of their curriculum. These were: to be healthy, stay safe, enjoy and achieve, make a positive contribution and achieve economic well-being.

Excellence and Enjoyment 2003

Excellence and Enjoyment (DfES 2003b) claims to promote excellence in teaching 'the basics' and enjoyment through the broader curriculum. The existing National Numeracy Strategy (1999) and National Literacy Strategy (1998) conflated into one document, the Primary National Strategy (PNS) (DfE 2003). The PNS again aimed to promote high standards which should be achieved through a rich, varied and exciting curriculum. It aimed to build on the literacy and numeracy strategies but to give teachers more chance to take control of their teaching. There was more flexibility for schools to adopt ways of working that suited them. Testing and target setting was all part of the PNS and assessment for learning developed out of this report.

Towards a new curriculum

The Children's Plan (DCSF 2007) announced a root and branch review of the curriculum and this was to be headed by Sir Jim Rose, another author of the so-called Three Wise Men Report (DES 1992). Running concurrently with this was a review by Robin Alexander and a team of researchers, The Cambridge Review. This is a more philosophical and research-based report, published as *Children, their World, their Education* (Alexander 2010). Neither review became policy.

Where to next?

The Cambridge Review (Alexander 2010) provides firm research evidence that, despite these intense pressures, primary schools are highly valued by children and parents. Primary schools were seen as largely happy places which consistently celebrate the positive, while not, as some claim, neglecting the '3 Rs' and 'those who regularly make this claim are either careless of the facts or are knowingly fostering calumny'.

 Reflective task: perspectives on the curriculum

In role as a 5-year-old, a 10-year-old, a parent, a teacher or a member of a Local Education Authority, present your case for the primary curriculum you would like and why. Present in turn to the group. At the end of each presentation, the group should critically evaluate the curricula presented.

 Summary

This chapter outlined changes in the philosophy, curriculum, organisation and accountability in primary schools moving from the 1800s to the ideas espoused in the Plowden Report, then to more centralisation, beginning with the Education Reform Act of 1988 and the creation of education fashioned by the concept of market forces and economic growth and measured attainment. Against this constantly changing background, the chapter aimed to encourage readers to understand the need to develop, defend and implement robust personal and professional philosophies which will enable them to respond to changes with professional integrity.

Supplementary information on legislation, Alexander (2010), The Final Report of the Rose Review (DCFS 2009) an overview of the implications for classroom practice of legislation described in this chapter and an additional reflective task and bibliography can be found on the website related to this book, pp. 3–7.

 Questions for discussion

1 Do we need Ofsted or is there an alternative? Consider: teacher stress, cost, standards, accountability, closure of schools, improvement.
2 Consider the areas of reform in the 1988 Education Act: the National Curriculum, national testing at 7 and 11, league tables, religious education and collective worship, local management of school budgets (LMS), governing bodies, Ofsted and Grant Maintained (GM) status. How have these had an impact on our schools over the last 20 years?
3 Discuss your ideas about what you want your classroom environment to look like, types of grouping you would try and the balance of time you would place on each subject.

Further reading

Alexander, R. (ed.) (2010) *Children, their World, their Education: Final Report and Recommendations of the Cambridge Primary Review*. London: Routledge. Available at: www.primaryreview.org.uk/Downloads/Finalreport/CPR-booklet_low-res.pdf
This comprehensive report is intended to be a discussion document. It raises fundamental and thought-provoking questions about the direction in which primary education should head in the future and provides a wealth of up-to-date research evidence to inform the discussion.
Plowden Report (1967) *Children and their Primary Schools*. Report of the Central Advisory Council for Education (England). London: HMSO.
This report raises challenging questions about the way primary education could have gone and the way it went over the last 40 years and whether the reasons given for this were convincing.

References

Alexander, R. (ed.) (2010) *Children, their World, their Education: Final Report and Recommendations of the Cambridge Primary Review*. London: Routledge.

Blair, T. (1996) Speech to the Labour Party Annual Conference, 1 October, Brighton.

Blair, T. (1997) Speech to the Labour Party Annual Conference, 30 September, Brighton. Available at: www.prnewswire.co.uk/cgi/news/release?id=47983 (accessed 29 September 2010)

DCSF (2007) *The Children's Plan*. London: DCSF.

DCSF (2009) *The Independent Review of the Primary Curriculum: Final Report*. London: DCSF.

DES (1978) *Primary Education in England: A Survey by Her Majesty's Inspectors of Schools*. London: HMSO.

DES (1980) *A Framework for the School Curriculum*. London: DES.

DES (1981a) *The School Curriculum*. London: DES/HMSO.

DES (1981b) Circular 6/81. London: DES/HMSO.

DES (1985) *Better Schools: A Summary*. London: DES.

DES (1988) *The National Curriculum*. London: HMSO.

DES (1992) *Curriculum Organisation and Classroom Practice in Primary Schools* (Three Wise Men Report). London: DES.

DfEE (1997) *Excellence in Schools*, White Paper. London: DfEE.

DfEE (1998) *The National Literacy Strategy*. London: DfEE.

DfEE (1999a) *The National Curriculum for England*. London: DfEE.

DfEE (1999b) *The National Numeracy Strategy*. London: DfEE.

DfES (2001) *Schools – Achieving Success*. London: DfES.

DfES (2003) *Excellence and Enjoyment: A Strategy for Primary Schools*. London: DfES.

DfES (2003a) *Every Child Matters*. London: DfES.

DfES (2003b) *Excellence and Enjoyment*. London: DfES.

Galton, M., Simon, B. and Croll, P. (1980) *Inside the Primary Classroom* (The ORACLE Report). London: Routledge and Kegan Paul.

HMI (1980a) *Framework for the School Curriculum*. London: HMSO.

HMI (1980b) *A View of the Curriculum*. London: HMSO.

HMI (1984) *Parental Influence at School: A New Framework for School Government in England and Wales*. London: HMSO.

Morris, M. (ed.) (1988) *Education, the Wasted Years? 1973–1986*. Lewes: Falmer.

Plowden (1967) *Children and their Primary Schools*. Report of the Central Advisory Council for Education (England). London: HMSO.

QCA (1999) *The National Curriculum: Handbook for Primary Teachers in England, Key Stages 1 and 2*. London: QCA.

TEGAT Report (1988) *Report of the Task Group on Assessment and Testing*. Chaired by Professor Paul Black.

Warnock Report (1978) *Report of the Committee of Enquiry into the Education of Handicapped Children and Young People*. London: HMSO.

CHAPTER 2

PHILOSOPHY OF EDUCATION AND THEORIES OF LEARNING

Hilary Cooper

By the end of this chapter, you should be able to:

- understand the kinds of questions educational philosophers ask, how they discuss them and why it is important for you to practise engaging in the kinds of enquiries which underpin this book

- understand the relationship between educational philosophy and theories of how children learn

- have a basic understanding of key learning theories and of their implications for teaching and learning

- be aware of the contribution neuroscience is making to our understanding of learning.

Introduction

You will see from Chapter 1 that, for a variety of reasons, the aims of education and the degree of political influence and central control over all dimensions of education are dynamic; they change as society changes. Teachers have had little encouragement recently to question what or how to teach. And 'primary education suffers more than its share of scare-mongering and hyperbole, not to mention deliberate myth-making' (Hoskins and Nothen 2009 p. 5). The report continues: 'Isn't it time to move on from the populism, polarisation and name-calling which for too long have supplanted real educational debate and progress? Children deserve better from the nation's leaders and shapers of opinion'. The Professional Attributes for Qualified Teacher Status do not expect you to explore questions about the aims, purposes and value of education but to 'deliver' the curriculum, with little responsibility for professional discretion. Yet if children's lives are not to be at the mercy of political whim, it is essential that teachers learn the skills of robust critical evaluation, based on their reading, experience and reflection, so that they develop strong personal philosophies about what, how and why we teach children, in order to interpret changes in ways which are professionally valid and have integrity. It is important to learn scepticism, and have a concern about the larger questions and a deep understanding of what we teach, to have time to reflect, research and study. This chapter aims to help you do this. First, it gives an overview of the questions philosophers have asked about education in the past, and ask currently, and shows you how to engage with them. Then it links these to theories about how children learn.

What is primary education for?

This is a fundamental philosophical question. Discussing a broad set of aims will prevent you from narrow thinking about what children can and should do. And it is essential that, having begun to discuss educational aims, through reading this chapter, you use these to shape what you do as a teacher and what children you teach experience in the curriculum, teaching and assessment. Since the beginning of state education until the Rose Review (DCSF 2009), the 'basics' have generally been seen as central to primary education. But what is basic in the twenty-first century? How can we empower children to find meaning in their lives? Independence and empowerment are achieved through exploring, knowing, understanding and making sense, through imagination and dialogue, through constructivist approaches. And before you can educate your pupils, based on these aims, you must learn to empower yourself.

The long tradition of educational philosophy

Plato to Rousseau

Since Plato in the fifth century BC and Aristotle in the following century, philosophers have considered the aims, processes and content of education and the relationship between education and society, and their ideas remain relevant today. Plato and Aristotle saw education as holistic, balancing the practical and theoretical. Avicenna (980–1037 CE) (in Goodman 2005) said that children should discuss, debate and learn from each other. John Stuart Mill (1859) also wrote of the importance of contesting and defending ideas. Jean Jacques Rousseau (1762) saw education as developmental, changing in response to pupils' needs, and based on learning from the environment.

Spencer to Steiner

Spencer (1851) advocated moving from concrete to abstract. Heywood Cooper (1892) championed the rights to education of women and ethnic minorities. Froebel (1895) emphasised learning through play and seeing children as the centre of their own worlds, and Montessori (1914) was confident that young children could make decisions for themselves and that they should learn from their environments. Dewey (1916) wrote about the social and moral nature of schooling, and Steiner (1919) believed in the freedom of teachers to shape their own curriculum.

Educational philosophy over the last 50 years

A section on the long tradition of educational philosophy from Plato to the early twentieth century can be found on the website linked to Chapter 2.

As philosophies proliferated and since everyone was now entitled to education, it became necessary to examine more critically what was meant by education and what it should aim to achieve. R.S. Peters (1966, 1967) and Hirst (1965, 1974) made a major contribution to showing how this might be done, through analysing concepts related to education which are often 'fuzzy' and which people may understand differently and by critically analysing and arguing about claims made for education. Peters asked, as Socrates had, questions such as: What is worth knowing? What do we mean by an educated person? Is the education system fair? Who knows best what children should learn? Is education different from training, teaching different from learning? How? These are questions which are complex and have no single answer or dictionary definition, and in an open society they must be argued over. Peters explored such questions by asking: What do you mean by this question? How do you know? To explore these questions, we need to collect a range of different examples, drawing on our experiences and reading. Can we find some key principles which will allow us to interpret the constantly changing demands made of us?

Using this process, Peters' conclusion to the question, 'what is an educated person?', was essentially: someone who has been changed, by their knowledge and understanding, in the way they look at the world around them; has a body of principles for organising knowledge (subjects or areas of learning), can make connections between areas of knowledge, and cares about what they know and understand. Do you agree?

But this concept of an educated person raises questions. Is it possible to be educated if you excel in only one area of knowledge? Does being educated involve only knowledge and understanding or does it include, for example, behaviour? Can everyone be educated if we accept this definition? Should they be?

Peters claimed that this process of conceptual analysis was free from politics and had universal significance, identifying certain values and ideals, irrespective of culture and society. Matthew Arnold had said that education should convey the best that has been thought and said. But is that still appropriate? Educational aims must be relevant to the culture, society and world in which children live and knowing only 'the best' may not reflect their own worlds. Yet should they have access to it?

By 1973 Peters accepted the criticisms of Dearden et al. (1972) and McIntyre (1998) that this was not the case, and that educational aims, values and methods are inevitably embedded in society and change with society. Hirst (1998) and Hirst and White (1998) agreed that Peters' analytical approach could not produce universal answers but was part of an evolving tradition and that the process of analysis must be closely linked to practical problems. Subsequent educational philosophers, for example Rorty (1979), took a more Aristotelian approach to addressing philosophical questions, based on a conversational style and pragmatic, practical discussion of current issues.

Contemporary educational philosophers take a rich variety of approaches to examine current educational policies and questions. Self-determination or autonomy are still seen as an important educational aim but in the context of maximising opportunities to choose, while recognising social responsibilities (Hogan 1997; Walker 1999; Winch 1999). There is a growing interest in the links between political philosophy and the notion that before we ask, 'What is education?', we need to say 'What are the values of this society?' For what our society values underpins discussion of educational issues such as: multiculturalism, identity, education and religion, inclusion, education for citizenship and for democracy, the curriculum, educational methods, organisation and assessment, education, the role of adults in the classroom, governance and who controls schools, education and moral practice and behaviour, personal and social development. For example, Hirst (1974) considered what the curriculum should consist of, a continuing contentious issue. Pring (2001) explored educational issues through the lens of moral questions and Crick (2000) discussed the nature of citizenship education. Pendlebury (2005) explored feminism and education. You will learn how to engage with such questions in the following chapters of this book.

How does philosophical questioning enable us to achieve our vision within changing political constraints?

Education embodies values and ideals. Most student teachers I have known have been highly motivated by a vision of the kind of teachers they want to be. They have ideas about what they think is valuable and how it might be achieved. But visions vary. For example, interviewees often talk of their aim to help children 'to be creative', 'to love art or books', 'to be independent'. But when such aims are analysed in a group they become controversial. They are all based on value judgements about what the student thinks is important, which not everyone agrees with. They involve concepts which are abstract and are understood in different ways. What exactly is meant by 'creative', 'loving books', 'independent'?

When philosophical discussion becomes a habit, it enables us to take responsibility for developing our own practice with integrity. It allows us to react against outside mandates. We stop accepting simple solutions to what we know are complex problems. It stops us being knee-jerk in reaction to change by enabling us to define and work towards what we value. It allows us to ask what values and beliefs underpin our work and to use these as the basis for interpreting our responses to change and refining our practice. We can set our personal goals rather than simply respond to those we are given. This constitutes professionalism. Philosophical analysis allows us to dissect slogans such as 'education for democracy', or for 'citizenship', 'equal opportunities', 'learning to learn', 'collaboration'. Once we do this, we realise that such slogans are by no means self-evident or beyond criticism.

    Reflective task

Begin to tease out your own philosophy by asking, 'What should be the aims of education in the UK today?' Then answer Peters' question: what do you mean by this? Then give any evidence from your reading and experience to support your claims.

Share your list, directly or through a discussion board, with a partner or group of colleagues.

Do people disagree about any of the aims? If so, why?

Identify any aims shared by several people.

Is it possible to create a list of key principles which underpin some of the aims?

Draft the first statement of your personal philosophy of education. As you read through this book, you will add to this, modify it and add your responses to the many other philosophical discussions you will have.

Philosophy of education and educational theory

Another response to the need to provide mass education explored what is involved in the process of learning, by seeking to define systematic rules, based on the evidence of observed behaviour. In psychology, hypotheses are tested in experiments and, if confirmed to a reliable degree, suggest theories. These theories inform practice and through practice the theory is refined. There is an expectation, today, that teaching should be a research-based profession. All teachers can, and should, reflect on how learning theories impact on their teaching in different contexts, consider in what ways they might develop, evaluate or modify theory practice links and share their reflections through professional discussion and professional publications.

Theory in education cannot be as reliable as scientific theory but is nevertheless genuine theory. An enormous amount of data has been accumulated about, for example, how children learn, although there is no single theory but several overlapping theories. The dominant theories over the last century were Behaviourism, in which the teacher controls the learning, Constructivism, in which the teacher supports the child in constructing their own learning and Hierarchies of Needs, which identify conditions necessary for learning to take place.

Behaviourist theories

During the first half of the twentieth century, the dominant theory about how children learn was behaviourism. The central idea is that most of human behaviour, like that of animals, is susceptible to simple, mechanistic explanation. It ignores the fact that language significantly distinguishes us from animals.

Classical conditioning

Behaviourism begins with classical conditioning, Pavlov's finding that dogs which salivate at the sight of food (an unconditioned stimulus), when presented with food accompanied by an oral signal, learned to salivate in response to the signal when no food was present (a conditioned stimulus). This is classical conditioning. Don't we still train young children to stop talking when they hear the wind chimes, a special tune, a hand clap? But the uses for this classical conditioning are limited.

Operant conditioning

Thorndike (1903) put a rat in a cage with a lever which it pressed to release food. However, when the food was replaced by shocks the rat stopped pressing the lever – hence, there are responses to reward and punishment. This is known as operant conditioning because the animal (or person) has to do something which has an associated consequence. And don't we give stars or points or 'golden time' and praise to encourage good work or behaviour and 'traffic lights' to warn against, then punish undesired work or behaviour? Don't we apply Ferster and Skinner's (1957) 'different intermittent schedules of reinforcement': fixed intervals for some rewards (marbles in a jar at the end of the week), fixed ratio schedules (names on the board, four times and you stay in), varied ratio schedules which reward only after a number of positive responses, variable interval schedules (rewards given irregularly to keep the children on their toes)?

Implications of behaviourism for teaching and learning

Behaviourist theory was largely unquestioned during the first half of the last century. Teaching was seen as instructing and training, transmitting information, without understanding the connecting principles and rationale behind the information, which was often piecemeal and not necessarily considered of immediate use or intrinsic interest, but necessary to know later in life. This attitude to education was instrumental and materialistic. Since behaviourism aims to mould behaviour and depends only on observed behaviour, it is not concerned with the inner life: emotions, the child's world, relationships between pupils or teacher and pupils, ideas and concepts. It is hardly likely to change children's views, knowledge or understanding of the world or their relationships or teach them to make decisions or take responsibility. The teacher's function is to manipulate and it is difficult to see this as moral. It leads to the teacher deciding on the curriculum irrespective of children's interests, on the pace, which aims at the middle, involves much rote learning and makes no differentiation for individual needs.

Constructivist theories

Constructivist theories explore the mental processes involved in learning. They see learning as an active process in which the learner is motivated to ask questions, based on experience, and tries to explore the questions and find answers. Piaget was the first to explore the processes of learning, generally focusing on individual children. Vygotsky and Bruner saw learning as a predominantly social activity. Although a great deal of subsequent research has explored and criticised aspects of their work in different contexts and in some cases modified it, their approach to learning underpins the thinking of educationalists today, especially in England and, it can be argued, reflects a society which values the individual and is essentially democratic.

Jean Piaget (1896–1980)

Stage theory   Piaget's wide-ranging empirical studies make three major contributions to the enquiry into how learning takes place (Piaget and Inhelder 1969). First, he saw learning as occurring in four main successive stages, characterised by qualitatively different thinking processes:

The *sensori–motor stage* is dominated by exploring through the senses: children like to feel things, to draw in their own dribble(!) and shake a rattle to make a noise.

The *pre-operational stage*, Piaget says, is dominated by perception and egocentricity: children are happy to talk to themselves without needing to convince others. Their thinking is dominated by what they perceive. A smaller person (or tree) is younger than a taller one. I've certainly seen children convinced that a small middle-aged student is much younger than a taller 20-year-old. It is fascinating to try out Piaget's claims in the classroom with children of different ages. At the pre-operational stage, dominated by what children see, they think that a large empty box must be heavier than a small box containing heavy weights or that a litre of water changes in quantity when poured into a differently shaped container. But they begin to reason at the pre-operational stage, for example to classify objects according to one characteristic, as in putting all the blue bricks together.

At the *operational stage*, learning is defined by reasoned thinking. A child can take in information from the outside world, retain it and apply it to new situations, and apply rules. Children can 'conserve' information, understanding that objects or sets of objects stay the same even when moved around or changing shape. A line of six counters remains six counters, when scattered; when matched one to one (correlation) they form two equal sets of three, the basis of multiplication and division, or divided into unequal sets (four and two), of addition and subtraction. They can use equal units to calculate mass, weight, volume, classify sets into subsets, for example sort a set of blue bricks into subsets of shape and size (class inclusion); sort 'yellow flowers' into daffodils, dandelions, primroses. Children learn to use the word 'because' to make causal statements.

At the *formal reasoning stage*, Piaget concluded that it is possible to bear in mind and compare a number of variables, to systematically test hypotheses and to discuss ideological and abstract ideas.

Piaget: progressing through the stages   A child takes in information from experience of the environment to build schema – these are mental maps to make sense of the world (assimilation). New information is added to this map which continues to make sense until this schema is challenged by information which does not fit into it. The child has to adjust the schema to encompass the contradictory information (accommodation). Everything in the water tray floats – but now put in the toy car. The previous rule no longer makes sense. Put some more things into the water tray to try to find a new rule – 'heavy things' sink? Children, Piaget says, try to balance the process of applying previous knowledge and changing schema to account for new knowledge (equilibrium). (For an excellent overview of Piaget's work, see Flavell 1963.)

Piaget evaluated   Recent neuroscience has contested Piaget's stage theory, challenging a sequence of qualitively different kinds of thinking, which ignores the possibility of intervention and social interaction to accelerate learning. Neuroscience suggests that children learn to think in much the same way as adults but lack the experience to make sense of what they find. It involves networks of neurons involving seeing, remembering, deducing and social and emotional aspects of learning. And yet there is a basic logic to the progression Piaget outlined and if you try out some of his ideas, about conservation for example, his basic findings are reinforced. The important thing about Piaget is that he was the first person to explore the process of learning.

Lev Vygotsky (1896–1934)

Concept development and the Zone of Proximal Development Vygotsky's empirical research (1962) emphasised the importance of social interaction and language in learning. He also explored the way in which concepts are learned through trial and error. We saw from Piaget's work that concepts are categories of words/ideas which have something in common. There are hierarchies of concepts: concrete concepts such as chairs or tables, and higher-order concepts into which they fit as sub-sets such as furniture. Sometimes there are three levels with an abstract concept which cannot be visualised (e.g. gun, weapon, power or family, village, community). All language is an organisation of concepts, identifying shared properties through the use of language and trial and error. All small furry animals are dogs – until you encounter a cat. Concepts form the building blocks of thinking and are learned through communication. This reflects the emphasis we now put on discussion in classrooms. Children support or contest each other's ideas, give examples and reasons. In this way they take each other's thinking forward and can reach levels of thinking none of them could on their own. In the early years, this process of forming categories of things which have common properties is evidenced in tiles of different colours, sizes and shapes and hence concepts, which children can group in different ways. This activity stems directly from Vygotsky's research into concept development. He passed around tiles which differed in shape, colour and thickness and asked participants to identify a nonsense word/a new concept which had two criteria in common, so creating, through trial and error, a new concept (e.g. thick and yellow, it is 'guk').

Vygotsky (1978) suggested that progress in thinking and in doing takes place through the 'Zone of Proximal Development' (ZPD), when a learner is supported by a 'slightly more able other' until he can complete the task independently; this underlines the current emphasis on pairs and partners in classrooms. Support might also be through differentiation in resources provided for different pupils, whether a teaching assistant, books at different levels of difficulty or mathematics apparatus. Differentiation, another strategy to promote learning by providing tasks at levels individual children can engage with, is reflected in this way. Vygotsky thought that children are not naturally motivated to learn academic subjects and that the motivation to do so comes from the environment for learning provided by the teacher and the satisfaction experienced in having learned something in response to this.

J.S. Bruner (1915–)

The first of Bruner's three interacting contributions to explaining the learning process is emphasis on the importance of providing materials in a form which enables pupils to engage with what is being taught – differentiation again. Although he does not see these 'modes of representation' (1966) as entirely successive, he suggests that resources and experiences may be kinaesthetic, explored through physical engagement, iconic, presented as visual images or symbolic, diagrams, maps, mathematics and language.

Second, Bruner (1963) pointed out the need to identify the key concepts, questions and methods of answering them which are at the heart of each discipline or subject. And, third, Bruner said that, having identified the concepts and questions at the heart of each discipline, we need to structure progression in learning the key concepts, questions and ways of answering them (the spiral curriculum, 1966), so that a child, from the very beginning, can engage with the essential questions and processes of every subject. The English National Curriculum (1999) made a good attempt to do this.

More recently, Bruner (1986) has written about the importance of culture – beliefs, values, symbols, shared meanings and cultural narratives – in determining how individuals make sense of the world and hence the importance of educators being aware of the thinking and diverse experiences pupils bring to bare on their learning.

Social constructivism and play

Piaget, Vygotsky and Bruner all extended their theories to consider the learning processes involved in play. Piaget (1951) suggested that play helps to overcome egocentrism since children may encounter conflicts of interest and so realise that others have goals and ideas too. It is a means of accommodating and assimilating reality. A child may imagine that a wooden brick is an aeroplane, 'assimilate' the brick into his existing schema of aeroplanes, seeing no problem in that its shape has no resemblance to an aeroplane, but may also role play the experience of seeing a street fire, in a serious attempt to 'accommodate' the reality of what he saw.

Vygotsky (1978) saw the Zone of Proximal Development as relevant to play, in that, through play a child can achieve a level of thinking far higher than she can outside play. The child may, for example, wish to ride a horse. There is no horse so she might use a stick as a symbol for a horse and hence be able to ride. In order to separate the idea of a horse from a real horse, the child uses the stick as a 'pivot' for moving towards thought which is not constrained by situations. This releases the child from the constraints of the objective world to enter the world of ideas, imagination, interpretation and will.

Abraham Maslow (1908–1970)

Maslow originally worked with Thorndike and, while studying monkeys, observed that some needs take precedence over others. This idea led to the construction of his theory of a Hierarchy of Needs (1943) (see www.google.co.uk/images). This is concerned with motivation to learn, and the needs which must be satisfied in order to do so. First, basic physiological needs such as the need for air, food, drink, shelter, warmth and sleep must be met before we can learn effectively. At the next level, security, stability, safety and order are necessary. Then affection and relationships with family and others. If these needs are met, we can achieve, take responsibility and develop self-esteem. And when this has been achieved, we reach a level which Maslow calls 'self-actualisation'. There has been much discussion about what this actually means but essentially it is self-fulfilment, the ability to be autonomous, to accept one's self and others and act with humility and respect, to be spontaneous and creative. Later, Maslow added three more categories of need: esteem needs; cognitive needs (the need for knowledge and meaning); and aesthetic needs (appreciation of beauty). Above self-actualisation, he perceived the need to help others to achieve self-actualisation. Maslow's sequence of needs and his methodology and the claim that only a few people ever reach self-actualisation have been criticised. Some children certainly succeed in spite of economic, social, environmental or emotional disadvantages – but many do not.

In this chapter, key learning theories have been outlined, but, as stated earlier, there are many more overlapping theories of learning which can be explored (see http://emtech.net/learnin_theories.htm; http://learning-theories.com).

Reflective task

In groups, if possible, research the work of one of the theorists outlined above. One person can find out the biography, another more about the theory, a third the empirical research on which the theory is based. Next, through group discussion, critically analyse the theory – what are its strengths and weaknesses? Evaluate the implications for classroom practice. As a group, present your findings and views to your colleagues and invite questions and discussion.

Summary

This chapter began by considering the kinds of questions educational philosophers ask and why it is important for you to engage in this process, followed by a look at the developments in the methods and scope of philosophical enquiry about education over the past 50 years. The second part of the chapter focused on empirical research into the *processes* of learning and the implications for all aspects of classroom practice. During the last 10–20 years neuroscience has begun to shed new light on the processes of learning. Website material discusses the potential of neuroscience to develop our understanding of the aims and processes of teaching and learning.

Questions for discussion

- Find out about approaches to teaching, learning and assessment in three politically contrasting countries. What seem to be the aims of the education system in each country? How is it embedded in the society? What appear to be the core values in each society and education system?
- Think of an area of expertise you have, not directly related to school (e.g. playing an instrument, performing a magic trick, cooking a particular dish, dancing). Write a lesson plan to show how you could teach this skill to a group of peers, using as many aspects of learning theories as possible. List the learning theories you apply and say why you used them. Present the lesson and invite your peers to identify the theories you applied.
- What are your most enjoyable experiences of learning something, in or out of school? What did they have in common? How can this inform your philosophy of teaching and learning?
- Critically evaluate a current policy.

Further reading

Aristotle (1968) *Aristotle on Education: Extracts from Ethics and Politics*. Translated and edited by John Burnet, first printed 1903, reprinted 1980. Cambridge: Cambridge University Press.

Bailey, R. (ed.) (2010) *The Philosophy of Education*. London: Continuum.
After initial chapters on the nature of educational philosophy, authors engage in philosophical discussion of such current issues as citizenship, educational opportunities and who should control education.

Matheson, C. and Matheson, D. (eds) (2000) *Educational Issues in the Learning Age*. London: Continuum.
This is also a series of essays on current debates on, for example, education and cultural identity, education and professionalism, education and effectiveness.

Palmer, J.A. (2001) *Fifty Major Thinkers on Education: From Confucius to Dewey*. London: Routledge.

Palmer, J.A., Cooper, D.E. and Bresler, L. (2001) *Fifty Modern Thinkers on Education: From Piaget to the Present*. London: Routledge.
Each of these succinct reference books gives an overview of each subject's work and basic bibliographical information, followed by critical reflection on the subject's thinking.

Pritchard, A. (2008) *Ways of Learning*. London: Routledge.
This book supplies details which teachers can make use of in their planning, linking theories of behaviourism, constructivist learning, multiple intelligences and neuro-science to practice.

References

Bruner, J.S. (1963) *The Process of Education: A Landmark in Educational Theory*. Cambridge, MA: Harvard University Press.
Bruner, J.S. (1966) *Towards a Theory of Instruction*. Cambridge, MA: Harvard University Press.
Bruner, J.S. (1986) *Actual Minds Possible Worlds*. Cambridge, MA: Harvard University Press.
Cooper, A.J.H. (1892) *A Voice from the South*. Available at: www.docsouth.unc.edu
Crick, B. (2000) *Essays on Citizenship*. London: Continuum.
DCSF (2009) *The Independent Review of the Primary Curriculum: Final Report*. London: DCSF.
Dearden, R.F., Hirst, P.H. and Peters, R.S. (eds) (1972) *Education and the Development of Reason*. London: Routledge and Kegan Paul.
Dewey, J. (1916) *Democracy and Education: An Introduction to the Philosophy of Education*. Available at: www.ilt.columbia.edu
Ferster, C.B. and Skinner, B.F. (1957) *Schedules of Reinforcement*. New York: Appleon-Century-Crofts.
Flavell, J. H. (1963) *The Developmental Psychology of Jean Piaget*. Princeton, NJ: Van Nostrand.
Froebel, F. (1895) *The Pedagogies of the Kindergarten*. New York: D. Appleton and Company.
Goodman, L.E. (2005) *Avicenna: Arabic Thought and Culture*. London: Routledge.
Hirst, P.H. (1965) 'Liberal Education and the Nature of Knowledge', in R.D. Archambault (ed.) *Philosophical Analysis and Education*. London: Routledge and Kegan Paul.
Hirst, P.H. (1974) *Knowledge and the Curriculum: A Collection of Philosophical Essays*. London: Routledge and Kegan Paul.
Hirst, P. H. (1998) 'Philosophy of Education: The Evolution of a Discipline', in G. Haydn (ed.) *50 Years of Philosophy of Education*. London: London University, Institute of Education.
Hirst, P.H. and White, P. (eds) (1998) *Philosophy of Education: Major Themes in the Analytical Tradition*. London: Routledge.
Hogan, P.J. (1997) 'The Politics of Identity and the Epiphanies of Learning', in W. Carr (ed.) *The Routledge Falmer Reader in Philosophy of Education*. London: Routledge, pp. 83–96.
Hoskins, D. and Nothen, S. (eds) (2009) *Introducing the Cambridge Primary Review*. Cambridge: University of Cambridge Faculty of Education. Available at: www.primary review.org.uk/Downloads/finalreport/CPR-booklet_lo-res.pdf

Maslow, A. (1943) 'A Theory of Human Motivation', *Psychological Review* 50(4): 370–96.

McIntyre, A. (1998) 'An Interview with Giovanna Borradori', in K. Knight (ed.) *The McIntyre Reader*. Cambridge: Polity Press, pp. 255–66.

Mill, J.S. (1859) *On Liberty* (republished 2008). Charleston, SC: Forgotten Books.

Montessori, M. (1914) *Dr. Montessori's Own Handbook*. Whitefish, MT: Kessinger Publishing.

Pendlebury, S. (2005) 'Feminism, Epistemology and Education', in W. Carr (ed.) *The Routledge Falmer Reader in Philosophy of Education*. London: Routledge.

Peters, R.S. (1966) *Ethics and Education*. London: Allen and Unwin.

Peters, R.S. (1967) *The Concept of Education*. London: Routledge and Kegan Paul.

Piaget, J. (1951) *Play, Dreams and Imitation in Early Childhood*. London: Routledge.

Piaget, J. and Inhelder, B. (1969) *The Psychology of the Child*. London: Perseus Books.

Pring, R. (2001) 'Education as a Moral Practice', *Journal of Moral Education* 30(2): 101–12.

Rorty, R. (1979) *Philosophy and the Mirror of Nature*. Princeton, NJ: Princeton University Press.

Rousseau, J.J. (1762) *Emile*. Available at: www.gutenberg.org.etext

Spencer, H. (1851) *Essays on Education and Kindred Subjects*. Available at: www.gutengery.org

Steiner, R. (1919) *The Renewal of Education*. Available at: www.ebook3000.com

Thorndike, E.L. (1903) *Educational Psychology*. New York: The Science Press.

Vygotsky, L.S. (1962) *Thought and Language*. Trans. E. Hanfmann and G. Vakar. Cambridge, MA: MIT Press.

Vygotsky, L.S. (1978) *Mind in Society: The Development of Higher Psychological Processes*. Cambridge, MA: Harvard University Press.

Walker, J.C. (1999) 'Self-determination as an Educational Aim', in R. Marples (ed.) *The Aims of Education*. London: Routledge, pp. 112–23.

Winch, C. (1999) 'Autonomy as an Educational Aim', in R. Marples (ed.) *The Aims of Education*. London: Routledge, pp. 74–84.

CHAPTER 3

PLANNING, MONITORING, ASSESSMENT AND RECORDING

Suzanne Lowe and Kim Harris

By the end of this chapter, you should be able to:

- identify the teaching and learning priorities for your school context and make an informed, positive contribution to curriculum development

- confidently plan to provide learners with engaging and meaningful learning experiences which motivate and promote understanding and development of skills

- use a wide range of assessment strategies to inform future planning, develop learning and independence.

Introduction

Statutory curricula are dynamic and change to meet new needs and with new governments. This chapter introduces you to ways in which schools and teachers translate national requirements into long-term plans for their school, develop medium-term plans from the whole-school plans and use these to plan lessons on a weekly and daily basis. It explains how assessments of different kinds and for different purposes are integrally related to planning so that sequences of work continuously build on pupils' previous knowledge. It examines the decisions involved in planning and assessment and some of the controversial aspects of the process. This chapter will help you to adapt to changing curricula and statutory assessment requirements. It will not address in detail all of the professional attributes to which it relates. This overall framework will be applied to specific curriculum areas by subject tutors.

Different approaches to the primary curriculum

The National Curriculum

The National Curriculum (NC) was introduced following the Education Reform Act of 1988. It comprised a subject-focused approach which outlined the knowledge, skills and understanding that children should be taught within a particular subject and Key Stage. It included attainment targets against which children are 'measured'. *Excellence and Enjoyment* (DfES 2003) was introduced to support schools to adopt a more individual approach in delivering the curriculum. Since the NC's implementation, amendments have been developed over time, more recently the Primary Frameworks for Literacy and Numeracy, and Personal Social and Health Education (PSHE). Other areas, such as Inclusion and Special Educational Needs were addressed in more detail through *Removing Barriers to Achievement* (DfES 2004a). These additions gradually overloaded and narrowed the curriculum.

Examining Key Stage 2 as a focus, the teaching of Literacy and Numeracy took approximately 50 per cent of the weekly timetable. There was a minimum legal requirement to teach RE each week for around 1 hour. Other curriculum subjects then followed in 'priority' order, with Science and PE each given 2 hours per week. This left the remaining curriculum areas of Information and Communication Technology, History, Art, Design and Technology, Geography, Modern Foreign Languages, Music and PSHE to be addressed in the remaining time.

A cross-curricular approach to the National Curriculum

Some schools attempted to redress the balance by using a cross-curricular approach rather than teaching discrete subjects. In using a cross-curricular approach, it is important to ensure that there is breadth across the curriculum and that *all* the necessary curriculum objectives are taught. One of the key advantages of a thematic approach is that it is thought to be a more contextually based approach to learning, by encouraging children to make connections between different areas of learning. In addition, many believe that this promotes deep learning and supports transference of skills, knowledge and understanding.

A concern in some schools is that children may not transfer the skills learned in, say, literacy into other subject areas. Conversely, some teachers believe that depth of subject knowledge can only be taught through discrete subject teaching and are concerned that a surface approach to the curriculum may be the result of a thematic approach.

Reflective task

Consider your personal views on this issue of subject-based teaching versus theme-based teaching. Are these *values*-based judgements? Are they linked to how much worth we apportion to each subject? Do you believe it is necessary to prioritise basic skills over the arts and humanities? In your experience so far, what do you believe to be the 'best' approach? Why? What strategies do you have to address the potential issues?

It is possible and important to interpret changes in statutory requirements mediated by your own professional philosophy; this chapter will give you strategies for doing this, in terms of planning and assessing what is taught and learned, with confidence.

Some international comparisons

The examples below illustrate the impact government agendas can have on teaching and learning in the classroom, particularly on the curriculum content and how it is organised. A focus on wider curricular agendas can give us a global perspective on education priorities, although the examples provided present a narrow view in terms of global priorities as they are all from more economically developed countries.

US educational priorities, outlined by President Obama, are:

- to extend the school day and year as, he states, American children spend a month less in school than children in South Korea
- early education

- introducing national standards as opposed to state-defined standards
- rewarding successful teachers while pushing out ineffective ones
- holding students and parents responsible for their education.

UK priorities, following the change of government in May 2010, are:

- improving literacy
- raising pupil attainment
- extending parental choice
- freeing teachers from bureaucracy
- improving discipline
- closing the widening gap between the richest and the poorest (Michael Gove, May 2010)
- the introduction of 'free schools'
- a rise in the number of academies.

Swedish schooling has the following key elements:

- the 'free schools' system began in the 1990s
- pre-school is available from age 1
- 'formal' timetabled schooling starts at age 7
- the National Curriculum with local elements is devised by municipalities
- there is teacher and school autonomy for teaching strategies
- there is a nationally valid timetable stating the number of hours per subject over all nine years of compulsory education – 6665 hours – but each municipality/school decides on the distribution of hours and in what year a subject is introduced.

Source: http://eacea.ec.europa.eu/education/eurydice/documents/eurybase/national_summary_sheets/047_ SE_EN.pdf [accessed 17.10.10]

The Independent Review of the Primary Curriculum

An alternative curriculum design was proposed following the Independent Review of the Primary Curriculum (IRPC) (DfE 2008), commissioned by the Labour government. The Rose proposal outlines 'a design for the curriculum which promotes challenging subject teaching alongside equally challenging cross-curricular studies' (p. 4) but 'insists that literacy, numeracy and ICT must be prioritised' (p. 6). An additional emphasis is placed on the importance of talk, as Rose considers the 'prime skills of speaking and listening to be essential in their own right and crucial for learning to read, write, to be numerate and, indeed, to be successful in virtually all of the learning children undertake at school and elsewhere' (p. 6). A further recommendation from the IRPC is a restructuring of the curriculum into six 'areas of learning':

- Understanding the arts
- Understanding English, communication and languages
- Historical, geographical and social understanding
- Mathematical understanding
- Understanding physical development, health and well-being
- Scientific and technological understanding.

'The areas of learning capture the essential knowledge, key skills and understanding that children need to develop as they progress through their primary years' (QCDA 2010 p. 16).

The Cambridge Review

The Cambridge Primary Review (Alexander 2010), supported by the Esmee Fairbairn Trust, is based on extensive research undertaken between 2006 and 2009. This comprised an investigation into the views of the general public on primary education including suggested changes, as well as 31 research reports investigating 10 key themes. Chapter 14 focuses on the curriculum and Chapter 16 on assessment. The final report recommends a coherent statutory framework of aims, as a basis for developing non-statutory programmes of study encompassing 12 educational aims and eight domains of knowledge, skill, enquiry and disposition, which would occupy 70 per cent of curriculum time. In addition, the report suggests that 30 per cent of the overall framework and programmes of study should be locally proposed and non-statutory.

In 2010, the coalition government abolished the Qualifications and Curriculum Authority (QCA), which had advised on the implementation of the National Curriculum, and rejected the Rose Review in order to develop its own educational policies.

The way forward?

It is worth considering that the Rose Review and the Cambridge Review proposed a reorganisation of the curriculum into areas or domains rather than maintaining a separate subject-specific focus. Whatever the curriculum, especially given the current expectation that teachers and schools will be given more control of the curriculum, and acknowledging that change is likely to occur throughout a teacher's career, it is likely that schools and teachers will increasingly need to make decisions about how different curricular areas can be linked in meaningful ways.

There are many opinions on and rationales for this (Barnes 2007; Rowley and Cooper 2009). One suggestion might be some units of work 'blocked' and taught intensively over a short period of time, for example. Would there be an advantage in this? Another consideration could be the extent to which the local community and expert visitors could be utilised to enhance children's learning within a thematic curriculum. Some schools have worked with local archaeologists, for example, or with a local firm of architects, builders, the National Trust, theatre – even fashion designers – or with a children's writer, ballet dancer, artist, musician. What contribution can parents or grandparents make to a wider and more diverse curriculum? Even within the constraints of recent years, many schools have developed exciting curricular opportunities, so be brave and 'think outside the box'.

Applying your philosophy to mediate statutory requirements

Epistemology is the branch of philosophy concerned with different ways of knowing and considering what are the most valid ways of knowing. How can we get beyond our personal opinions to something we can feel has validity? Some things we know because they are based on reason. Other things we know from experience. We think we know how children learn based first on reason, on what we have learned from research and from the authoritative experience of others about learning. In addition, we have our empirical knowledge – what we observe about the children in our classrooms. We develop our personal educational philosophy based on a combination of what we learn from scholarly authorities and our personal experience. We may therefore find ourselves in agreement with the current prevailing ideology of education or at times find ourselves teaching in ways which we fundamentally believe to be misinformed. It is vital that we adopt the view presented by Pollard:

> Professional ideologies are always likely to remain strong among teachers – they represent commitments, ideals *and* interests. Reflective teachers should be open-minded enough to constructively critique their own beliefs, as well as those of others. (Pollard 2008 p. 94)

As Government education policy changes in response to what is believed to be necessary for future generations' learning needs and workforce requirements, so curricular change is necessary and ITE (Initial Teacher Education) changes to reflect this.

There is an ongoing tension related to the prioritisation of literacy and numeracy above other areas of the curriculum, with some teachers believing it is important for children's education to focus on core subjects and others believing that core skills can be taught contextually through other subjects.

Discussion at staff meeting

Amy: I prefer to teach my literacy skills when the children are learning other subjects so they have a context. So this week we are looking at the structure of newspaper reports and writing up our activities in groups to make a report for Year 2, to let them know about what happens in Year 3 when they come to visit.

Andrew: No, I prefer to teach the skills separately. How can you tell how much each child understands about the newspaper features? Once we have learned the skills in literacy, then we use them in history to write about the Ancient Egyptians.

Amy: If I do it that way, I don't feel I have enough time to give quality teaching to all the subjects. I find a more thematic approach works better for me.

Barbara: But how do you make sure you plan for all the individual needs? In my class, some children prefer the 'joined-up' thematic approach but others really seem to thrive when they can focus on one subject at a time. So I plan from knowing my children, their prior knowledge, and then what I am to teach is tailored to that. So sometimes I plan to teach in a theme, sometimes not.

This discussion explores some of the issues facing teachers today. *How* to teach areas of the curriculum can be dependent on teachers' own philosophical belief of how children learn or on school approaches to learning and ethos. Changes to the curriculum at national level will resonate with some teachers and not with others. Planning a successful learning experience then depends on the children, the teacher, the school and its community, all within the context of a wider curriculum.

Reflective task

Consider your initial observations of planning and assessment practices. How did the school organise the curriculum?

How did this fit with your own emerging professional philosophy of education?

As you progress through your training, revisit these questions in light of your developing knowledge and understanding.

What are the children going to learn or what am I going to teach?

Planning and assessment or assessment and planning – which comes first? There is no definitive answer. It is like the proverbial 'chicken and egg'. Many beginning teachers become involved in what they need to teach rather than focusing on what the children will learn. If governments define prescriptive and crowded curricula, teachers may be led to 'covering' the objectives, for example 'delivering the literacy objectives' rather than fostering a love of literature or focusing on 'facts' to be learned rather than the excitement of enquiry-based learning.

This leads us to consider *what is* knowledge?

Kinds of knowledge

Biggs (2003 pp. 41–3) gives a theoretical analysis of the kinds of knowing which can result from the need to 'get through the prescribed curriculum' and the kind of knowing which changes the way we tackle problems and look at life leading to learning which is deep and transformative:

- demonstrating what you know, without necessarily understanding it (declarative or propositional knowledge) – for example, rote learning, repeating times tables, delivering the curriculum, learning that 'area' is length times breadth
- using such knowledge to solve problems ('functioning knowledge') – for example, planning a class party, solving problems in maths or science, applying your formula for area in a context
- knowing what comes next in a sequence without understanding why (procedural knowledge) – for example, following through a series of lessons as outlined in a 'scheme' or unit as written, or knowing that after area comes teaching of volume
- using what you know in order to make informed judgements, which is by far the most important kind ('conditional knowledge') – for example, you know the area of carpet needed for your classroom, but now you consider the use of the room, the children and alternative solutions.

Reflective task

You may wish to refer to Chapter 2, if you have not already looked at it, to link this discussion with the aims of education and the political dimensions and to consider 'just what society's aims and values are'.

Planning for learning

Levels of planning

The statutory curriculum is mediated and interpreted at different levels through statutory curriculum and policies which are then translated into a whole-school curriculum plan and then further broken down into policies.

In addition, all schools have an individual ethos which is comprised of their philosophy and values and this is what makes every school different. When you walk in, you get the 'feel' of the school from the environment (displays, welcome, orderliness) and as a student you need to adapt to this as quickly as possible, although when you are a member of the teaching team you contribute to the ethos and to the development of the whole-school curriculum plan and policies.

Whole-school plan

Whatever the statutory content, schools must translate it into whole-school plans for their school. For example, looking at the National Curriculum requirement to teach 'significant people in British history' at Key Stage 1, teachers often taught about Florence Nightingale, Grace Darling or Mary Seacole, George Stephenson or Isambard Kingdom Brunel. What are the reasons for these decisions? Locality of the school is a consideration alongside available resources and the personal skills and knowledge of the teaching team. It is also possible to respond to the enthusiasms and interests of the children in your class, although this is more usually at lesson level than for longer-term planning.

Reflective task

Now consider your own knowledge – which famous British people do you feel you would like to teach the children in your class about? What else do you need to know other than the chosen person's story? Use relevant statutory requirements to devise a medium-term plan. You should include assessment opportunities and identify some strategies. Also consider how you may use this to teach thematically. How might a school come up with a long-term plan? What would it be based upon other than statutory requirements? Your answer should include contextual links, such as local geography or history.

The whole-school curriculum plan is developed from national requirements and the school ethos and priorities. This is usually organised in Key Stages/age phases and is often referred to as the 'long-term plan'. In this, you can observe the cyclical 'spiral' nature of the curriculum with subject areas being revisited throughout a child's time in school. Also, cross-curricular links or themes can be identified and the long-term plan ensures all areas of the curriculum are taught at appropriate times and in relevant detail across the age phases.

Long-term plan

A school long-term plan for Year 4 might look like this.

Year 4/ Curriculum area	Autumn 1	Autumn 2	Spring 1	Spring 2	Summer 1	Summer 2
Science	Moving and growing	Keeping warm	Solids, liquids and how they can be separated	Circuits and conductors	Friction	Habitats
History	Ancient Greeks	Ancient Greek ideas today			King Henry VIII and the Reformation	The lives of the rich and poor in Tudor times
Geography			A village in India (for whole term)			
ICT	Writing for different audiences	Developing images, repeated patterns	Collecting and presenting information		Modelling effects on screen	Branching databases
Art		Journeys	Take a seat		Viewpoints	
D and T	Storybooks			Torches		Light it up
Music	Play it again	Ongoing skills and Christmas	Class orchestra Ongoing skills		Dragon scales Ongoing skills	
PE	Dance Gym	Net/wall skills	Swimming and invasion games	Net/wall skills	Dance Gym	Striking/fielding games
RE	How and why do Hindus worship at home?	Celebrations/ Christmas journeys	Why is Easter important for Christians?	What is faith?	What religions are represented in our neighbourhood?	
MFL (French)	Portraits		Les Quatre Amis		Ça pousse!	On y va
PSE/YCDI ('You can do it' scheme)	Rights and responsibilities Circle time and YCDI	YCDI	Developing our environment Circle time and YCDI		Diversity YCDI	Differing perspectives (rainforest) YCDI

Figure 3.1   Example of a Year 4 subject-based approach to the curriculum

Reflective task

Some of the areas lend themselves to a cross-curricular approach and would be taught in this way. Examine Figure 3.2 to see which lessons you would teach using this approach.

   The children at this school were taught about electricity in Y2, Y4 and then again in Y6. This illustrates the spiral nature of the curriculum with subjects being revisited to 'build' on prior knowledge and allow for consolidation of learning through experience. After each unit of work has been taught, teachers would make a 'summative' assessment to ascertain the level of individual understanding. Formative assessment is used regularly to inform planning and support learning. We will return to this later.

Medium-term plan

To help deliver specific areas of the curriculum, the whole-school long-term plan is organised into medium-term plans which are targeted at specific year groups and often for specific half-term, theme or 'unit' periods. The long-term plan can be delivered in cross-curricular themes or subject-specific chunks or a mixture of the two as decided by the school management team to best meet the learning needs of the children. Barnes (2007 p. 184) states that 'a medium term plan should show the proposed relationship between key questions and attention to specific subject-based skills and knowledge. It must show progression towards a questioning stance and the development of ever-deeper understanding'. The medium-term plan (unit of work) should also show when assessment is to take place and begin to make clear the differentiation strategies to be used across the 'unit of work'. These should include a range of approaches to assessment to enable all learners to demonstrate their successful learning. We will discuss differentiation and assessment later in the chapter.

Weekly plans

Short-term plans are often called 'weekly plans'. From these, an individual lesson plan can be constructed. These are necessary to ensure that all areas of the curriculum are taught effectively and in adequate depth to enable children to learn. Although weekly plans are meant to outline specific activities and sessions throughout the week, they need to be flexible so that you can respond to changes, in order to extend children's learning. The different levels of mediation/interpretation at each level are shown in Figure 3.2.

Individual lesson plans

Each school will have a particular approach to the individual lesson plan with a preferred proforma. Your Initial Teacher Education provider may also have a recommended

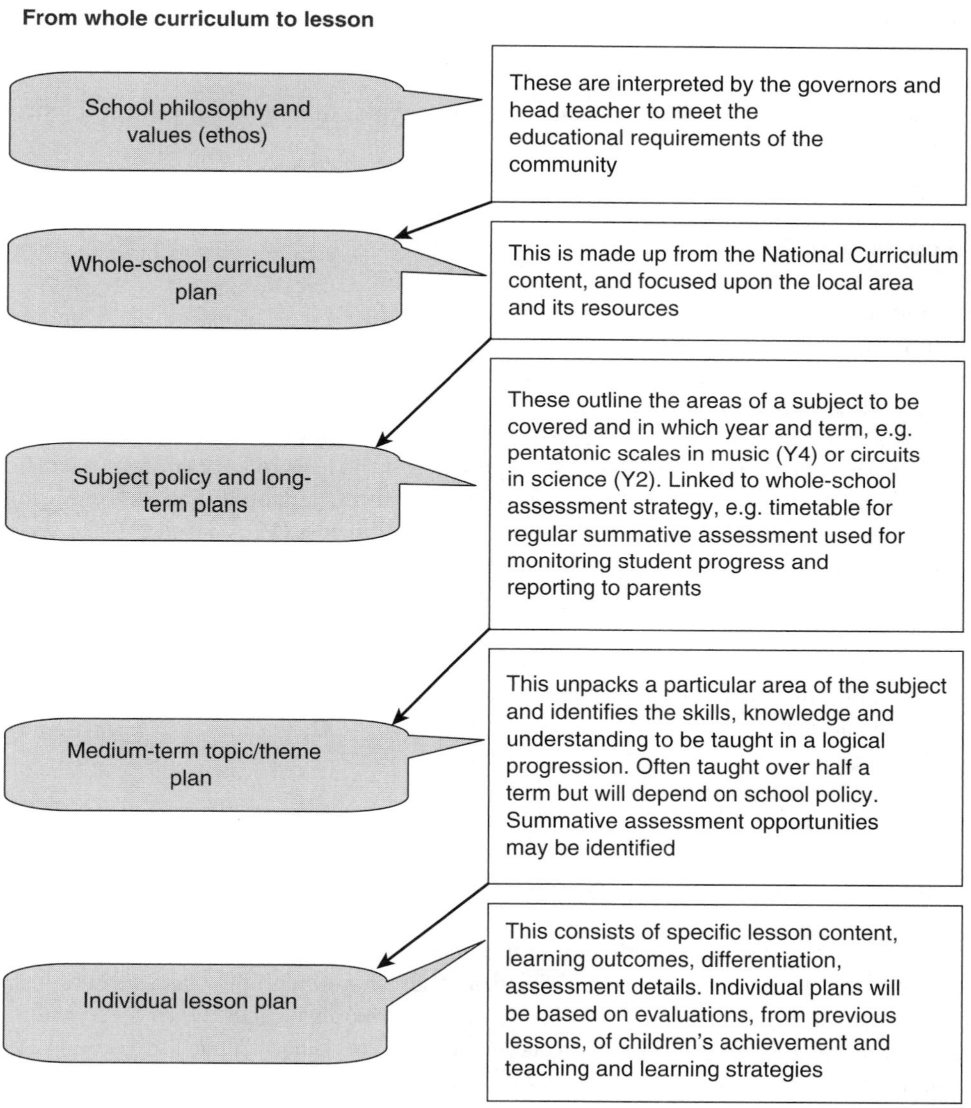

From whole curriculum to lesson

School philosophy and values (ethos)

These are interpreted by the governors and head teacher to meet the educational requirements of the community

Whole-school curriculum plan

This is made up from the National Curriculum content, and focused upon the local area and its resources

Subject policy and long-term plans

These outline the areas of a subject to be covered and in which year and term, e.g. pentatonic scales in music (Y4) or circuits in science (Y2). Linked to whole-school assessment strategy, e.g. timetable for regular summative assessment used for monitoring student progress and reporting to parents

Medium-term topic/theme plan

This unpacks a particular area of the subject and identifies the skills, knowledge and understanding to be taught in a logical progression. Often taught over half a term but will depend on school policy. Summative assessment opportunities may be identified

Individual lesson plan

This consists of specific lesson content, learning outcomes, differentiation, assessment details. Individual plans will be based on evaluations, from previous lessons, of children's achievement and teaching and learning strategies

Figure 3.2   Showing the different levels of planning and the stages at which teachers can interpret the statutory curriculum and policies to reflect the philosophy of the school and teachers

format. So rather than confuse you with a table to be completed, we thought it more important to identify the key elements which should be included on an individual lesson plan.

General information

- Year (e.g. 4)
- Class – number of students, plus may require gender numbers, i.e. male and female
- Teacher
- Time of lesson and duration.

Lesson-specific information

- Title of lesson (usually taken from medium-term plan)
- Intended Learning Outcomes
- Previous assessment information (if any is available)
- Current assessment opportunities and strategies
- Activities (these should be linked to the learning outcomes and the assessment – the more aligned with each other these are, the better the learning opportunities will be)
- Differentiation – this is generally into at least three attainment/ability levels and should include reference to any IEP (Individual Education Plan) strategies for specified children. However, some activities may be better differentiated by outcome
- Groupings – these may be based on partners, mixed ability or friendship or ability. There are good reasons for any of these groupings but it is essential to be clear about why you have chosen a particular grouping for a particular activity and to not keep the same groups all the time. Why?
- Key vocabulary
- Key questions
- Possible misconceptions
- Resources, including staff (other adults)
- Plenary or series of mini-plenaries, to correct misunderstandings, consolidate learning, or introduce next learning steps.

Teachers use the statutory curriculum and national strategies to devise ILOs (Intended Learning Outcomes) for each lesson. These are then shared with the class, sometimes in the form of 'We Are Learning To …' (WALT) or child-friendly notices. From these and the discussion that follows, 'Success Criteria', which may be called 'What I'm Looking For' (WILF), can be constructed. As each child is an individual then how they will learn and be able to demonstrate this learning may be evidenced differently. The ILO may be differentiated for differing groups of ability within the class, and consequently there will be a similar number of differentiated success criteria. Personalisation of approach to enable individualised learning is perhaps too idealistic a goal for every teacher in every lesson if it is the teacher who has the 'control' and determines what is learned. However, through self-determination and personalisation of the success criteria, children can be encouraged to be involved in the lesson outcomes. This does come with a caveat though. Whilst children perceived to be 'gifted and talented' and those confident in the curriculum area in question may relish this 'challenge', there may be some children whose self-esteem is too poor for them to believe they can achieve in any way. Giving this group of children the opportunity to set realistic, attainable yet high standards may take some encouragement and support until they become comfortable and confident in this area. Good planning based on prior knowledge (from assessment) will ensure allocation of the correct resources (including staff) to support the children in their early steps until they become more confident in this approach. A useful approach may be through adding a context to the lesson by presenting a 'This Is Because ...' (TIBS) aspect to help children understand how the knowledge and/or skills they have learned in the lesson may be of wider use.

Homework

A further area for consideration is the planning of homework. Many primary schools expect children to at least undertake reading, literacy and/or mathematics tasks at home. The amount increases with age, and the frequency is variable although weekly spelling homework and daily reading are still fairly common. Some teachers and many parents believe that homework is a useful extension to the school day and if parents are supportive then this may well be the case. However, 'obstacles such as limited space, insufficient backup from adults, and limited access to computers, have led some to query the government's belief that homework can raise attainment and narrow the achievement gap' (Alexander 2010 pp. 83–4).

Thought needs to be given to the content of the homework. Is it to be carried out independently by the child, or with the support of their parents or carers? Do they have the support of parents and carers and the necessary equipment at home to be able to complete the homework successfully?

When work is returned, judgements need to be made about how much the child has understood independently and how much they may have been supported. For this reason, it is important to have additional evidence of learning by the child before conclusions are reached about their understanding and achievement.

Differentiation

Planning should include 'differentiation'. This is the term used to explain what happens when the teaching and learning are specifically targeted and made different, to meet the needs of all children within the class. This will include varied aspects of education: learning, social, emotional and any physical needs. In any classroom of children, there will be a range of abilities – whether this is linked with understanding of concepts, skill levels or factual knowledge. For example, there are children for whom English is an Additional Language (EAL), and these who have physical, social or emotional barriers to learning. Because of this expected range of abilities (for want of better terminology), which may well alter for individual children across the curriculum, teachers should aim to plan specifically to support children to succeed at the differentiated levels.

In addition to this, there are children who require a more individualised approach to their learning, which may involve an Individual Education Plan to meet their specific needs.

Children who need help in addition to classroom differentiation are identified as needing support at School Action (SA) level. The school will allocate staffing and resources to support the child in their development and learning.

Teachers will need to use their thorough understanding of whichever statutory curriculum requirements apply and its underlying principles with regard to inclusion *and* their knowledge of the strengths and needs of the individual child to plan with a flexible approach. This approach will in no way involve reduced expectations of achievement, rather a personalised approach with each child achieving appropriately.

Reflective task

Consider a class of children you have worked with at some point of your Initial Teacher Education so far. Can you identify a spread of abilities? What strategies did you and the class teacher use to remove any barriers to learning and help all children to achieve? How were these identified in your planning?

Strategies you may have noticed could include grouping (classroom organisation), support, outcome, task or resource. If so, make notes about how well you feel these worked for the child, the teacher, other children.

Logically, as planning involves many aspects to ensure inclusion and achievement by all, assessment must also be varied and differentiated in approach to allow all children to demonstrate their strengths. As Wearmouth puts it, 'students' sense of themselves as having the potential to be effective in the community of practice of learners may be constructed and/or constrained by the forms of assessment that are used with them' (2009 p. 93).

Overview of planning process

Long term planning

A long term plan must show how progression is planned for across the Key Stage and across Key Stages, by breaking down progression into yearly plans, in ways which reflect both national requirements and the school's vision.

Medium term planning

A medium term plan sequences units of study in ways which reflect the long term plan, based on what pupils have learned, irrespective of year group. Learning objectives must be differentiated and include both content and process. It should outline related activities the pupils in your class will engage with, the resources to support them and the teaching approaches you will use. Assessment opportunities should be shown, in line with the school policy and again teaching and learning should reflect both national requirements and the vision of the school.

Short term planning (lesson plans)

Lesson plans are derived from the medium term plans. Each plan should have clear learning objectives, and lessons should be sequenced, each building on the previous lesson. Each lesson plan should identify teaching approaches which will interest and engage the pupils, key vocabulary which must be made explicit and assessment opportunities, whether questioning, observation, product, peer or self-assessment. They should state how learning might be taken beyond the classroom, to consolidate or extend learning and say how the lesson will be reflected upon in order to inform the next lesson. Again lesson plans must reflect the vision for your school.

Lesson evaluations

These should focus first on the learning and then on the teaching, leading to an end product which informs the next planned teaching. A further area to consider is children's attitudes to, and enjoyment of, the learning. These are professional judgements which will support both teacher knowledge of an individual child and inform future planning decisions.

 Case study

An example of this is a surprise event which helps you rethink your teaching strategy. In a music lesson with a Year 4 class of 20 boys and 9 girls, the children were listening to Saint-Saëns' *The Carnival of the Animals*, identifying how the musical elements combined to create the effect and help us relate this to particular animals. The children used language to describe how the music represented the animals, and described the mental images the music evoked. Part way through the lesson, the 'surprise' happened, as a group of boys asked if they could dance to illustrate the movement of the animals in addition to describing the musical elements which contributed. The assumptions this teacher made when planning had not included the boys wishing to dance. The children's desire to respond in this way impacted on future planning to include more opportunities for dance.

An evaluation of each lesson taught will support the teacher's knowledge through identifying children who have achieved the ILOs, those children who have achieved more than expected and those who have yet to fully achieve the ILOs, along with any children who have misconceptions which will need to be addressed. Teachers will also evaluate how children responded to the teaching strategies used and which learning strategies children relied upon. Resources, learning environment and classroom management are also areas for consideration due to the impact they have on a lesson. It is important also to obtain feedback on your teaching from the children, for example with young children through drawing or role play, by consulting a focus group of children you perceive to be having problems, or by pupils commenting on an aspect of their learning through analysing video of a lesson.

Purposeful lesson evaluations and record keeping are useful tools to aid memory and impact upon future planning. Therefore they need to be 'user-friendly'. In most situations, making annotations on the planning sheet is an acceptable form of record keeping for day-to-day evaluation. This should be clear and specific to aid planning for the next appropriate lesson.

Teachers and schools have differing methods for recording children's achievement through records of progress and attainment; it is usually the medium-term end of unit summative assessments which go to build up this record.

Reflective task

When next on placement, ask your school for a copy of the long-term plan and a subject-specific or themed medium-term plan and then try to see how an individual lesson you have observed (or taught) fits into the big picture. Evaluate the lesson to identify the strategies needed to teach the next lesson to the same class. Which misconceptions need to be corrected? What will the gifted and talented children learn? How will you differentiate appropriately?

The relationship between planning and assessment

Assessment contributes to and derives from effective planning. Any activities planned for children should be assessed either formally or informally in order to support and extend children's learning. There are several different types of assessment and each one has its advantages and disadvantages. One issue to consider is who the assessment is for and this will inform the type of assessment chosen.

Is the assessment for:

- the children, to inform their future learning? Comments need to be age-appropriate and shared in a format that the children can understand, for example annotating their work, verbal feedback.

- parents, to let them know how their children are doing. This will probably be in the form of a written report but could also be verbally when appropriate. There is a legal requirement for an annual written report for parents but many schools supply more. Parent evenings or open days are a good opportunity for verbal reporting.
- yourself, the class teacher, to inform your future planning, to inform reporting to parents, to identify specific difficulties in individual children, to support SEN provision. This could take a variety of formats although most schools have an assessment policy that will stipulate the minimum requirements expected and also outline strategies for best practice. You may want to support this by developing your own individual records in an indexed file of some description.
- the school, to meet the requirements of the School Improvement Plan (SIP) and School Development Plan. Until recent government changes, this may also have included the SEF (Self Evaluation Form).
- government agencies, for statistical information, for example Statutory Assessment Tasks.

Summative assessment

Assessment at the end of a theme, topic or unit of work is generally summative, giving an indication of how much the child has learned through studying that area. This form of quantitative data can be used to produce evidence that children have been working at a particular level or can help to identify individual or group difficulties within the class. Records could include tick sheets linked to learning objectives, multiple-choice tests or grouping children according to guiding statements. For example: some children/most children/a few children will .... and highlighting children's names.

For children in the Early Years Foundation Stage, summative assessment has been in the form of the Early Learning Goals, which is a set of criteria to be reached by the end of the Foundation Stage of schooling. The record for each child is kept in the Foundation Stage Profile.

Summative assessment through standard assessment tasks

Recently, national summative assessments (Standard Assessment Tasks, SATs) have taken place at the end of Key Stages 1 and 2. They have been teacher marked at KS1, while the KS2 SATs have been externally marked. The results (products), reported to schools, Local Authorities and parents, formed the contentious league tables. There is a level of accountability through this process although many children, parents and teachers feel an unnecessary degree of 'stress'. There is a body of opinion that believes that 'teaching to the test' limits validity in the actual accreditation of knowledge, skills and understanding attained. Many secondary schools throughout England carry out further testing for Year 7 children which they claim gives a more accurate understanding of the children's ability than the SATs.

The SATs are currently limited to the curricular areas of Literacy and Numeracy, and Alexander (2010 p. 498) believes that:

> While the assessment of literacy and numeracy is essential, a broader, more innovative approach to summative assessment is needed if children's achievements and attainments across the curriculum are to be properly recognised and parents, teachers and children themselves are to have the vital information they need to guide subsequent decisions and choices.

Arguments against national standardised assessments include the view that they can be interpreted to identify weak or ineffective teaching rather than supporting children's learning. There is a further limitation associated with externally marked summative assessment in that they are dependent upon pencil and paper methods of assessing which therefore focus on a child's literacy ability rather than being a true reflection of the child's ability in the subject under test. The questions that can be asked in this form of testing and external marking may lead to narrow answers limited to factual knowledge or short answers which need a good examination technique to complete well.

Other criticisms suggest that testing on a particular day can disadvantage children who are ill or have had some sort of upset that affected their performance at a specific time. In this case, formative assessment is essential in order to develop an overview of each child over a longer period of time. Perhaps one solution is to make several wider-stroke summative assessments across the broad curriculum, at the end of a topic or unit of study, either as a result of cumulative formative assessments or by assessing a product resulting from the topic or unit. This could be by making a summative statement about a book or file of work on the topic, a piece of drama which has drawn on what is learned in a history topic, a series of art works using different techniques, a musical composition resulting from a sequence of lessons. A further consideration when assessing is how a teacher can assess a child's enjoyment or attitude to a piece of art or music, dance or drama. It is possible through observation and discussion to understand how much a child is enjoying and their attitude to it; self or peer evaluations of work by children can also give an insight. This is an area where formative assessment is a valuable source of information.

Formative assessment

Formative or ongoing assessment provides a broad overview of a child's achievement over a period of time. It generally focuses on the whole child and includes both academic and pastoral aspects, enabling teachers to identify children's personal interests and ways of learning. Recording methods include observation, questioning, pieces of work, self-assessment or a combination of these.

Questioning

Questioning from the teacher can be 'open' where the pupil can give explanation and detail in the answer or 'closed' when the expected response is generally limited to factual knowledge and is correct or incorrect. Questions can be targeted towards specific children or groups during a lesson for the teacher to assess ongoing understanding and engagement, or can be used at the start or end of a lesson to review learning and check for misconceptions. There is a further level of questioning which needs flexibility in planning and this involves 'enquiry-based learning' with questions generated by children. Often they will suggest areas for research or discovery, or ask questions for clarification when they are motivated and engaged in the tasks at hand. This may originate with something they have learned during the lesson or outside school. It can be difficult to assess imagination and enquiry, yet these are key skills within society and should be encouraged. Good subject knowledge is essential to support learning. However often children do not need to be told the answer to their questions, they need to be taught how to find the answer and how to weigh the validity of the answers they have found.

Transference of skills, knowledge, understanding and personal development

Teachers need to engage in ongoing formative assessment to allow and encourage transference of knowledge and skills and to continue children's development of skills, knowledge and understanding. For example, children collaborating in a music activity not only learn about music – they are also learning to collaborate and are developing social skills. These skills are generic and transferable into other areas of the curriculum and crucial to their future success as adults. So teachers need to be aware of the attainment of each child not only in skills, knowledge and understanding across the curriculum domains but also in relation to their personal development. This will enable best practice when planning as a holistic approach to each child's strengths and areas for development will help promote a more cohesive classroom environment, thus further promoting learning and enabling children to reach their potential.

Evidence to inform and support judgements

A further consideration is the need for 'evidence' in assessment to support the teacher's judgements and to show any interested parties how these were arrived at. To balance this with fair and varied assessment methods which promote learning is a significant skill. Assessment methods for formative assessment use can include: observations, questioning, peer or self-assessment against known criteria, discussion, poster creation, concept maps (some are more appropriate at different ages). But, significantly, it is the feedback that is received that helps children know what they need to do next; this needs active engagement by the child in their own learning.

Feedback and Assessment for Learning

Black and Wiliam's (1998) research into assessment led to the development of 'Assessment for Learning' (AfL), sometimes called formative assessment. Figure 3.3 shows the key principles of AfL.

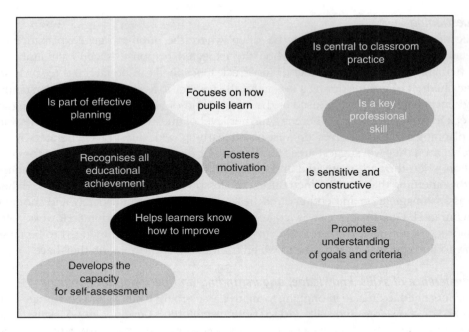

Figure 3.3　Assessment for Learning principles

For further information, please see www.ttrb.ac.uk/ViewArticle2.aspx?ContentId=15313

Black and Wiliam found that the use of strategies including sustained and relevant feed-back, and peer and self-assessment for the pupils improved the learning of the pupils involved. The use of feedback should be separate from grades or levels and lead to developing independent learning strategies for the children. However, there is some concern over how effective this has been in the classroom.

Platforms for children to use self-assessment could include:

- whole-class discussions
- one-to-one reviews
- paired comments
- choosing a question to respond to
- writing/responding at the end of a piece of work
- pupils doing first marking
- writing self-evaluative logs and journals.

Criticisms of this approach could include issues related to time management for the teacher and pupils and a need for it to be embedded as a whole-school approach. There may be subjective views of attainment and variety in teachers' professional judgements. How do children 'know' what the next necessary step is to accurately set their own targets? The Department for Education and Skills' National Strategy documentation (2004b) promotes the use of AfL in schools but also includes grades. This can lead children to focus on the grade/result and then not use the improvement suggestions to their best advantage. This is an example of a focus on the product of learning rather than the process of learning.

As we improve our understanding of how learning happens through research, literature and professional dialogues, for example, how we teach to facilitate that learning also changes. Black and Wiliam's (1998) work shows that AfL works best when children begin to self-assess efficiently and engagement with learning increases. This could be considered to be as a result of a deconstruction of the 'mystique' surrounding teaching, and a laying open or more transparent consideration of the skills. Children no longer simply 'receive knowledge' in the form of facts to be memorised from the teachers as in Victorian schooling and rote methods. Skills are not taught only as though one method is correct, for example in handwriting, or in strategies in mathematics.

The planning, teaching and assessment cycle

Regardless of the assessment strategy adopted by schools, a clear connection between planning, teaching, assessment and recording is essential in order to effectively manage and extend children's learning. Figure 3.4 outlines the planning, teaching and

Assessment cycle

Evaluation of prior achievement

Short-term planning
Making learning objectives specific and concise, related to previous attainment

Evaluation of how specific children in the class learn

Recording evidence of pupil's attainment
Some outcomes from assessment briefly recorded on short-term plan and used to inform next lesson

Planning, teaching and assessment cycle

Activities
Relate directly to objectives and are differentiated to suit different abilities

Assessment
Opportunities are built into the lesson using a range of strategies to assess a group of pupils or an individual child e.g. discussion, observation, marking, self-assessment, testing

Evaluation of achievement

Evaluation of engagement, attitude, misconceptions

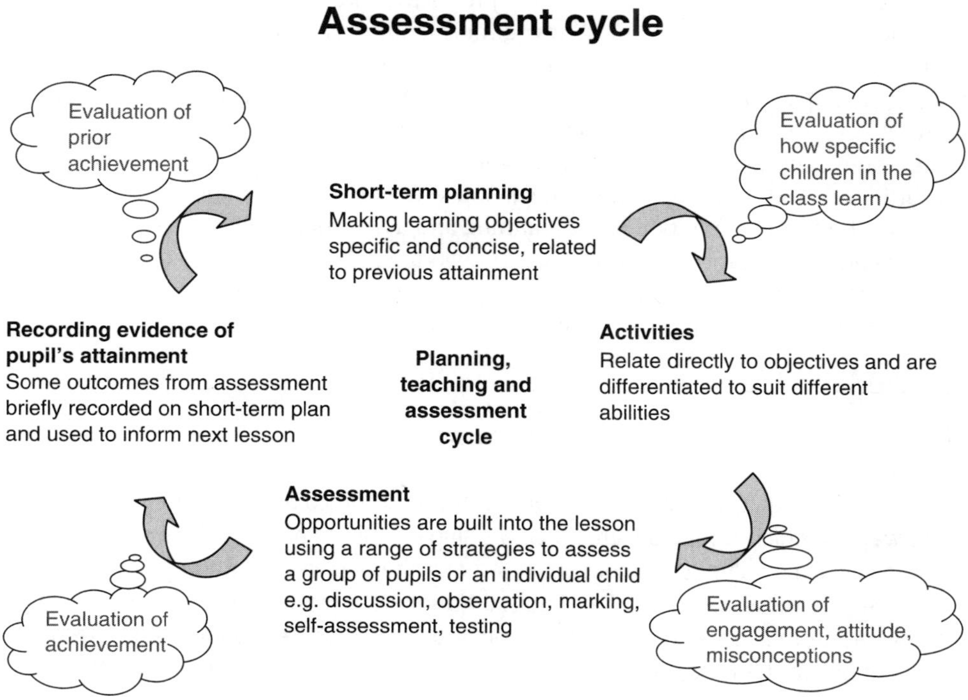

Figure 3.4   Showing the assessment cycle, with an explanation of how the key parts of the planned lesson fit together

assessment cycle at the heart of effective teaching. Good planning for children's individual needs is dependent on knowing 'where they are' so that challenge can be incorporated into activities alongside appropriate scaffolding. Therefore, accurate and detailed assessment and recording is a key element of good teaching in order to identify next steps in learning, misconceptions to be addressed and effective differentiation.

Formative assessment throughout each lesson

Ongoing evaluation of the learning *throughout a lesson* is vital. The use of questioning and observation to collate an accurate picture of children's (or a child's) depth of understanding related to the learning outcomes will be needed to inform your teaching. This could be through adding a mini-plenary to redirect or extend the class's learning, through specific questioning or teaching to correct a misconception, through adding a resource to support learning, to name a few actions you may need to take. Good lesson planning based on accurate assessment and evaluations, coupled with secure subject knowledge, is necessary to facilitate effective learning. They allow the teacher to be flexible in response to the needs of the children and to have confidence in a range of teaching strategies that are best suited to the group of children being taught.

One of the difficulties in writing this chapter is the integrated nature of planning and assessment. We have tried to show how good planning is based on meaningful assessment and that accurate assessment comes through good planning. To avoid confusion, we have perhaps reinforced the separation of the two areas in your mind although we believe assessment and planning to be intricately linked.

The complexity of planning and assessment practice is linked to the discussion we had earlier on kinds of knowledge. You can know the facts of what and how to do it, you can know the sequence but effective planning and assessment will only come when you have reached the point of 'conditional knowledge', allowing you to make informed judgements. The following chapter will show the importance of classroom organisation and the learning environment in promoting children's learning.

Summary

This chapter began with an overview of the statutory curriculum, then discussed different ways in which it may be structured, as single subjects or through cross-curricular approaches, the value judgements involved and the impact of changing government priorities on these decisions. The English National Curriculum was compared with curricula in other developed countries and with proposed developments, the recommendations of the Rose Review (DfE 2008) and the Cambridge Review (2010).

A consideration followed of the many decisions which teachers must make in order to mediate national requirements, at the levels of long term, whole school planning, medium term planning, daily planning and lesson planning. The importance of integrating planning and assessment at all levels, through a cyclical process, was explained and different types, methods and purposes of assessment were discussed. Methods of differentiation and the importance of embedding these in planning and assessment were explained. Finally, the process of needing to reflect, on both the teacher's teaching and pupils' learning was explained, in order that both may be taken forward.

Questions for discussion

1 What are the key points to remember when planning a successful lesson? Make your own list of everything you consider to be 'key', then prioritise this and assign a number (1–5) to each of your five most significant factors, 1 being most important. Talk with a peer and consider your decisions – do you have the same priorities? Discuss this with a larger group of your peers. Why are there differences or similarities?
2 We asked you to consider your own philosophy of learning and teaching and how this may impact upon your planning. Now consider how this will impact on your assessment methods. Discuss it with your colleagues.
3 How does the creativity agenda fit with planning and assessment? How can you be creative in a subject-based curriculum? Is teaching in this way more or less 'creative' than teaching through themes?

Further reading

Alexander, R. (ed.) (2010) *Children, their World, their Education: Final Report and Recommendations of the Cambridge Primary Review*. London: Routledge.
Chapter 16 gives a thorough overview of assessment practices in primary schools. Pages 83–4 highlight some of the complexities involved in the homework debate.

Goodhew, G. (2005) *Meeting the Needs of Gifted and Talented Students*. London: Network Continuum.
For ITE generalist students and educators, it is a useful resource to focus on an aspect of inclusive practice termed 'a bit of a Cinderella' by Goodhew in the introduction. From

the necessary discussion relating to the difficulty in coming to a definitive definition of the terms 'gifted', 'talented' and 'exceptionally able', Goodhew uses a variety of sources to develop shared understanding for the purpose of the book, examining a variety of perspectives. Perhaps the most relevant chapter in relation to planning and assessment is Chapter 4 which discusses classroom practices.

Jacques, K. and Hyland, R. (2007) *Professional Studies: Primary and Early Years*, 3rd edn. Exeter: Learning Matters.

Many chapters of this accessible book will support and extend your developing understanding of planning and assessment practices, especially Chapters 2–4 and 14.

References

Alexander, R. (ed.) (2010) *Children, their World, their Education: Final Report and Recommendations of the Cambridge Primary Review*. London: Routledge.

Barnes, J. (2007) *Cross-Curricular Learning 3–14*. London: Sage.

Biggs, J.B. (2003) *Teaching for Quality Learning at University: What the Student Does*. Society for Research into Higher Education, Buckingham: SHRE and Open University Press.

Black, P.J. and Wiliam, D. (1998) *Inside the Black Box*. King's College London School of Education.

DfE (2008) *Independent Review of the Primary Curriculum: Interim Report*. London: DfE.

DfES (2003) *Excellence and Enjoyment: A Strategy for Primary Schools*. London: DfES.

DfES (2004a) *Removing Barriers to Achievement: The Government's Strategy for Special Educational Needs*. London: DfES.

DfES (2004b) *The Primary National Strategy*. London: DfES.

Pollard, A. (2008) *Reflective Teaching*, 3rd edn. London: Continuum.

QCDA (2010) *The National Primary Curriculum Handbook*. Great Britain: QCDA.

Rowley, C. and Cooper, H. (eds) (2009) *Cross-Curricular Approaches to Teaching and Learning*. London: Sage.

Wearmouth, J. (2009) *A Beginning Teacher's Guide to Special Educational Needs*. Maidenhead: Open University Press.

Websites

http://webspace.ship.edu/cgboer/epist.html (accessed 12 July 2010)

www.ttrb.ac.uk/ViewArticle2.aspx?ContentId=15313 (accessed 12 July 2010)

National Centre for Excellence in the Teaching of Mathematics: www.ncetm.org.uk/resources/21510

CHAPTER 4

CLASSROOM ORGANISATION AND THE LEARNING ENVIRONMENT

Jan Ashbridge and Jo Josephidou

By the end of this chapter, you should be able to:

- discuss the key factors to consider when providing for an appropriate learning environment

- consider how theory and research impact on how the learning environment is designed

- reflect critically on learning environments you have observed on placement and question assumed practice

- examine how your own values and attitudes as a teacher can impact on the learning environment and the children's learning.

Introduction

In this chapter, we discuss a classroom scenario in order to explore the reasons why learning environments are complex, significant and shaped by a teacher's personal educational philosophy. Constructivist learning theories are drawn on to suggest starting points for creating effective learning environments which promote independence, social skills, self-esteem, positive attitudes to learning and give children a sense of ownership of their environment.

Different perceptions of the learning environment

The authors felt the best way to approach this was by giving you an insight into how the learning environment could be perceived by a child and by a teacher.

The child's voice

'It's in-time!'

Whistle goes and it's time to go into school but first I need to line up. If I'm really quick then I can get to the front. I make it in time but then Sally pushes ahead of me and stands on my toe. I dig her in the ribs with my elbow just as Mrs Jones is coming around the corner to collect us. Oh no, trouble again before I've even got into the classroom. I hate hanging my coat up because everyone pushes and the coat pegs are too near together. I get trampled on so I try to hang back until everyone one else comes back. Trouble again, I'm late.

'It's register time!'

I sit on the carpet quickly but then I realise that my name has been put on the amber traffic light and I'm really worried. Am I going to miss playtime? If I sit really still and listen Mrs Jones will put my name back on green but then I feel the cold, hard floor digging into my bottom and I realise that the Velcro on my left shoe has stuck to the carpet. I'm concentrating so hard on sitting still so the Velcro doesn't make a noise that I miss my name being called and I'm in trouble again.

'It's handwriting time'

Once register is finished it's handwriting time. I'm on the Yellow table. Books are ready in the middle of the table and the pencils are sharpened in the yellow pot. I try to get comfortable on my chair because I know I am not allowed to get up until the big hand is on the 6. Oh no, I should have gone for a wee when I was hanging my coat up. I know I have to look at the handwriting display and practise the letters on the yellow balloon. My teacher calls it being in-de-pen-dent. Red group have to practise the letters on the red balloon. Mrs Smith always comes to help Yellow table but she calls the letters differ-ent names to Mrs Jones and I get a bit confused. Rosemary gets a sticker because she is holding her pencil beautifully. Sometimes, near the holidays, we are allowed to play in the role-play area and with the sand and water. The holidays seem a long way off.

The teacher's voice

'Going into class'

The bell is about to go. Time to go and get the children in from the playground. You'd think by Year 2 they could make a straight line. Look at Sally, she's always at the front standing so smartly, having the maturity to ignore the little boy behind her who's trying to push in front. I'm so glad we line them up, it makes it so much easier. I have worked very hard on training the children to make them independent and most of them manage to sort themselves out quickly and come back to the classroom to sit quietly on the carpet. They know my expectations.

'Taking the register'

Simon is back 3 minutes after everyone else. I won't tell him off because I don't want to lower his self-esteem but I quietly get up and move his name from the green traffic light to the amber. The children sit beautifully for register and show really good listening. Everyone sitting still, all eyes towards me. I don't have to remind them, I just have to point to the good listening checklist on the wall.

'Handwriting practice'

It's good to start the morning off with handwriting because they can all get on with it quietly whilst I hear readers. To make sure they can be independent I have prepared all the resources and put them out ready on the table for the children. The activity is care-fully differentiated and all children know what level they are working at. My colour coding system works a treat. I have directed Mrs Smith to Yellow table today as they need an extra bit of input. Those who finish quickly will get 15 minutes to choose a free activity.

Reflective task

Read the above scenarios and note down the key themes and issues where mis-matches in perceptions are apparent:

- What has the environment taught the child?
- What does the teacher believe the environment is teaching the child?
- How does the environment do this?

The importance of the learning environment

The learning environment is a complex and ever-changing place. It is a physical area with resources and furniture and has to fit in children and adults comfortably. It is an emotional environment too, where people form relationships, learn rules and develop attitudes, beliefs and values relating to themselves, each other and the world they live in. It is a place where children learn not only the curriculum but begin to understand their strengths, weaknesses and how they measure up to the others around them. Boundaries are set and particular behaviours are expected. It is not only where children learn but where children learn to learn. It is vital then to give much consideration to the way that it looks, feels and operates from a range of perspectives.

Organising the learning environment

The learning environment of the classroom is first and foremost a place where effective learning needs to take place. A key characteristic of this is where clear aims are agreed and teaching is purposeful. Theories of cognitive development tell us that for children to learn effectively they need to be actively involved in their learning: creating and constructing new knowledge in ways that are meaningful to them. It stands to reason, therefore, that the environment in which they are to do this must reflect their ways of learning and their individual needs. It must allow them to develop the skills they need to become independent learners and also to interact with the environment and resources as well as with each other in ways that make constructing knowledge purposeful and motivating. In order for this to happen, children need to be seen as central to the learning process not only in planning but also in the creation, organisation and management of the learning environment.

The scenario

Let us take the scenario above and consider what the teacher was trying to achieve. She is aiming to make the children in her class as independent as possible. She has done this through ensuring that the children know what is expected of them, ensuring that all necessary resources are easily accessible and that carefully differentiated work is provided along with additional adult support for those who may need it. The children are able to complete the activity with the minimum of fuss and noise. She aims to make them aware that their behaviour affects others and that they should respect the right of those others to be able to get on quietly. The clear ability grouping and the associated classroom display support this. She has set the environment up to enable the children to be able to learn by themselves.

Constructivist theories, classroom organisation and the learning environment

Exploration and stimulating experiences

What do theories of cognitive development have to tell us about the learning environment and how can they shed light on what happens in the scenario above? If we take the work of Piaget, we can see that his influential ideas about children needing developmentally appropriate activities are reflected in many classrooms, especially in Foundation Stage and Key Stage 1, although the same principles, differently interpreted, apply in any primary classroom. Piaget believed that the environment and children's interactions with it and within it are the key to children's learning and it is through engagement and exploration of real, concrete experiences that they are able to learn and develop. Piaget felt it was important for children to have stimulating activities, opportunities for symbolic play and an environment to actively explore (Daly et al. 2006). We can see that despite the teacher's good intentions, these opportunities are not offered and perhaps the learning needs of the children are not being met.

Social interaction and talk

Vygotsky focused more on the role of the adult in guiding children's learning. He also saw how important social interactions and language were to children's intellectual development. His work has influenced teachers and encouraged them to provide children with a challenging environment and activities. They also provide opportunities to work alongside adults and more knowledgeable others, including peers, to extend their understanding within the 'zone of proximal development'. More recent research has also stressed the importance of children developing effective communication skills with a broad cross-curricular vocabulary. This ability to articulate their thoughts helps them to make links in their learning and therefore their thinking (Daly et al. 2006).

Planning for exploration and talk

In the situation described above, although the children are grouped together, social interaction between the group or between groups is not encouraged; nor does the task given to the children encourage constructive talk. The way that teachers organise the physical environment (tables, chairs, etc.) sends out messages to the children about what kind of activities they are likely to be engaged in. Where children are all sitting looking at the front, they expect that the teacher will be talking to them and that they will be expected to focus their attention there and that any activity will probably be of an individual nature. When children are sitting around a table together, it appears that a more social and collaborative way of learning is expected and children will interact. It appears in the example above that there is a mismatch between the organisation of the classroom and the task given to the children. Social grouping is a valuable tool for teachers in supporting learning but it is very often used simply for convenience as a seating arrangement (Moyles 1992 p. 18). Conflicting messages such as this can be avoided by keeping the environment flexible and making the organisation match the task.

Effective adult interventions

In our scenario, the children on the Yellow table have access to a teaching assistant. She is available to scaffold the children's learning, helping them to achieve with support what they could not do unaided. This idea, first introduced by Wood, et al. (1976), requires the adult to match their interventions to the needs of the individual child and decide what sort of support is necessary (Doherty and Hughes 2009 p. 270).

Effective groupings

Vygotsky's model of social constructivism could perhaps best be played out where children were seated in mixed ability groups. This provides opportunities for 'less able' children to work within their zone of proximal development having input from a more knowledgeable other. 'More able' children who take on this role of more knowledgeable other can, therefore, both consolidate and articulate their learning. Gnadinger (2008) demonstrates in her research that peer collaboration is an effective learning strategy for children. In addition, other research has shown that higher achieving children who work in ability groups actually have their potential limited rather than enhanced, as they 'develop a crystallized view of their ability which may lead them to avoid challenges which are necessary for effective learning' (Dweck and Legget 1988 cited in MacIntyre and Ireson 2002 p. 250).

Moving around

All that we know about children's cognitive development tells us that active learning and problem-solving approaches can be beneficial. They enable children to engage with their learning in individual ways depending on their preferred way of learning and thinking. Active learning involves problem solving and this requires children to move around, talk, collaborate and gather resources. Any environment for learning needs to facilitate these approaches and teachers need to be sure they know the children well enough to be able to anticipate these needs and reflect them in the organisation of the classroom.

Reflective task

Consider the information above and your own experiences of classroom environments. What do you think a classroom for children of a given age needs to look like, in order to support children's learning as described? How might your use of the learning environment be reflected in your planning?

Encouraging independence and autonomy in the learning environment

Return to the scenario

Classroom layout and organisation

Let us return to the scenario. Consider for a moment what messages the classroom layout and organisation is giving to the child:

- How does he think that the class teacher wants him to use the environment?
- How does he think that the teacher views learning?
- How independently is he able to think and learn in this environment?
- What skills is he learning?
- What do you think the teacher's priority was for his learning?

Classroom organisation reflects your educational philosophy

Waterson (2003) claims that the classroom needs to reflect the way in which an individual teacher intends to organise and teach the children. It sends messages to the children about how they are going to learn and what their part in that learning is likely to be.

Much of what happens in primary classrooms is directed through print in the form of worksheets, over-reliance on schemes and lots of written recording. These are quite individual acts which do not necessarily develop children's critical thinking skills or their creativity – skills that are required if children are going to become independent and autonomous learners (Bowles and Gintis 1976). If we as teachers have abandoned the notion of the child as a 'tabula rasa' or 'empty vessel' (Kehily 2010 p. 5) onto which we transmit relevant knowledge, then surely as class teachers we should be encouraging those skills which enable the children to think for themselves and therefore to take some control over their own learning.

How much better it is not only to teach children, but also to ensure that our learning environment encourages the consolidation of skills such as 'information processing, reasoning, enquiry, creative thinking, [and] evaluation' (DfEE 2000 p. 22). We want to plan for and provide as many opportunities as possible for children to develop skills of metacognition, the ability to think about thinking (Goswami 2008 p. 295). If the children's learning is determined by how much we as teachers allow them to learn, then how limited will their learning be?

Encouraging independence

What do children actually need in order for them to become independent learners? The authors would argue that a good place for teachers to start is by overtly giving children the permission to learn in this way. Even so, the skills required for independent learning do not develop by themselves and need the teacher to provide structure and support.

Children need to be clear about what they are learning and how they are able to engage with this learning. If aims and objectives are shared clearly and reinforced through displays and resources, ambiguity is avoided and children are then able to focus on the task in hand. Teachers' own beliefs and attitudes about learning are thrown into stark relief at this point. As Alexander (1992) points out, 'notwithstanding the classroom layout and organisation, they are but the framework within which the acts and interactions central to teaching and learning take place' (Moyles 1992 p. 11). The objectives that teachers choose, the way they are shared and the ways that teachers expect that learning to be carried out, will influence the ability of the children to work in independent and autonomous ways just as much as the physical environment.

Teachers who believe that knowledge is a 'public discipline' (Kendall-Seatter 2005 p. 97) will create a classroom where the interactions and the environment focus on transmission of knowledge, whereas if knowledge is seen as being 'a fluid act of interpretation' (Kendall-Seatter 2005 p. 97) then a very different ethos pervades. Autonomous and independent learners have control and ownership over their learning. This needs to be supported by and negotiated with the teacher, who will use classroom interactions and the environment to encourage collaborative working and more meaningful contexts for learning.

Organisation of resources and classroom layout

If this is to succeed, the emotional and physical environment must be equally supportive. Resources must be easily identifiable, relevant and available, as well as flexible enough for the children to use them in the way that they need to. The physical layout of the room also needs to be flexible enough for children to work in ways that are appropriate for the task in hand. Planned opportunities for paired and group work, along with careful differentiation of tasks, are required in order to build up the skills to enable children to learn with and from each other and their environment.

The scenario again

In our scenario, the teacher believes that she is enabling independence, and within the context and purpose of this particular task, it could be argued that she is. The learning for the session is explicit to the children but it is tightly controlled by the teacher. If this is representative of other teaching and learning interactions within this classroom, then children become at risk of 'learned helplessness'. Children become accustomed to accepting extrinsic motivation and organisation and are not able to succeed without it. They do not have the necessary strategies. The teacher in our situation has created an environment where children have little need to be independent: they are lined up, sat down, moved to tables and given a specific task with specific resources. It is all organised and done for them. This teacher believes it is for the benefit of the children but in reality it could have more to do with convenience for herself. Children do not have to consider others or the effect of their behaviour as they are closely monitored. It is perhaps for this reason in the only part of the scenario where the children are not under the direct supervision of the teacher, in the cloakroom, that there is a breakdown of order. Children have not been helped to think independently and behave autonomously. These skills enable children to be resilient, to tolerate and adapt to new and different ideas and experiences and to stay engaged with things that are outside their comfort zone.

Reflective task

Think about a classroom that you have spent time in. Make notes on:

- the routines
- the types of tasks
- the resources used and the ways they were organised
- the physical layout used in the classroom.

(Continued)

(Continued)

Put these into two columns – those that supported independence and autonomy and those that hindered it. How can you ensure that your learning environment encourages those skills that support independence and autonomy?

Supporting positive behaviour through the learning environment

Disruptive behaviour, whether low level or with greater impact, will of course always
hinder effective learning so it is important to consider how our learning environment
may help the children to choose appropriate behaviours which enable all to make good
academic progress. Ecological psychologists note that the learning environment is
important for children and that it can affect their behaviour (Bronfenbrenner 1979;
Gump 1987; Pointon and Kersher 2000 cited in Pollard 2008). Learning dispositions can
be influenced by the environment. An environment that is scruffy and untidy will not be
respected by the children. If it is dull or cold, then they will not be happy about being
there. If it is cluttered, it can make children feel stressed and overwhelmed, whereas a
tidy, organised environment can help children to feel calm and positive, ready to learn
in a place where there is a perception of order and structure (Cowley 2006). This can be
achieved through carefully organised stations or areas of provision so children know
how, and where, to access equipment. Signs, labels and displays will help to clarify these
areas. Interactive displays are an effective learning tool which, alongside the use of music,
sound and light, can encourage interest and focus engagement with the environment.

A sense of ownership

Learning environments are places where a complicated mix of factors come together –
local community values, parental expectations, religious values, children and their attitudes, and so on. McNamara and Moreton (1997) cited in Kendall-Seatter (2005)
showed that where children were actively engaged in their classroom a higher level of
involvement was ensured and shared ownership, shared values and mutual respect
were fostered.

Looking at the scenario, the child did not seem to feel any sense of ownership over
the environment he was in. He was not involved in setting it up nor does it appear to
consider the ways in which he needs to behave in order to learn effectively. Too many
classrooms are sterile laboratories where the children are fenced in by table arrangements and not allowed to move from their places unless it is a key transition time.
Everything is put in front of them – paper, pencil and books – so that they have to make
few decisions or interactions with peers and adults.

The authors would argue that the classroom should be more like a workshop, a
bustling busy place with children moving between different areas collecting resources

independently, sometimes standing, sometimes sitting, sometimes even working on the floor. Sometimes it may look messy – workshops are full of very busy, productive people. This positive engagement appears to be the key to encouraging appropriate behaviours. It has been suggested that children should not only be involved in designing their classroom environment but also in working with teachers and architects in redesigning old buildings and in creating new ones (Alexander 2010 p. 355).

Evaluating engagement with the environment

As teachers, how can we tell if children are able to engage with an environment? Do the children sit still for too long? Are they uncomfortable? Do children know what is expected of them? Are instructions clear? Can they get the resources they need? What should they do if they finish the set task? What strategies can they use if they get stuck? Are they bored? Is the work too easy or too hard? Can they make decisions about their learning? Are they able to choose how to approach a task? Can they talk to their peers about their learning?

The scenario

Let us consider the scenario again. The child knows that he is expected to sit still for quite some time. He is also aware that he finds this difficult. Ouvry (2000 p. 23) asserts that 'the most advanced level of movement is the ability to stay totally still, which requires entire muscle groups to work in cooperation with balance and posture'. The struggle to do as he knows he should requires him to concentrate on the issue of staying still and as a result he misses other information. What is he engaged with? At all points, he is trying very hard to behave and this has a detrimental impact on his ability to engage with the learning he is being presented with. The teacher's perception of his behaviour is very different to his own desire to behave appropriately within the constraints of the environment she has created. How could the teacher have set the environment up differently to enable a more positive experience for this child?

Creating a work-centred atmosphere

Where the teacher creates a work-centred atmosphere, classes tend to behave better (Docking 2002). There is, however, a wide range of advice and research about how this is best achieved. Plowden (1967) advised teachers to put children in mixed-ability groups in order to promote active, problem-solving discussion. Later studies showed that although teachers grouped children, they were usually directed to work individually. The group situation but individualised nature of the task meant that children were often found to be off task and talking inappropriately (Whedall and Glynn 1989). In 1995, a study by Hastings and Schwieso found that primary children concentrated better in rows where disruptive children were less distracted. There was no eye contact to disturb them and the better they behaved, the more positive reinforcement came from the teacher. So are rows the answer? Probably as primary teachers, something inside us recoils at the idea! Why is this? Could it be that we really do believe that children learn better in a social environment and that our training tells us that it cannot be right that teachers' requirements for conformity and rules should override the child's need for 'understanding and engagement in high quality learning tasks' (Holt 1982 in Pollard 2008 p. 309). We need, therefore, to be challenged to provide a flexible environment where the needs of the children, the classroom, the tasks and experiences, groupings, levels of challenge, boundaries and routines, and expectations all come together to support children's positive behaviour. A challenge indeed!

Encouraging self-esteem and emotional development through the learning environment

Few would disagree that the learning environment may also have a powerful impact on the child's self-esteem and emotional development. Without a doubt, the class teacher in the above scenario will have spent many long hours planning and resourcing her delivery of the curriculum but one wonders how much time was spent planning the hidden curriculum and how to 'manipulate the environment' (Child 1997 p. 265) to offer opportunities to make the children feel valued, safe and that they have a contribution to make.

Case study

Simon's low self-esteem was reinforced by the seating arrangements, the use of wall displays and his observation of rewarded behaviours. Teachers are fond of using and applying the label of low self-esteem and may take up a one-woman/man crusade to help re-educate parents or offer strategies to develop self-esteem in the home, but how do we know that Simon did not arrive at school aged 4 ready to conquer the world and it is actually school that has taught him he is failing?

Our understanding of brain development informs us that a child under stress is unable to learn effectively. If you re-read his perception of the scenario, you will note that there were many issues for Simon in his environment which were sources of stress for him and which could have prevented him from learning. Sometimes empathetic teachers or teaching assistants will recognise stress issues for children but may inadvertently impact on their achievement and therefore self-esteem even more by removing challenge from tasks they are required to do and encouraging the 'learned helplessness' we have already made reference to. Kendall-Seatter (2005) speaks of the necessity to provide environments which are 'low-stress-high-challenge' (p. 59) to ensure achievement for all children regardless of ability.

(Continued)

Simon's concerns will not just be with how his teacher perceives and values him but the opinions of his peers will also be of great importance to his positive self-esteem. The 'ripple' action (Jacques and Hyland 2003 p. 161) set into motion by the classroom teacher as she sets up the learning environment to reflect her own values and beliefs about learning and children will continue until all children included in that environment cannot help but be influenced by them. There will be a shared, if unspoken, understanding that some children are failing, therefore 'lesser', whilst others are successful and 'apart' and will always continue to be so. The failing children, the 'Simons' of this world, may feel they are powerless to move from the level in the hierarchy they have been assigned by the learning environment, the teacher and their peers and it is, thus, once they have decided there is no point any longer in trying, that disaffection may set in. If, on the other hand, the ripple that the teacher, through the environment, sets in motion is an inclusive one that demonstrates that all children are valued for the unique and individual talents and attributes they bring, all children will see themselves as learners regardless of their ability.

Children's perceptions of their place in society

The environment will dominate the children's understanding of their own role and place in society regardless of the teacher's discourse. This is why, as classroom teachers, it is so important to get it right and leave nothing to chance. We may feel we have a group of learners but in reality we have a group of individuals (Kendall-Seatter 2005 p. 62).

Summary

To conclude, the authors believe that for effective learning to take place the environment needs to be flexible enough to be created around the needs of children. However loud the teacher's voice may be, the environment will always be able to shout louder, declaring to every child in that class the values and attitudes of that teacher. Children pick up these subliminal signals, adapting their behaviour accordingly where possible to fit into the requirements of their environment. Our challenge to you whatever your level of experience is to think hard about your underpinning values and attitudes towards teaching and learning and to create, within the limitations in which you find yourself working, an environment that will demonstrate to the children what you truly believe learning is.

Questions for discussion

- Children's voices: how might teachers find out how children feel about and respond to the learning environment they provide?
- How might children at each Key Stage be involved in creating their own learning environment?
- How might learning in the classroom be linked to learning outside the classroom at Key Stage 1? At Key Stage 2?
- What might your ideal learning environment at either Key Stage be like? What might be the constraints in creating this environment?

Further reading

Hewitt, D. (2008) *Understanding Effective Learning: Strategies for the Classroom*. Maidenhead: Open University Press.
This book explores these important concepts by examining learning in a range of classroom settings and drawing on evidence from teachers and pupils, through interviews and observations. The focus is two-fold: to understand learning in the classroom, and to develop practices which will support learning.

Roffey, S. (2010) *Changing Behaviour in Schools*. London: Sage.
Taking an holistic approach to working with students, the author provides examples of effective strategies for encouraging pro-social and collaborative behaviour in the classroom, the school and the wider community. Chapters look at the importance of the social and emotional aspects of learning, and ways to facilitate change.

Skinner, D. (2010) *Effective Teaching and Learning in Practice*. London: Continuum.
Based on excellent summaries of recent research on teaching and learning, this book presents a clear framework around which teachers can build their classroom practice. It provides an excellent starting point for new entrants to the profession as well as a source of reflection for their more experienced colleagues.

References

Alexander, R. (1992) *Policy and Practice in Primary Education*. London: Routledge.
Alexander, R. (ed.) (2010) *Children, Their World, Their Education: Final Report of the Cambridge Primary Review*. London: Routledge.

Bowles, S. and Gintis, H. (1976) *Schooling in Capitalist America*. London: Routledge and Kegan.

Bronfenbrenner, U. (1979) *The Ecology of Human Development*. Cambridge, MA: Harvard University Press.

Child, D. (ed.) (1997) *Psychology and the Teacher*, 6th edn. London: Continuum.

Cowley, S. (2006) *Getting the Buggers to Behave*, 3rd edn. London: Continuum.

Daly, M., Byers, E. and Taylor, W. (2006) *Understanding Early Years Theory in Practice*. Oxford: Heinemann.

DfEE (2000) *The National Curriculum Key Stages* 1 and 2 (revised edition). London: HMSO.

Docking, J. (2002) *Managing Behaviour in the Primary School*, 3rd edn. London: David Fulton.

Doherty, J. and Hughes, M. (2009) *Child Development: Theory and Practice 0–11*. Harlow: Pearson.

Gnadinger, C. (2008) 'Peer-mediated Instruction: Assisted Performance in the Primary Classroom', *Teachers and Teaching* 14(2): 129–42.

Goswami, U. (2008) *Cognitive Development: The Learning Brain*. Hove: Psychology Press.

Gump, P. (1987) 'School and Classroom Environments' in I. Altman and J.F. Wohlwill, *Handbook of Environmental Psychology*. New York: Plenum Press, pp. 131–74.

Hastings, N. and Schwieso, J. (1995) 'Tasks and Tables: The Effects of Seating Arrangements on Task Engagement in Primary Classrooms', *Educational Research* 37(3): 279–91.

Jacques, K. and Hyland, R. (2003) *Professional Studies: Primary Phase*. Exeter: Learning Matters.

Kehily, M. (ed.) (2010) *An Introduction to Childhood Studies*, 2nd edn. Maidenhead: McGraw Hill.

Kendall-Seatter, S. (2005) *Primary Professional Studies: Reflective Reader*. Exeter: Learning Matters.

MacIntyre, H. and Ireson, J. (2002) 'Within-class Ability Grouping: Placement of Pupils in Groups and Self-concept', *British Educational Research Journal*. 28(2): 249–63.

McNamara, S. and Moreton, G. (1997) *Understanding Differentiation*. London: Taylor and Francis.

Moyles, J. (1992) *Organising for Learning in the Primary Classroom*. Buckingham: Open University Press.

Ouvry, M. (2000) *Exercising Muscles and Minds*. London: The Early Years Network.

Plowden Report (1967) *Children and their Primary Schools: A Report of the Central Advisory Council for Education (England)*. London: HMSO.

Pollard, A. (2008) *Reflective Teaching: Evidence-informed Professional Practice*, 3rd edn. London: Continuum.

Waterson, A. (2003) 'Managing the Classroom for Learning' in K. Jacques and R. Hyland (eds) *Professional Studies: Primary Phase*. Exeter: Learning Matters, pp. 74–85.

Whedall, K. and Glynn, T. (1989) *Effective Classroom Learning: A Behavioural Interactionist Approach to Teaching*. Oxford: Basil Blackwell.

Wood, D., Bruner, J. and Ross, G. (1976) 'The Role of Tutoring in Problem Solving', *Journal of Child Psychology and Psychiatry* 17: 89–100.

CHAPTER 5

THE ROLE OF THE ADULT

Jan Ashbridge and Jo Josephidou

By the end of this chapter, you should be able to:

- discuss the many roles of the teacher in the education and care of children

- examine how teachers work with other adults within and beyond the classroom to develop effective practice which will impact on children's achievement

- consider how positive relationships between adults and children can impact on their learning

- reflect critically on the values and philosophies you hold regarding the education of children.

Introduction

In this chapter, metaphors are used in order to help you to explore, extend and challenge your perception of your role as a teacher. The first metaphor considered is the teacher's role as a partner with a range of other adults: parents, teaching assistants, other teachers, professionals from outside agencies and the local community. Then other dimensions of the teacher's role are explored: supporting the development of the whole child, facilitating and scaffolding learning, pastoral care, inspiring learners and in coordinating all these roles.

    Reflective task

Imagine yourself in your first classroom with your first class of children. Take a mental photograph of the picture this creates in your head. Now describe this image to a peer.

Describe the following:

- What you are doing?
- What are the children doing?
- Is there anyone else in the classroom?
- What are they doing?

It will be interesting to see whether the image you have described has changed by the end of this chapter.

Teachers are a cog in a much bigger mechanism. It is easy to focus only on the cogs immediately around us, where it is obvious how they affect our work and how we affect them. Understanding the bigger picture is a key way of beginning to grasp the main issues in partnership working and avoiding the appearance of a 'muddled system of education and care' (Penn 2008 p. 193).

    Reflective activity

Who are we in partnership with?

In small groups, write down on separate sticky notes all the different professionals who might be working alongside a teacher in their work and who may influence their practice. What different ways can you find in which to group them? By role? By sphere of influence? By the immediacy of their impact on the teacher's work?

On a large sheet of paper, draw the teacher in the middle – can you organise your sticky notes around them? Who seems nearest, who seems less important?

This activity should have illustrated the number of people that teachers work with. A study of roles and responsibilities (adapted from Siraj-Blatchford et al. 2002 p. 7) found the following roles and responsibilities in today's primary schools:

- teaching assistant (and equivalent learning support assistant, nursery nurse, therapist)
- pupil welfare workers (education welfare officer, home–school liaison officer, learning mentor, nurse and welfare assistant)
- technical and specialist staff (ICT network manager, ICT technician, librarian, science technician, technology technician)
- other pupil support staff (bilingual support officer, cover supervisor, escort, language assistant, midday assistant, midday supervisor)
- facilities staff (cleaner, cook, other catering staff)
- administrative staff (administrator, finance officer, office manager, secretary, personal assistant to the head teacher)
- site staff (caretaker and premises manager).

This list is considerably extended when we add colleagues within the school and the community and multi-agency working.

We cannot examine all of these partnerships and the defining teaching role in primary schools is that of the generalist teacher but the number of people with whom teachers need to communicate effectively is huge.

Working with others: the teacher as partner

Partnership with parents and carers

Perhaps the key partnership teachers must engage in is with parents and carers. Parents are statutorily responsible for their child's education, are legally entitled to state a preference for a particular school and have a legal right to parental representation on the governing body. As a result of this, they are major stakeholders in children's education and are able to influence school policy. This responsibility is shared as when a child is at school, teachers are *in loco parentis* and have a common-law duty to promote children's safety and well-being as well as their education (Children Act 1989).

What might be some of the stumbling blocks to effective partnership with parents?

	Perceived power balance	Openness and honesty	Poor communication	Judgemental attitudes	
Lack of understanding	Poor listening		Lack of trust	?	?

Parents know their children better than the teacher ever can. They are the children's first educators and have vital information on what the children enjoy, how they learn, etc. Most learning happens outside school (Dean 2000 p. 140), and this needs to be recognised and valued by those within the school too.

Opportunities to share information with parents

Teachers can usually think of many ways to share information with parents. Before the first, nervously anticipated 'parents' evening', you may have met many of the parents informally at the beginning or end of the school day. You may have written notes to them about school events or out-of-school visits. You may have been encouraged to invite them to a meeting at the beginning of term to introduce yourself, explain what the children are going to be learning about and why and to discuss how they may like to be involved. If you have managed initial encounters with parents in a friendly and professional way, this will be a good basis for meeting them on more formal occasions to discuss their children's progress. Some schools invite parents to meetings to learn more about how the school teaches, for example, reading or mathematics, so that they can be more involved in their children's learning. But this is not a partnership if you do not also learn from the parents.

Opportunities for parents to share information with teachers

Even confident parents may feel threatened by meeting a teacher to discuss their child's progress, attitudes, social skills and behaviour. Less confident parents may have had poor experiences of school themselves and feel insecure or alternatively confrontational. How might parents feel about sharing family information with a teacher? How can you help parents to feel confident in telling you about their children? What might you want to know, and why?

Parents' contributions to school life

How can parents contribute to the life of the school? Through your formal and informal communications with parents, you may find that they have special expertise, through their work or their interests, which would enrich an aspect of your teaching. Some parents are eager to 'help in class'. Can there be difficulties in welcoming this and, if so, how could they be resolved? Some parents may have little English. How might you involve them in helping in school? How might you make parents from different cultural backgrounds feel included in school life?

 Reflective task

In pairs: one person thinks of a child they have taught who was finding school difficult in some ways. The partner, in role as the class teacher, needs to find out why. Role play a meeting between parent and teacher. Share what you both know

(Continued)

and feel about the child and agree how you can work together to support her. Then share your thoughts about the difficulties encountered and how well both partners negotiated them. Share the role play with others. Compile a list of ways in which you might work in partnership with parents to support a child.

This relationship has considerable influence over the way parents feel able to support their children's learning, resulting in a shared purpose, understanding and belonging for all (Dean 2000 p. 151).

Social events with teachers and parents

Partnerships can be strengthened by situations in which parents and teachers work together on a more equal footing to support the school. One head teacher set up a number of projects more enterprising than the 'school fete', themed dance evenings and fancy dress parties, although these were greatly enjoyed. The projects included a school garden, the construction of an 'adventure fort' and a pet shed. Children, teachers and parents worked together on these projects. The fort project was particularly successful in involving dads, some of whom did not live at home.

True partnership with parents cannot flourish where respect and power are not equal. Home–school communication is a complex process in which 'issues of control and power are present and shape the forms of communication'. However, when effective communication with parents is achieved, 'the contribution that parents make to their child's learning is often rich and varied' (Alexander 2010 p. 81).

Partnership with teaching assistants

The same skills are required to work alongside the other adults in the classroom. Teaching assistants and other support staff often have a slightly different relationship with children and families and can, therefore, add another perspective to planning and to supporting children's needs. Involving them and using their knowledge and experience can ensure more effective learning outcomes for the children and can create a more responsive and motivated team approach in the classroom.

It was the intention that the considerable increase in teaching assistants and other support staff between 2003 and 2006, as a result of 'workforce reform', should strengthen teaching and learning, by using the full potential of teaching assistants (TAs), allowing them to take on wider and deeper roles, and allowing schools to focus on the individual needs of every child. Higher Level Teaching Assistants (HLTAs) were, under the supervision of the teacher, to be involved in planning, teaching and assessment as well as teaching and learning and to work with whole classes without the presence of the teacher.

How to work with teaching assistants in ways that will realise these opportunities involves decisions about how best to use their expertise in ways that meet the needs of children in your class, and the ability to forge mutually supportive relationships. It is essential that teachers include teaching assistants in planning, monitoring and assessment, medium term, weekly and daily and this requires time. They also need to be clear about what their role is within what the teacher is planning, with an individual, a group or the whole class and how they are going to monitor and assess this. They may have particular areas of curriculum expertise to contribute, in art, or music or dance, for example. But the most important aspect of working effectively with your teaching assistant is to develop a mutually supportive relationship so that you enjoy working together.

Partnership with other teachers

A school is a community, a collaborative, inclusive community for learning. This community creates and conveys values, attitudes and purposes. Relationships between teachers and the ways in which they behave have an important impact on the ethos of that community. They are models which children notice. A positive and mutually agreed and shared whole-school philosophy, shared values, mutual respect and support are a powerful, formative influence on children and on the community. Whole-school policies and planning contribute to the school ethos.

Within schools, there are teams which must work effectively with each other and the school community: management teams, curriculum leaders, Special Educational Needs coordinators, year group teams, Key Stage teams. And there is evidence that if all these groups work effectively, this has an impact on all aspects of children's learning.

Partner with local schools
In rural areas particularly, schools work in local clusters to share resources and expertise and to support each other. It is important that they work together cooperatively rather than submit to government encouragement of competition.

Partner with global colleagues
Many teachers also think that it is important to develop the global dimension of education and liaise with teachers and schools in other countries and continents. This demands sensitivity, for example when resources and opportunities are unequal.

Working in partnership with professionals in other agencies

Primary Health Care Trusts
In 2000 Primary Care Trusts (PCTs) replaced the former Health Authorities. The PCTs work with families, children and schools. Teachers therefore may work with the PCT

services such as: disabled children's teams, child development teams, health visitors, health education programmes, occupational therapists, speech therapists, physiotherapists, community parent schemes, children's mental health teams.

Behaviour and Education Support Teams

These multi-agency teams were set up in partnership with schools in 2002 to promote well-being and positive behaviour, attendance and to raise attainment through early intervention.

The 2004 Children Act

In 2003 the Every Child Matters initiative was introduced. This became part of the Children Act 2004. It was intended to secure the well-being of all children and in particular those in danger of abuse. Local authorities were to provide 'joined up' education and care services with multi-agency cooperation. Schools were to work with health care agencies, social services, family law and criminal justice agencies and services concerned with the arts, recreation and sports. These include public, private and voluntary agencies.

Children's trust boards

In 2007 the government announced that children's trust boards would be set up. These were to consist of representatives from schools and the other integrated services and would be held responsible for child protection measures.

Implications for teacher as partner

It has been complex to manage multi-agency work and some schools have been criticised for lack of involvement, but where it has been successful children and parents have benefitted. It has been suggested that agencies should liaise with clusters of schools. However multi-agency work develops in the future, its success will depend on teachers being prepared to work with other professionals and to share information and expertise.

Extended schools

Extended schools were created to provide all children with access to a variety of clubs and sports and adults access to education classes and parenting support. The aim was that by 2010 all children should have access to an extended school. Teachers are not required to contribute to extended schools, but may choose to.

Partnership and the community

'To establish itself as a thriving cultural and communal site should be the principal aim of every school' (Alexander 2010 p. 500). The community of the school – its pupils and their families, and often the school staff – are part of the wider community. So the wider curriculum needs to gain meaning by starting with that community, its geography, its history, its opportunities for creating art, music, drama and all kinds of writing related to the community and the people who lived and live there.

Then children need to learn about citizenship through taking an interest in and contributing to their community. This might involve discussing a proposed development, making suggestions to the town council about changes they would like to see, attending council meetings, becoming aware of sustainability and environmental issues, contributing a display in the local library (if there still is one) or presenting a performance at an old people's home.

Parents can contribute in all sorts of ways. One Year 1 class had a 'teddy museum'. Children brought in their teddy bears and wrote brief information labels. Parents did the same with their teddies. In another school, in groups, children from each KS2 class were helped by parents to prepare a lunch related to a theme they were learning about, then invited a member of the community, perhaps a librarian or nurse or policeman, to share their lunch. Parents may demonstrate skills or hobbies or talk about their interests or working day.

People from local businesses can enrich the curriculum in all sorts of ways, perhaps inviting children to make a positive contribution: making designs for a new flower bed in the park, or a new building in town, or a new recipe for the sandwich bar. Alexander (2010 p. 276) suggests that community curriculum partnerships should be convened by the local authority, including representatives from schools and the community and experts in contributory disciplines and involving consultation with children. This community curriculum would include elements agreed collectively by the schools, with each school responding in ways which build on and respect the lives of their children.

Having discussed the multifaceted role of the teacher as partner, let us now consider the multifaceted role of teacher as teacher.

The developing child: teacher as signpost

Children's learning is often seen as a journey. Children move along a path from the early years, through the primary school and on to high school and beyond. Along the way they develop, they grow, they learn. Careful planning ensures that the children's itinerary takes them to visit a variety of different places and experience a range of situations.

The teacher's role here is perceived to be to lead and manage the curriculum at a number of different levels and in a variety of ways. As seen in the previous chapter, the environment and its careful management and use is key to effective learning and teaching. Children need to be kept safe, resources organised and accessible, and social interactions, groups and tasks carefully considered and appropriately employed.

It is interesting here to note who is making the decisions about these issues. Many of these management decisions are taken for the benefit of the adult. The image of a signpost offers us a slightly different perception of the role of the teacher. It is one where some of the control over decisions about learning is given to the children. They are able to indicate a choice of where they want their learning to go, how they want to engage with it, and how much time they need to master it. It is still very much about moving children on and supporting their progress but with a key difference: the children are more involved in the direction their learning may take them.

In order to be able to respond appropriately to children in this situation, teachers need to understand that 'teaching and learning [are] a continuous unfolding of related knowledge, skills and understanding' (Hayes 2004 p. 151). We cannot simply give children complete free choice over what and how they learn. We need to have an overview. Continuity of learning is 'achieved when there is a discernable thread of knowledge, skills and understanding' which runs through different learning experiences (2004 p. 151). Aiming for this will enable us to be effective signposts, allowing children to progress smoothly along their learning journey.

Facilitating learning: teacher as magician

Magic moments

Sometimes the classroom teacher glimpses small nuggets of gold when a child grasps and articulates a concept in a way the teacher had not considered before. Or a group of children display a skill or ability beyond that same teacher's expectation. Or the wisdom of children as opposed to the knowledge of adults is allowed to take centre stage so that the classroom becomes a real learning community. By being the catalyst, the facilitator of all these events, the teacher could be forgiven at times for feeling as if they were a magician, an alchemist, a producer of gold.

Catering for individual differences

The teacher as magician is there to do the seemingly impossible – to facilitate learning for all. The successful teacher will do this by being very clear about the individual learning needs of the children. Some children learn more effectively by having their learning introduced in small steps, while others like to view the bigger picture and proceed from there. The wise teacher will not seek to impose strategies that may not work for all children and will not succumb to the flawed opinion that because they themselves learnt successfully in one way then so will all children. Some children will disengage much more quickly than others so the teacher as magician will seek to captivate their attention for as long as possible by creating an exciting learning environment, rich with stimulating and purposeful activities and opportunities to succeed.

A learning community

The teacher as magician will be clear about learning outcomes, will know that at the end of the show the white rabbit has to come out of the hat, but at the same time will read her audience and be flexible about how this outcome is achieved. Audience participation is encouraged because by encouraging interaction between teacher and children and children and children, the effective teacher is aware that a learning community is being constructed which everyone can both contribute to and learn from. Talk and questioning are used to extend learning rather than a focus for 'guess what is in the teacher's head' type activities.

Transformative learning

It could be argued that indeed the analogy of the magician does stand up as a description of the teacher. Just as the magician can change the silk handkerchief into the white rabbit, so can the class teacher bring about real transformation and change. On the other hand, just as the magician's is an illusion of change, so too can the education system support the illusion of change by the introduction of strategies, the massaging and analysis of statistics and data, teaching to tests which inflate key assessment results rather than impact any lasting change, growth in knowledge and skills or transformation. Just as the magician puts on a show to bring a real sense of wonder and excitement to his audience, so too does the classroom teacher, at times, draw her audience in, sometimes to entertain, sometimes to enthral, at other times to turn the mundane and simple into spectacles worthy of the children's attention.

Pastoral care: teacher as gardener

We cannot afford to ignore the social and emotional development of the children. Children who are happy at school, who share good relationships with both adults and peers in that environment, are children who will make good progress academically. So this is why we turn now to the analogy of the teacher as gardener, carefully considering and providing the best possible environment and conditions for the children to thrive and grow in all areas of their development.

Praise

Teacher praise has always been an effective motivator for children though Child (1997 p. 119) reminds as that it must be used carefully if it is to have any impact, otherwise it can become meaningless and limiting. Moyles too warns us to be careful about how we offer it: 'praise may appear to make children work harder, but what was the cause of any reluctance to do so in the first place?' (2001 p. 69). Instead, many would argue that appropriate behaviours should be considered the norm, not something to be rewarded and that the present fashion for acknowledging teacher pleasure through constant bestowing of certificates and stickers actually decreases children's intrinsic motivations and undermines them as learners.

Lifelong learners

Teachers who are aware that their role is much more than a transmission of knowledge will work hard to plan for resilient lifelong learners who are enthusiastic about learning because they know they have the freedom to make mistakes, seeing mistakes as necessary stepping stones on the way to academic success. They will look to provide opportunities for children to build on and demonstrate their strengths rather than focusing on the child's weaknesses within the rigid framework of assessment 'where the threat to self-esteem is ever present' (Cockburn and Handscomb 2006 p. 45).

Fostering independence

The teacher is an expert at asking questions of the children but it may be pertinent for her to ask herself about how it feels to be a learner in the classroom environment she has created. Do the children feel quite dependent on the teacher for their learning or are they confident enough and skilled enough to see and use their peers 'as a resource'? (Moyles 2001 p. 13). Children who are strong and healthy, not just physically and cognitively, but also emotionally resilient need the correct conditions or learning environment to grow and thrive.

Scaffolding learning: teacher as bridge

Teachers are curriculum makers. They take their detailed knowledge of the frameworks and statutory expectations of children, combine this with an understanding of children's needs, their development and their current skills and understandings and create an environment with meaningful and challenging learning experiences for all. This professional responsibility means that we are ultimately accountable for the learning situations that we create for the children in our class and for the children's responses to these in terms of learning and progress. Teachers are constantly using their professional judgement but must be able to justify their decisions.

Progressing learning

A bridge is something that gets you from one side of a gap of some kind to the other. As classroom teachers, we aim to support children as they travel from their current knowledge to concepts and skills as yet unknown and unexplored but perhaps anticipated and eagerly awaited. In supporting children from one side of this gap to the other, we need to have our eyes fixed firmly on the connection, the learning itself and on the process of connecting. To get this right, we must return again to theories of cognitive development. These can give us an insight into the way that children make connections and what we can do to make these as strong as possible. In this way, we can interpret the curriculum in appropriate ways for specific groups of children.

Siraj-Blatchford et al. (2002) argue that it is this bringing together of children and adult in a learning situation that enables co-construction of knowledge where both are engaged and involved. Their research showed that where adults and children were engaged together in these 'sustained shared thinking interactions' (Siraj-Blatchford et al. 2002 p. 10) a high level of intellectual challenge enabled children to make good progress in their learning.

Interventions

It would seem, therefore, that we support children's learning and their interpretation of what they are experiencing through careful scaffolding and sensitive yet challenging adult interventions. These interventions which are designed to make connections between existing understanding and new knowledge form part of a complicated process. On their own, children may not be able to make these connections or could make inaccurate ones. Enabling children to bridge this gap will lead to 'principled understanding' (Edwards and Mercer 1987 p. 95 cited in Myhill et al. 2006 p. 87), where children make deep, meaningful, conceptual connections in their learning.

Listening to children's voices

The challenge for the teacher is to enable and support all children to make these connections when each child has a 'uniqueness and individuality of … prior knowledge … that has to be incorporated into a classroom setting' (Myhill et al. 2006 p. 85). The answer seems to lie in listening to children and their thoughts and ideas rather than more formal recapping of previous curriculum coverage and relating this to a current learning focus which narrows children's thinking rather than provoking 'speculation and extend imagination' (Siraj-Blatchford et al. 2002 p. 47). The types of questions used by teachers are instrumental in helping children to truly explore their prior knowledge and also to share their understanding and begin to construct an extended understanding together.

The inspiring teacher: teacher as superhero

Modelling

Children's media are full of superheroes. They are enthralled by characters with super powers and look up to champions of good over evil. For many primary school children, their teacher can be a superhero figure. When trainee teachers are asked to consider how they perceive the role of the teacher, they will often use the term 'role model' but what exactly are they implying by their use of this phrase? Certainly, the idea of modelling is a key theme that runs through issues surrounding effective teaching and learning at primary level. The effective teacher models a range of skills from how to solve mathematical problems to how to deal with conflict in the playground and then supports the child in their own interpretation of this modelling until finally the child has the confidence and is ready to use these skills independently. This view of children and their 'guided participation' (Rogoff cited in Penn 2008 p. 49) mirrors practices in cultures across the world where the child is viewed as competent and ready to learn skilled adult activity, and also links with the work of Bruner and Vygotsky already discussed. The effective teacher may also feel that not only is their role one of modelling for children but also for other adults working in the classroom and, at times, parents and other teaching colleagues. We can disseminate excellent practice by allowing others to observe us at work, by the way the learning environment we have created speaks of our values and expectations and by articulating clearly and explicitly why we have chosen to adopt certain strategies and philosophies.

The metaphor of the superhero was chosen because this is a powerful, inspirational figure, a defender of children who will ensure that their learning needs are at the forefront of everything the teacher does. However, it is important to recognise that these same children are strong, competent individuals who need an advocate to fight their corner rather than a rescuer to come and save them.

▢   Summary: teacher as conductor

As we have explored, the role of the teacher is complex and multifaceted. It requires partnership with a wide variety of others. We need to have excellent knowledge of child development and subject knowledge. We must understand how to facilitate learning, how to scaffold learning, how to nurture the whole

(Continued)

(Continued)

child, how to inspire. At some points, we can feel like a conductor, orchestrating children's learning experiences, their responses, the curriculum, resources, routines and other adults. This wider view is important as it ensures that we can pull all this together into a holistic, coherent experience with each child expressing themselves and performing positively.

 Questions for discussion

- For many children, their socio-economic circumstances are a barrier to learning. In what ways can a school 'make a difference' in spite of this?
- It has been suggested that children should have specialist subject teachers rather than generalist class teachers in the primary school. Do you agree?
- In most European countries, subject knowledge is included in the field of Professional Studies but there is less emphasis on pedagogy. What are the advantages and disadvantages of this?
- It has been said that multi-agency working and classroom assistants are a threat to teachers' professionalism. Do you agree?

Further reading

Eaude, T. (2011) *Thinking Through Pedagogy for Primary and Early Years*. Exeter: Learning Matters.
This user-friendly text encourages readers to consider how children learn, and how teachers can best support their learning. It begins by asking 'what is pedagogy?' and goes on to examine the wider context, including how language and education impact on pedagogy.

Muijs, D. and Reynolds, D. (2010) *Effective Teaching*, 3rd edn. London: Sage.
This book encompasses the latest research on effective teaching and learning. Appropriate for all age groups, it provides a comprehensive overview of what is now a large body of knowledge on effective teaching.

Pritchard, A. and Woollard, J. (2010) *Psychology for the Classroom: Constructivism and Social Learning*. London: Routledge.
A discussion of interactive approaches to teaching, this book provides a background to research in constructivist and social learning theory, offering a broad and practical analysis which focuses on contemporary issues and strategies, including the use of e-learning and multimedia.

References

Alexander, R. (ed.) (2010) *Children, Their World, Their Education: Final Report and Recommendations of the Cambridge Primary Review*. London: Routledge.

Child, D. (1997) *Psychology and the Teacher*, 6th edn. London: Continuum.

Cockburn, A. and Handscomb, G. (2006) *Teaching Children 3 to 11*, 2nd edn. London: Paul Chapman Publishing.

Dean, J. (2000) *Improving Children's Learning*. London: Routledge.

Hayes, D. (2004) *Foundations of Primary Teaching*, 3rd edn. London: David Fulton.

Moyles, J. (2001) *Organising for Learning in the Primary Classroom*. Buckingham: OUP.

Myhill, D., Jones, S. and Hopper, R. (2006) *Talking, Listening, Learning: Effective Talk in the Primary Classroom*. Berkshire: OUP.

Penn, H. (2008) *Understanding Early Childhood: Issues and Controversies*, 2nd edn. Maidenhead: McGraw Hill.

Siraj-Blatchford, I., Sylva, K., Muttock, S., Gilden, R. and Bell, D. (2002) *Researching Effective Pedagogy in the Early Years*. Nottingham: DfES.

Part 2

INCLUSIVE DIMENSIONS OF PROFESSIONAL STUDIES

In Part 1 you were introduced to the philosophy underpinning this book and to the broad foundations of Professional Studies: planning and assessment, classroom organisation and ethos and the significance of relationships with children and adults. Part 2 builds on these foundations by focusing on a range of themes which have in common the concept of inclusion, the need to take into account children's individual needs. These depend on their levels of ability and matura- tion, social, cultural and ethnic backgrounds, personal and social development. You will consider inclusive teaching and learning strategies which will enable you to provide children with equal opportunities to learn and to meet their potential. And you will realise that each of these themes involves informed value judgements about how best to proceed.

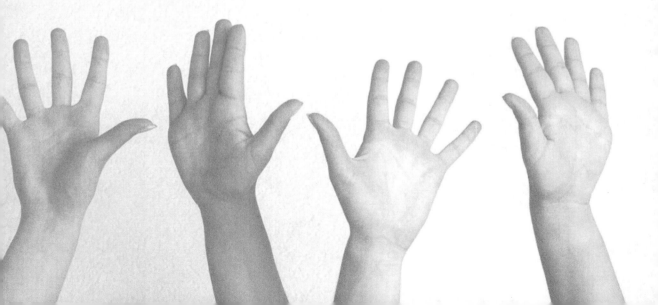

CHAPTER 6

REFLECTIVE PRACTICE IN THE EARLY YEARS: A FOCUS ON ISSUES RELATED TO TEACHING RECEPTION-AGE CHILDREN

Lin Savage and Anne Renwick

By the end of this chapter, you should:

- have an informed understanding of controversial issues related to teaching 4–5-year-olds in reception classes

- have some understanding of the importance of the play-based curriculum and how to protect it in mixed-age classes, the importance of creative and innovative practice and how to develop this

- have some understanding of the importance of developmentally appropriate approaches to teaching 3–5-year-olds and of how to do this

- have some understanding of theories underpinning the teaching of 3–5-year-olds

- understand some international perspectives on early years education.

Introduction

This chapter will focus on issues related to teaching reception-age children. It will address several controversial issues such as school starting age, the entitlement to a play-based curriculum and different pedagogical approaches to early reading. The chapter will focus on the need for reception teachers to develop an evidence-based personal philosophy and to use this to develop innovative and creative teaching practice, which extend young children's learning in a manner appropriate to their age and stage of development.

Through reflective, enquiry-based activities, readers will be encouraged to consider issues particular to teaching reception class children, including how to protect the entitlement to a play-based curriculum for reception-age children in mixed-age classes. Some consideration of the QTS standards and their interpretation and application for teachers of children aged 3–5 will be included. Theoretical models and international perspectives will be drawn upon to encourage a consideration of education in the wider context.

Some challenges and issues

Adapting to a new environment

As the leader of the first class in a child's statutory education, the reception teacher has particular challenges and issues to consider. Children arrive in the reception class having had a variety of diverse experiences prior to beginning statutory school. While a reception class is likely to include many children who have had some nursery or pre-school experiences, it is possible that some children will be leaving their home and family for their first experience of the wider world. Settling children successfully at the beginning of their school life is a skill many student teachers do not get an opportunity to practise in training, but is a crucial aspect of the reception teacher's role, and can heavily influence a child's attitude to school and disposition for learning.

The chances of a child's successful adjustment to school can be increased by the adoption of certain transition strategies, such as home visits, familiarisation with the buildings and close communication with parents throughout the process (Fabian and Dunlop 2002). Margetts (2002) has noted that children who have difficulties adjusting to school in the early days are more likely to experience difficulties in adjustment throughout their schooling; this reinforces the responsibilities of the teacher in this crucial period.

Dealing with differences in maturation

Additionally, in this age range the 11-month gap between a September and August born child can amount to approximately a quarter of the child's life span and developmental stages of individual children can be extremely varied. The only way to deal with this wide range of experience and development is to start where the children are. The reception teacher will need to be skilled in observation and child development in order to begin to make sense of the range of experiences of the children she is responsible for, and to learn about their abilities, needs and motivations in order to plan appropriately for their learning experiences.

Good practice includes:

- practitioners with a sound knowledge of child development
- regular use of a variety of observation approaches, used to build individual profiles of children
- observation used to inform planning of appropriately matched learning experiences.

The importance of relating to parents and carers

Relationships with parents and carers are an important aspect of the reception teacher's work. There is a rare opportunity, while the children are young and brought to school, to have daily contact with parents and carers. This can create the climate for forming the all-important relationship between home and school which will hopefully last through-out the child's primary education. Research (Desforges 2003; Sammons et al. 2007) indicates that parents and home learning have the most significant impact on children's attainment, and understanding and working with parents is, therefore, a central concern for reception class teachers.

In addition to the possible anxieties of children adapting to new surroundings, the reception teacher has, also, to be mindful of the feelings and views of the child's parents. There are occasions when difficult separations are not only about the child's needs; some parents can require significant support during the early days and weeks of leaving their children at school. Parents' preoccupations and anxieties in these early days are often focused on school dinners, toileting behaviours and social aspects of transition, and reception teachers need to recognise the significance of the child's holistic experi-ence of the school environment and be versed in communicating sensitively with parents about children's learning in its widest sense.

Good practice includes:

- offering home visits to meet families in their own environment
- clear and user-friendly information packs
- planning for parents to stay and settle children
- use of a noticeboard for informing parents
- allocating time to listen to parents.

A meeting of cultures

In trying to analyse the specific issues inherent in the challenges and issues for reception-age children and teachers, it can be useful to analyse the various cultural perspectives impacting on the reception class experience. The child's first encounter with school life involves the meeting of a number of cultures which may be typified by different values and beliefs, different traditions, behaviours and rules.

At least three specific cultures meet and impact on the reception-age child: the culture of the home, what we will refer to as the culture of 'early years provision' and the culture of the primary school. Of course, there are also additional cultures impacting on the child's situation such as the community and national cultural influences but in this chapter, the three cultures outlined above will provide the focus for reflection and analysis.

The culture of the home

Children's home lives will, of course, vary considerably, but some significant generic aspects of home life might be:

- family traditions and routines
- cultural and religious identity
- the amount and quality of attention from key adults
- relationships with older or younger siblings
- the home environment – the amount and quality of space, familiarity and ownership of space and key objects (e.g. own room, toys, cup, plate, etc.)
- freedoms (e.g. to sleep, eat, drink when need to).

It can be too easy to underestimate the impact of arriving in a building which is completely unfamiliar and unlike 'home'. This has been brought to the attention of the authors on many occasions, for example when children look around the room wide-eyed and ask, 'Where's your bed?' or emerge from the school toilets having washed their hair.

Fabian (2002) refers to this experience for the child in terms of a 'physical discontinuity', which, in transition is accompanied by 'social discontinuity' as the child adjusts to different key adults and larger social groups of children.

The culture informing early years provision

In this section, we refer to the culture informing early years provision which has developed in England over the last two centuries, stemming from the work of early pioneers such as Susan Isaacs and Margaret McMillan and informed by more recent research such as *Researching Effective Pedagogy in the Early Years* (Siraj-Blatchford et al. 2002) and *Effective Provision of Pre-School Education* (Sylva et al. 2003). The early years community has a strong body of researchers, writers and practitioners with a well-researched and deep-seated set of principles. These have informed the statutory Foundation Stage curriculum, ethos and documents of the last decade and include:

- commitment to a curriculum which starts from observations of the child rather than specific curriculum content to be taught
- providing a curriculum which uses play as a vehicle for planning meaningful learning experiences
- planning a curriculum appropriate for the child's developmental stage
- a focus on active learning which deepens conceptual understanding
- the equal importance of all areas of learning when planning learning experiences
- the centrality of partnership with parents and families
- an emphasis on using the environment to facilitate learning, including the outdoors
- a balance between adult led and child initiated activity
- the interlinked nature of education and care
- routines such as small group times with key workers, snack time, singing and story sessions.

Children's experiences of early years provision before entering reception will reflect the principles outlined above in varying degrees as quality varies. The current statutory Early Years Foundation Stage (DCSF 2008) curriculum applies to children until the end of their reception year and should be the guiding ethos for the reception teacher. In some reception classes this is not evident in practice.

A report published in 2004 by the Association of Teacher's and Lecturers, entitled *Inside the Foundation Stage: Recreating the Reception Year*, concluded:

> There is a demonstrable gap between the quality of children's experiences in the reception classes in our sample, the *second year* of the Foundation Stage, and the quality of their experiences in the *first year* of the Foundation Stage in our best nurseries and family centres as highlighted in other research, e.g. Bertram *et al*. 2002; Whalley 1994. (Adams et al. 2004 p. 19)

 Reflective task

Summarise the main findings of the EPPE (Sylva et al. 2003) and REPEY (Siraj-Blatchford et al. 2002) reports as though you were explaining them to:

- A KS2 colleague
- A parent
- A health or other integrated services practitioner.

(Continued)

(Continued)

What would be the key points you would want to communicate to each of these people? Role play a conversation in order to extract key points.

The culture of the primary school

Here we consider the culture of the wider primary school and some of its principles, traditions and routines in order to raise awareness of some of the tensions, which can have an impact on reception-age children and their teachers.

The statutory documentation for the primary curriculum in England is currently the National Curriculum. As in early years provision the ethos of different primary schools can differ considerably, but external factors have impacted on the culture of the English primary school with certain generic consequences.

Some features of the primary school culture include:

- a curriculum presented in 11 discrete subjects
- a curriculum focus on subject knowledge and content
- priority given to core subjects (English, Mathematics, Science and ICT)
- the current and historical impact of the primary strategies
- standard assessment tasks which inform school league tables
- routines such as assembly, undressing and dressing for PE, playtimes, school dinners.

Practice in reception classes can vary a great deal and we have found it useful in explaining and analysing this with regard to the cultural perspectives model outlined above. In different schools, the meeting of the cultures outlined above will favour some cultural perspectives and associated values more than others and practice will reflect the dominant ethos.

The Early Years Curriculum Group, a nationally recognised group of early years specialists, identified a number of factors that have placed constraints upon the adoption of the early years ethos in reception classes (EYCG 2002).

These factors include:

- the false assumption that the earlier children learn something, the more high achieving they will later become
- fear of the inspection process, which has resulted in a strong emphasis on literacy and numeracy targets
- the top-down pressure of Year 2 SATs, which has created inappropriate expectations about early success in particular aspects of literacy and numeracy

- confusion about the principles of early years pedagogy, and an erosion of the practitioner's commitment to the importance of play as a vehicle for learning. (Adams et al. 2004 p. 12)

Reflective task

Consider a reception class in a school you are familiar with – to what extent do the three cultures outlined above impact on practice? Draw a diagram representing the interplay of the three cultures outlined in this chapter and the dominant influences in a reception class you have experienced.

In mixed-age classes, the pressure to pursue the primary school values and routines is even stronger than with a straight reception class. This has been resisted by some teachers who have planned for Key Stage 1 children using some of the principles of early years provision. Attempts to bring the primary provision closer to the early years culture have been made, with the introduction of the Continuing Learning Journey (QCA 2005) training and, to some extent, the Primary Curriculum (2009), which reconfigured discrete subjects into areas of learning. England has not been as successful in this as Wales, where the Foundation Phase refers to the 3–7 age phase. The imposition of daily phonics sessions suggested in the *Letters and Sounds* (DCSF 2007) document, discussed below, and the failure of the 2010 coalition government to adopt the primary curriculum, may well signal a shift to dictates that adopt an approach closer to the primary school culture with very young children.

Good practice in mixed-age classes includes:

- using active learning and play-based activities inside and out to deliver the 5–7 curriculum, including tasks differentiated to provide the full range of challenge
- expecting older children to work independently at times and interacting with younger children in child-initiated play situations
- planning mixed-age group work for some curriculum delivery.

Reflective task

Consider the 2007 QTS standards, available at: www.tda.gov.uk/training-provider/itt/qts-standards-itt-requirements/guidance/qts-standards.aspx

(Continued)

(Continued)

How does achieving the QTS standards support potential reception class teachers in their crucial role in settling new children into school?

Analyse the extent to which the QTS standards, including the language adopted, reflect the early years ethos and training needs of a reception teacher. Compare the QTS standards with those for Early Years Professional Status available at: www.cwdcouncil.org.uk/assets/0000/9008/Guidance_To_Standards.pdf

Would you like to amend the QTS standards in any way in the light of this comparison?

School starting age: international comparisons

The statutory age at which a child begins formal schooling varies across the world and has become an area of controversy within the UK. Even within the UK, there are differences, with children in Northern Ireland beginning at 4, while England, Scotland and Wales have official statutory starting ages of 5, though many begin reception at 4. In most other European countries, age 6 or 7 is the norm (Sharp 2002). Debate and discussion centres around the quality of the provision accessed by these young children and its appropriateness for their age and stage of development. In those countries with a later school starting date, most children will have access to some form of pre-school provision in a nursery or kindergarten.

The formality, structure, expectations and demands on the children, of each country's curricula, whether prescribed or not, varies considerably. When comparing England with the rest of Europe and indeed other countries around the world, it becomes apparent that as a society we impose a statutory curriculum and assessment process on our children at a younger age than most (Bertram and Pascal 2002). However, in international comparisons of later achievement, UK children do not perform significantly better than those starting school at 6 or 7 (OECD, PISA).

The recent reviews of the Primary Curriculum (Alexander 2010; Rose 2009) have only served to fuel the debate. While Rose suggests an earlier school starting age of 4, Alexander proposed 6 as a more appropriate starting age, saying that anxiety focuses on the fact that, at the age of 5 – against the grain of evidence, expert opinion and international practice – children in England leave behind their active, play-based learning and embark on a formal, subject-based curriculum. For many, this process begins at 4. The report continues to say that there is overwhelming evidence that children of this age need structured play, talk, interaction with others and that this is particularly true for children from disadvantaged homes. (For the key recommendations of the Cambridge

Review, see Alexander 2010 p. 491.) Yet the Labour government's commendable investment in the early years collided with its 'standards agenda' and downward pressure from KS1 and 2. Formal schooling at too early an age has been counter-productive, resulting in England's appallingly large attainment gap.

In England, one of the key findings from a review of recent international research and policy on the issue of relative age highlights that 'pupils who are younger in the year group (known as 'summer borns' in the UK) do less well in attainment tests, are more frequently identified as having special educational needs and are more frequently referred to psychiatric services' (Sharp et al. 2009).

Sue Palmer has been drawing our attention to wider issues related to childhood in the twenty-first century and the 'dangers' children face in the modern world. Poor diet, lack of exercise and the dangers of television and computers, to name a few of her concerns, are all impacting on the quality of childhood (Palmer 2006).

A UNICEF report published in 2007 assessed the well-being of children and young people in 21 industrialised countries and gave the UK the lowest ranking (UNICEF 2007).

'A Good Childhood', a landmark report for the Children's Society, looks at the condition of childhood in the UK, drawing our attention to the higher levels of child poverty and lower levels of well-being experienced by children in the UK compared with their counterparts in Europe (Layard and Dunn 2009).

With children in the UK attending school from the age of 4 and amongst the youngest in Europe, there are significant implications and responsibilities for the reception teacher to ensure that the children's needs are appropriately met and that they are prepared for the pressures of the modern world. While protecting children from real risks, we must be careful to ensure that we do not produce children who are 'wrapped in cotton wool' with little resilience or ability to cope in the modern world (Gill 2009).

Creative and innovative practice, based on first-hand experience, which enables children's self-esteem as well as social and emotional learning to develop and thrive, must be key.

International inspiration from the world-renowned pre-schools of Reggio Emilia in Northern Europe, the Forest Schools of Scandinavian countries and Te Whāriki, the curriculum of New Zealand, with their emphasis on the social and creative needs of young children, have all influenced the development of recent practice within the UK.

Good practice includes:

- planning for children's developmental needs, abilities and interests, whatever the setting
- using the curriculum in a flexible way to ensure that children's needs and interests are met

- practitioners who use their developing knowledge of the experiences from other countries, to extend their own thinking and allow this to impact on the experiences they plan for children
- challenging our own thinking about the needs and interests of children
- allowing children to take the lead – this requires a confidence and underpinning understanding of child development
- listening to children, verbally and through observation, in order to create an environment that allows for creativity.

The importance of a play-based curriculum

The importance of play, indoors and outside, is generally recognised by early years practitioners as of crucial importance. It is well researched, documented and part of early years pedagogy. High involvement levels and the maximising of learning through child-initiated experiences are supported though the work of Ferre Laevers (2005). The recent statutory curricula have placed high importance on using play as the means through which children learn. The current EYFS (DCSF 2008) includes 'Play and Exploration' as one of the key commitments within the learning and development theme and recognises its importance: 'Children's play reflects their wide ranging and varied interests and preoccupations. In their play children learn at their highest level. Play with peers is important for children's development' (DCSF 2008). In planning for children's learning and development, reception teachers are required to ensure that this commitment is translated into practice. International influences, referred to above, reinforce the role of play and follow the interests of children in order to maximise learning.

The well-trained early years teacher will recognise its importance in delivering all areas of the curriculum and resist those top-down pressures associated with a concentration on literacy and numeracy. At the beginning of their school career, before they have acquired the formal skills of reading and writing drawn upon by so many primary lessons, the reception year requires a pedagogy of its own which builds on what children can do and develops fundamental skills in a meaningful context. The process of planning meaningful learning experiences that cannot, by their nature, rely on the skills of reading and writing, which have not as yet been fully mastered, presents a challenge to many trainee and experienced teachers.

It must also be recognised that children require a balance of child- and adult-initiated experiences in order for their learning to be maximised (Sylva et al. 2003; Siraj-Blatchford et al. 2002). There are skills and concepts, which need to be directly taught to children, through the support of a knowledgeable adult who has provided a suitable environment to support learning through play, while at the same time scaffolding children's learning in an appropriate way. Interactions in a well-organised and planned learning environment are essential. '"Sustained shared thinking" occurs when two or more individuals "work together" in an intellectual way to solve a problem, clarify a concept, evaluate an activity, extend a narrative, etc. Both parties must contribute to the thinking and it must develop and extend the understanding' (Sylva et al. 2003). This concept requires highly skilled adults to support children in an appropriate way. The challenge for reception teachers, and perhaps particularly when working in a mixed-age class, is to enable staff to contribute to these interactions within the areas of continuous provision. An emphasis only on direct teaching to small groups, or the whole class, will miss the opportunities for spontaneous interactions at the most relevant time for the child. In mixed-age classes, it can be all too tempting to allocate support for the reception children to those least qualified, or in some cases to volunteers. Challenges to provide an appropriate play-based curriculum, indoors and outside, may also include the lack of resources and the size of the space available to many reception classes. Where there is no access to an outdoor area enabling continuous free-flow of movement in both environments, teachers must think creatively in order to meet the requirements of the current curriculum of daily access to an outdoor environment.

Good practice includes:

- a well-planned, organised and resourced environment – indoors and outside – appropriate to the developmental needs of children
- practitioners who plan to extend and widen children's experiences, while enabling children to follow their own interests
- practitioners who engage, extend and develop creativity and critical thinking across the curriculum, allowing children to be independent in a safe, yet challenging environment.

Early reading

Children bring a variety of early reading experiences to the reception class in school. Some children may have few books in the home, while others have a whole 'library' of books in their bedrooms. Whatever their home circumstances, most children will have some experience of print in the environment, on television or a computer screen and those attending nursery or pre-school will have accessed books in these settings. Learning to read is a complex process and can be challenging for those with little prior experience of books or a secure language base on which to build.

The most appropriate age and method through which to teach children to read has long been a subject for heated debate. To date, there is no significant research that suggests that starting reading earlier produces long-term benefits (Suggate 2009) and, as suggested above, those countries who have later school starting ages do not suffer significantly in terms of reading competence – quite the opposite (OECD; PISA). Following the Independent Review of the Teaching of Early Reading (Rose 2006), teachers are currently strongly encouraged to adopt a 'synthetic phonics' approach and use the 'simple view of reading'.

Reception staff with weighty responsibility for the introduction of children to statutory education and in particular for the teaching of early reading, must be mindful that this experience can significantly impact on children's lifelong attitude to school.

Introducing children to fundamental skills is a complex process and it can be too easy for young children to feel like a failure before they even begin Key Stage 1. Pace and appropriateness of delivery are crucial and differentiation for different stages of child development is imperative.

As Rose (2006) suggests: 'the introduction of phonic work should always be a matter for principled, professional judgment based on structured observations and assessments of children's capabilities'. Parents want their children to succeed in school and can unwittingly communicate unrealistic expectations on young children of their potential achievements 'now they are at big school'.

Reception staff should ensure that 'best practice for beginner readers provides them with a rich curriculum that fosters all four interdependent strands of language: speaking, listening, reading and writing' (Rose 2006).

Good practice includes:

- teachers who protect children from the pressures of 'learning to read' before they are developmentally ready to do so
- a stimulating environment with an attractive reading area, containing a wide variety of reading materials, as well as books, story sacks and materials for storytelling
- adults who model the reading process and engage children in enjoyable reading experiences, including 'talk' about books and stories.

Different curricula will come and go but good practice will continue to require a focus on child development and provision, which is appropriate for individual children.

Developing an evidence-based philosophy

Earlier in this chapter, we used a cultural perspectives approach to consider differences in ethos that underpin practice variations in reception classes. Reception teachers can approach their role with more confidence and clarity if they have considered their own values and beliefs and how these will influence the ethos, guiding principles, behaviours and rules they wish to adopt with reception-age children.

It is important to inform a personal philosophy with evidence in order to support practice with rigour. There is a wealth of existing research on matters related to aspects of provision for children of 4 and 5 years of age in England. Additionally, a range of research from other countries can provide an interesting comparative view (Bertram and Pascal 2002). Some starting points to engage with this research can be found in the reference list below.

Classroom teachers are increasingly completing their own classroom research, in order to inform their philosophy and improve quality of experience for young children. Taking the 'teacher as researcher' approach in your reception class will enhance your own understanding of the issues particular to your context. The Centre for the Use of Research and Evidence in Education (CUREE) produces materials to support practitioners in developing evidence-based practice.

Reflective task

List some of the important values and beliefs that will guide your personal philosophy when working with reception-aged children.

Summary

In this chapter, we have introduced the reader to some of the controversial issues related to teaching 4–5-year-olds in reception classes. This included the tensions between formal and play-based learning and the importance of protecting an active approach to learning for children in mixed-age classes.

For young children to develop a positive disposition to school, their experience in the classroom needs to be exciting and inspiring. The reception teacher requires creative and innovative approaches to retain children's motivation and interest. Well-matched learning events, tailored to children's developmental achievements, are essential and this requires a sound knowledge of child development. The wealth of existing research can be drawn upon to develop an evidence base to underpin practice. Inspiration can be gained from the study of international perspectives on early years education.

The website related to this book gives further suggestions for web-based activities and reading.

Questions for discussion

- What training do you think would support potential reception teachers to induct new children into school?
- Considering the relevant research referred to the above regarding school starting ages, what age do you believe is most appropriate for children to start formal schooling?
- How can we promote a lifelong love of reading? What strategies should teachers deploy in order to develop enjoyment as well as skills in early reading?
- How would you organise the environment in a mixed-age class to support active and play-based learning?
- It has been identified that the development of thinking skills is an area that needs further development in early years provision (Siraj-Blatchford et al. 2003). What would you do in your own classroom to ensure the engagement of children in experiences that promote critical thinking?

Further reading

Linked to topics of interest, the following readings have been chosen because the authors are among the leading experts in the field.

Generic issues affecting early years' provision:

Duffy, B. and Pugh, G. (2009) *Contemporary Issues in the Early Years*. London: Sage. This book includes chapters written by several leading authors on current issues related to policy and research, practice and the workforce, and provides a sound insight into important influences on the current field of early years work.

Parents and home influences:

Melhuish, E. (2010) 'Why Children, Parents and Home Learning are Important', in K. Sylva, E. Melhuish, P. Sammons, I. Siraj-Blatchford and B. Taggart (eds) *Early Childhood Matters: Evidence from the Effective Pre-school and Primary Education Project*. London: Routledge, pp. 95–114.
This research emphasises the impact of home and parental interest in supporting children's achievements at school and will support early years practitioners in understanding the importance of their work with parents.

Whalley, M. (2007) *Involving Parents in their Children's Learning*. London: Sage.
Pen Green Children's Centre has completed some seminal work in teaching parents about child development and developing parents as partners in their children's learning. This book explains the work with parents in detail.

A play-based curriculum:

Bilton, H. (2010) *Outdoor Learning in the Early Years*. Oxford: Routledge.
A useful book to support setting up and extending outside provision and developing outdoor learning.

Bruce, T. (2004) *Developing Learning in Early Childhood (0–8)*. London: Sage.
This book includes practical ideas for supporting early active learning experiences.

Lindon, J. (1999) *Too Safe for Their Own Good*. London: NCB.
Reading this book will help you to consider your own position with regard to balancing risk and challenge in children's lives.

Moyles, J. (1989) *Just Playing?* Maidenhead: Open University Press.
This book will help you to pursue ideas introduced above about the value of play. It includes sections on play and progress to aid record keeping and the tracking of children's learning.

Early literacy:

Bayley, R. and Palmer, S. (2008) *Foundations of Literacy*, 3rd edn. London: Continuum Books.
A practical book full of inspired ideas for planning literacy in the early years.

Whitehead, M. (2010) *Language and Literacy in the Early Years 0–7*. London: Sage.
This book gives both a theoretical and practical perspective on teaching literacy for enjoyment, across the full early years age range.

References

Adams, S., Alexander, E., Drummond, M. J. and Moyles, J. (2004) *Inside the Foundation Stage: Recreating the Reception Year*. London: Association of Teachers and Lecturers.
Alexander, R. (ed.) (2010) *Children, their World, their Education: Final Report and Recommendations of the Cambridge Primary Review*. Oxford: Routledge.
Bertram, T. and Pascal C. (2002) *Early Years Education: An International Perspective*. Birmingham: Centre for Research in Early Childhood.
DCSF (2007) *Letters and Sounds*. London: DCSF.
DCSF (2008) *Early Years Foundation Stage*. London: DCSF.

Desforges, C. (2003) *The Impact of Parental Involvement, Parental Support and Family Education on Pupil Achievements and Adjustment: A Literature Review*. Research Report RR433. London: DfES.

Early Years Curriculum Group (EYCG) (2002) *Onwards and Upwards: Building on the Foundation Stage*. Oxford: Early Years Curriculum Group.

Fabian, H. (2002) *Children Starting School*. London: David Fulton.

Fabian, H. and Dunlop, A.W. (2002) *Transitions in the Early Years: Debating Continuity and Progression for Children in Early Education*. London: Routledge Falmer.

Gill, T. (2009) *No Fear: Growing Up in a Risk Averse Society*. London: Calouste Gulbenkian Foundation.

Laevers, F. (ed.) (2005) *Well-being and Involvement in Care Settings: A Process-oriented Self-evaluation Instrument*. Leuven: Research Centre for Experiential Education, Leuven University.

Layard, R. and Dunn, J. (2009) *The Good Childhood*. London: Penguin Books.

Margetts, K. (2002) 'Early Transition and Adjustment and Children's Adjustment After Six Years of Schooling', *European Early Childhood Education Research Journal* 17(3): 309–24.

Palmer, S. (2006) *Toxic Childhood: How the Modern World Is Damaging Our Children and What We Can Do About it*. London: Orion.

QCA (2005) *Continuing the Learning Journey*. London: QCA.

Rose, J. (2006) *Independent Review of the Teaching of Early Reading*. London: DfES.

Rose, J. (2009) *Independent Review of the Primary Curriculum: Final Report*. London: DCSF.

Sammons, P. et al. (2007) *Summary Report: Influences on Children's Attainment and Progress in Key Stage 2: Cognitive Outcomes in Year 5: Effective Pre-school and Primary Education 3–11 Project (EPPE 3–11)*. Research Report RR828. London: DfES.

Sharp, C. (2002) *School Starting Age: European Policy and Recent Research*. Slough: NFER.

Sharp, C., George, N., Sargent, C., O'Donnell, S. and Heron, M. (2009) *International Thematic Probe: The Influence of Relative Age on Learner Attainment and Development*. Slough: NFER.

Siraj-Blatchford, I., Sylva, K., Muttocks, S., Gilden, R. and Bell, D. (2002) *Researching Effective Pedagogy in the Early Years (REPEY)*. Nottingham: DfES.

Suggate, S.P. (2009) 'School Entry Age and Reading Achievement', *International Journal of Educational Research* 48(3): 151–61.

Sylva, K., Melhuish, E., Sammons, P., Siraj-Blatchford, I. and Taggart, B. (2003) *Effective Provision of Pre-School Education (EPPE)*. Nottingham: DfES.

UNICEF (2007) *Child Poverty in Perspective: An Overview of Child Well-being in Rich Countries. Innocenti Report Card 7*. Florence: UNICEF Innocenti Research Centre.

Whalley, M. (1994) *Learning to Be Strong*. London: Hodder and Stoughton.

Websites

Centre for the Use of Research and Evidence in Education (CUREE): www.curee-paccts. com

Forest Schools: www.forestschools.com/

OECD: www.oecd.org/home/0,2987,en_2649_201185_1_1_1_1_1,00.html

PISA: www.pisa.oecd.org/pages/0,2987,en_32252351_32235731_1_1_1_1_1,00.html

Reggio Emilia: http://zerosei.comune.re.it/inter/reggiochildren.htm http://www.reggioemilia approach.net/

Te Whāriki: www.educate.ece.govt.nz/learning/curriculumAndLearning/TeWhariki.aspx

CHAPTER 7

INCLUSION AND SPECIAL EDUCATIONAL NEEDS

Verna Kilburn and Kären Mills

By the end of this chapter, you should be able to:

- engage with fundamental questions concerning special educational needs as a contested concept

- develop your own values and demonstrate a commitment to social justice and inclusion

- construct and sustain a reasoned argument about some issues of inclusion, in a lucid and coherent manner

- demonstrate a clear understanding of the implications of whole-school issues relating to inclusion and special educational needs.

Introduction

Special Educational Needs (SEN) is an area that is simultaneously fascinating and complex. Although in historical terms it is a relatively recent expression, being brought to prominence through the Warnock Report (1978), in many ways it involves questions that are central to concepts of our humanity. What is the duty of the State to the individual? What compromises must the individual make to be part of a group? What is it to be different and who decides what the parameters of difference are? SEN has grown out of the fertile soil of politics, philosophy, medicine, ethics and pedagogy and all are set in a linguistic minefield.

This chapter considers interpretation of the terminology associated with inclusion and SEN. It considers changes in attitudes to children with SEN over the last century and the reasons for this, recent legislation on provision for children with SEN and the implications for teachers in primary schools. Throughout, there is a discussion of inclusion as a contested concept, the efficacy of the legislation, disparity between the ideology and practice and the complex and difficult decisions which teachers are involved in making. Case studies and activities involve readers in developing their own understanding of their roles in decision making and their views about problematic issues.

Why is discussion of inclusion issues complex and emotive?

It is not uncommon for students to be apprehensive before a school placement, and this anxiety may be increased by uncertainty about how to deal with children in the class who have SEN. This may be because of problems encountered on a previous placement, perhaps having a sibling with SEN, students themselves having experienced a Barrier to Learning in their own schooling or a student's own philosophy of education. The implications are that SEN is an area fraught with emotional and academic tensions. This is because responding to SEN involves not just academic and pedagogical skills but is also concerned with moral issues. By reflecting on the terminology you use and that others use, you can begin to participate in informed discussions of these issues.

 Reflective task

- In small groups, select a word from the following list:

Equality	*Inclusion*	*Disabled*	*Democracy*	*Management*
Special	*Diversity*	*Education*	*Labelling*	*Community*

(Continued)

(Continued)

- Write down the connotations of the term (words or ideas suggested by the word). (This should only take a few minutes and should reflect a quick, emotional reaction to the word.)
- Underline which connotations are positive and which are negative.
- Write a *short* definition of the term.
- Share all of this with a larger group and ask them to critique the definition.
- Which was the most difficult part of the activity?
- Are the definitions representative of the connotations?
- Which may have the most power?

According to Graber (2002), the use of some high-value words can distort an argument as their accompanying emotive power can hide the fact that there is little agreement over their definitions. This can not only obscure the argument, but lead to a manipulation of the feelings and thoughts of the reader/listener. This may be something in which politicians demonstrate a high level of skill (listen to a party political broadcast and notice the 'high-value words').

It is possible that the same difficulty is also encountered in the area of inclusion and education in general. We perhaps need more respect for the approach of the young child who asks 'What does it really mean?'

Words and meanings

The world of SEN contains sufficient of these emotive idioms to ensure a high level of anxiety in any student. Consider the following: handicap, disabled, impairment, Barrier to Learning, normal, segregation, integration … and this is not including the terms that are *definitely* not used in academic circles. The question arises as to why this is more prevalent in the area of inclusion than in other subjects? If I use the wrong term in mathematics or science, it may indicate a factual mistake or misunderstanding but may tell the other speaker little about my belief system or ethics. This is not true in SEN, which is value-laden. There are however, dangers in this because:

- the study of inclusion/SEN can be *ideologically* driven
- there is little agreement over the *definition* and use of the key terms.

Ideologies

The QTS standards give prominence to the values and attitudes expected of teachers and it has long been acknowledged that teaching should have a strong ethical and belief-based foundation. This may not be synonymous, however, with an ideological stance. According to Haralambos and Holborn:

> The term ideology refers to a set of ideas which present only a partial view of reality … it involves not only a judgement about the ways things are, but also about the way things ought to be. (2000 p. 19)

An ideology may be a partial, one-sided view, but one that is in harmony with the speaker's world view. Any cognitive dissonance is 'brushed under the carpet' in the mind. This may make life exceptionally difficult for the student as they need to constantly examine what evidence the author supplies (and what is omitted) and to be critical of the terminology used.

Definitions

The term inclusion has long been associated with children with SEN but it could be argued that it is relevant to all groups that are marginalised in and by our education system. There may be a strong case that educational failure is a form of exclusion as much as separate schooling. This could include, for example, children with English as an Additional Language (EAL), children in care, refugee children, traveller children and the division by ethnicity, gender, faith and social class into separate institutions. The UK has a growing number of different types of schools and the number seems set to increase in the near future. This expands on the argument from special versus mainstream schooling into a debate on whether we can have inclusive education while maintaining the myriad form of faith schools, private schools, academies, grammar schools, and so on.

Ainscow et al. (2006) clarify the difficulty of defining inclusion, by distinguishing between narrow and broad definitions; narrow referring to aspects of SEN, and broad to all aspects of marginalisation and diversity, but Armstrong et al. (2010) also point out the key dangers in stating:

> the meaning of 'inclusion' is by no means clear and perhaps conveniently blurs the edges of social policy with 'feel-good' rhetoric that no one could be opposed to. (p. 4)

Indeed, bearing in mind the statement in the National Curriculum that 'Education influences and reflects the values of society, and the kind of society we want to be' (QCA 1999 p. 10), then what possibility is there for inclusive education if the society it reflects is non-inclusive? Definitions of inclusion vary from the absolute, to be found in the statement by the Centre for Studies on Inclusive Education (CSIE):

> We fully support an end to all segregated education on the grounds of disability or learning difficulty, as a policy commitment and goal for this country … the existence of special schools represents a serious violation of students' human rights … (2002)

to the more hesitant one in the Fundamental Aims of the SEN Code of Practice (DfES 2001): 'the special educational needs of children will normally be met in mainstream schools or settings' (1.5).

It may not surprise you at this point, but there is also disagreement over the use and definition of the term SEN. According to the SEN Code of Practice (COP) (DfES 2001), children are deemed to have SEN if they have

> significantly greater difficulty in learning than the majority of children the same age
>
> or
>
> have a disability which prevents or hinders them from making use of educational facilities of a kind generally provided for children of the same age in schools within the area of the local education authority. (1.3)

At a NASEN (formerly the National Association for Special Educational Needs) debate (2009), however, some of the leading thinkers in the area held the view that the use of the term SEN was not only outmoded, but damaging (although in true academic style, there was little agreement). Norwich (2008) argued that the use of the term was problematic as it:

- led to negative labelling
- was poorly defined
- led to the expansion of SEN as a 'separatist industry'.

It is worth reading the debate in full as it gives a good picture of the complexity in the area.

The most common focus in SEN, however, is centred around the contentious issue of placement, usually on the argument of special versus mainstream provision. However, there is no clear division between those who may benefit from a full-time special school and those who may not, or in the levels of support pupils may need in a mainstream school. Norwich (2008 p. 136) outlines the full range of possibilities, which are shown in Table 7.1.

A historical perspective

The nineteenth century was essentially one of educational and social hierarchies. Children who were considered 'handicapped' were to some extent treated as the 'deserving poor' in that a charitable response was advocated to 'help the helpless', which was largely done by an act of separation. While it cannot be argued that this was not a vast improvement to the reaction of previous centuries, it was nevertheless set heavily in the deficit model; the fault lay in the child for not being 'normal' and not in the education being offered. In 1870 elementary education became compulsory, but only for children that could be thought to benefit from it. This excluded all those who

Table 7.1   Continuum of special education provision

MOST SEPARATE
Full-time residential special school
Full-time day special school
Part-time special and part-time ordinary school
Full-time special unit or class in ordinary school
Part-time special unit/class and part-time ordinary class
Full-time in ordinary class with some withdrawal and some in-class support
Full-time in ordinary class with in-class support
Full-time in ordinary class
MOST INCLUDED

(Norwich 2008)

were deemed to be imbeciles, idiots, and other groups who were either educated at a separate institution, or not at all.

Although segregated education has been widely rejected as discriminatory and unjust, it would be wrong to view the introduction of special schools as being motivated by any deliberate intent to exclude people with disabilities from the mainstream of society. Humanitarian motives were equally if not more important.

Medical/social models

The medical model is often known as the child deficit or within-child model. This has its origins in medical or psychological approaches where the *pathology* of differences was advocated (Clough and Corbett 2000). For example, assessment of an individual child would be carried out by a doctor or psychologist to determine the child's capabilities, 'but at the heart of these approaches was a view of the individual child as somehow deficient' (2000, p. 12).

The inclusion movement had its roots in the social model of disability, which holds that it is 'society's failure to adapt the environment to accommodate an individual's condition that is the disabling factor' (Kellett 2008 p. 163). The implication is that the problem is not the child's 'deficiency' but schools' failure to adapt teaching approaches, to sufficiently differentiate and to accept the culture of differences. These two approaches were supported with an almost religious fervour by what was becoming a simplistic split in philosophy, with each side becoming increasingly entrenched in a claim to the moral high ground and thus decreasing the possibility of acknowledging the more complex dilemmas and contractions that may have existed. It is now being proposed that the area may not be so 'black and white'. The term 'child deficit' influences the debate simply by its emotive connotations and may be rejected in favour of the previously mentioned 'feel good rhetoric of inclusion' (Armstrong et al. 2010 p. 4). This is not a plea to return to the era of labelling children as either deficient or uneducable, merely one to acknowledge the possible complexities. As McKay states, 'our job is not to make disability go away, not to pretend that it is not there. Instead, it is to respect its complexity, and to respond to it with honesty, vision and intelligence' (2002 p. 162). Many, including Lindsay (2003), now advocate an 'interactive model'.

It was only in 1970 that all children came under the aegis of education as, before that, any child who was deemed to be 'uneducable' was under the control of health authorities (Florian 2008 p. 202). There was growing dissatisfaction with the medical model, and echoing a growth of various national and international movements for social justice generally, in 1974 the Government ordered an enquiry into the education of 'Handicapped Children and Young People'. While it could be argued that the resulting Warnock Report (1978) was in some ways an epistemological break from previous thinking, Weddel (2008) is of the opinion that it merely 'caught up with recent thinking' (p. 127).

The Warnock Report

The main tenets of the Warnock Report (1978) were:

- One in five children would at some time require special educational provision.
- Eighteen per cent of these would be in mainstream schools (with the remaining 2 per cent being in special schools).
- Use of the term SEN (although this was not new: it was first used by Gulliford in 1971).
- Recognition that 'special educational needs arose from the context of the child's experience which includes family life and the quality of schooling' (Armstrong et al. 2010 p. 19).

Although this was a move away from the purely medical model, taking into account contexts, it still acknowledged the concepts of individual and institutional 'failure' and this reflected tensions in the dichotomy of the social/medical model.

Special Educational Needs and Disability legislation

The current law concerning SEN is contained in the Education Act (1996) and was amended in the Special Educational Needs and Disability Act (SENDA) (2001). This led to the revision of the 1994 Special Educational Needs Code of Practice (SEN COP). The fundamental principles of the Code of Practice (DES 2001, Section 7.5, p.7) are shown below.

The Code of Practice states that:

- children with SEN should have their needs met
- the SEN of children will normally be met in mainstream schools or early education settings

- the views of the child should be sought and taken into account
- parents have a vital role to play in supporting their child's education
- children with SEN should be offered full access to a broad, balanced and relevant education, including an appropriate curriculum for the Foundation Stage and the National Curriculum.

The graduated approach

- The approach recognises that there is a continuum of SEN.
- Where necessary, increasing specialist expertise should be brought to bear on the difficulties that a child may be experiencing.

School action

- When a class teacher identifies that a pupil has SEN, the class teacher devises interventions additional to or different from those provided as part of the school's usual differentiated curriculum offer.
- The class teacher remains responsible for working with the child on a daily basis and for planning and delivering an individualised programme – an IEP (Individual Education Plan) will usually be devised.
- The Special Educational Needs Coordinator (SENCO) in the school could take the lead in planning future interventions for the child in discussion with colleagues monitoring and reviewing the action.

School action plus

- SENCO and class teacher, in consultation with parents, ask for help from external services.
- Class teacher and SENCO are provided with advice or support from outside specialists.
- Additional or different strategies to those at school action are put in place – an IEP will usually be devised.

Critical success factors

- Those responsible for SEN provision take into account the views and wishes of the child.
- Professionals and parents work in partnership.
- Professionals take account of parents' views.

- Provision and progress is monitored and reviewed regularly.
- Statements are clear and detailed, specify monitoring arrangements and are reviewed annually.

Roles

As can be implied from the Code of Practice (DfES 2001), the voice of the child must be taken into consideration, as must the views of the parents. Obviously, the teachers, SENCO, teaching assistants (TAs) and, potentially, external services will also be required to not only give some input, but to work collaboratively. The Every Child Matters (ECM) agenda (DfES 2005) crystallised and formalised the need for multi-agency working, but it had existed in one form or another long before that, with varying degrees of success. It is likely that each person will come to this process with differing and perhaps conflicting perspectives, depending on which 'discipline' they belong to (Education, Health, Psychology, etc.), their personalities, stress levels, loyalties and knowledge.

At best, this diversity of approach and knowledge could lead to a problem-solving, holistic approach, where all knowledge is shared and respected. Conversely, it could also result in a hierarchical culture, where some points of view are held to be of a higher status and thus may have more power. There are some excellent journal articles discussing this point addressing the roles of the parent, child, SENCO and teaching assistant, some with potential solutions (see list of further reading).

Areas of need

There is an acknowledgement that these are not 'hard and fast' categories and that 'each child is unique' (7.52) but the Code of Practice (DfES 2001, Section 7.52, p.85) identified four areas of need:

- communication and interaction
- cognition and learning
- behaviour, emotional and social development
- sensory and/or physical.

It could certainly be argued that some formal system is needed to acknowledge that some pupils need more support than others, but it remains problematic.

In many ways, these four areas of function reflect the contradiction that Dyson pointed out (2001) between an 'intention to treat all learners as essentially the same and an equal and opposite intention to treat them as different' (p. 201).

Questions for discussion

- Does a child either 'have SEN' or not?
- What should you take into account?
- Can SEN provision ensure a broad, balanced, relevant curriculum?
- What classroom problems, and solutions, have you seen in schools so far?

Reflective task: barriers to learning

- In small groups, select a barrier to learning. This may be one of the more common ones such as dyslexia, dyspraxia, autistic spectrum disorder, visual impairment, hearing impairment, or a behaviour difficulty. (You need to treat ADHD as being contentious.) You may, however, wish to select one that you have already had some experience of in schools.
- Research this area (see further reading).
- Consider how you would use the following strategies to support a child in your class who has this barrier to learning. (You need to specify a particular age group.)

differentiation	use of resources	assessment
classroom grouping	use of other adults	provision on an educational visit
the creation of an inclusive culture in the class	communication with parents	involving the views of the child

- Feed back to the whole group. (A poster presentation may be an effective way of doing this.)

In completing this task, you may have found that the necessary range of knowledge, skills and roles was intimidating. Yet class teachers do this on a daily basis. It may help to bear in mind that your aim is competence and care, not divinity, and that no one gets it right all of the time. You should also not expect to be alone in this process. The teaching assistants, parents and the child can all help you come to a solution that benefits the whole child. This can also increase your expertise in reacting to all the children.

Case study

Read the following critical incident and, individually or with others, discuss the questions it raises.

Ben

Ben is 6-years-old, from a traveller family and has been admitted to your school recently: he is the middle of five children. His academic attainment is below that of most of the other children in the class, especially in written work. He rarely completes these written tasks and his work is generally untidy with his writing being typical of a younger child with letter reversals and immature spelling. He enjoys activities that are based on talking and giving verbal feedback to the group, teacher or class. Art and science lessons are a particular strength for him and he appears to have a good understanding of geography. In class, he is slow to settle into tasks and can be disruptive. Socially, his peer group describe him as a loner who prefers to seek out the company of his siblings during playtimes; the class teacher commented to other staff members that he had few friends. The class has a full-time TA, but Ben does not like working with her in withdrawal situations. His parents did not attend the open evening, but the mother brings Ben to school. She does not come into the classroom but will talk amicably to the teacher in the playground before and after school. What questions does this raise?

Critical incident

Ben is working with a group of another five children. He has just started to write and is getting restless. His writing is very slow and he repeatedly stops and wanders round the room. He then breaks his pencil and throws it on the floor. The TA approaches him, tells him to behave and to work at a small table with her. Ben swears at her and refuses. He is becoming increasingly upset and disruptive. When he is reseated at the table, the other children complain that they don't want him, stating that 'he can't do any work' and 'I don't want to sit next to *him*'.

Analysing the incident

There are many possible conclusions that can arise from analysis of this critical incident, but they tend to fall into four possible categories:

1 Ben has a form of Specific Learning Difficulty (SpLD). The observations that Ben has disproportionate difficulties with his written work compared to verbal tasks, has immature spelling, letter reversals and has devised task-avoidance strategies

(Continued)

(breaking the point of the pencil, 'wandering off') could lead us to think that Ben has dyslexia.

2 Ben does not have SpLD. His difficulties can be explained by his educational history and background. It is possible that an interrupted schooling has had an effect on his academic progress. If he is operating at an earlier stage of literacy, then letter reversals and immature spelling are representative of this and not dyslexia. If he is aware of this, then the ensuing tensions may explain his behaviour. If he also feels excluded because of his ethnicity, and so chooses not to interact with his peers at playtime this will give him the reputation of a 'loner' with other children.

3 Ben may come from a traveller culture, have had interrupted schooling *and* have dyslexia.

4 It may be explained by something totally different that only future information may shed light on.

You may want to explore the following questions:

- How could the incident have been avoided?
- What do you need to do next?
- What could explain the incident?
- What information do you now need?
- Does Ben have a special educational need?
- *Does* the problem lie solely inside Ben?
- What extra knowledge do you need?
- How will you involve the parents?
- How will you find out what Ben thinks?
- What will the role of the SENCO be now?
- How will you deploy the TA?

Summary of case study

In considering the case study, it should be becoming clear that not only are there many factors that can affect a child's progress, but that inclusion may be reliant on more than the interaction between the teacher and the child. What of the general culture of the classroom. Does Ben *feel* included by the other children? If not, what should the teacher do? How many of Ben's difficulties are 'within child' and does it make a difference at this stage? Much of the advice by the British Dyslexia Association (BDA) merely reflects good literacy teaching. The major focus may have to be on inclusion and not solely a 'medical approach' to SEN.

International perspectives

One way of appreciating that inclusion has social, political and cultural roots is to examine international perspectives.

The Cambridge Review (Alexander 2010) states that many of England's 800,000 pupils with special educational needs are still offered patchy and inadequate services, according to parents, teachers and local authorities and that, while the principle of inclusion has been accepted, the 'concerted effort the United Nations warned would be needed to make it successful has not been achieved'. The Review expressed concerns that pupils are being labelled and segregated unnecessarily by the type of school they attend and the experiences they receive when there and that they are therefore vulnerable to stereotyping and discrimination. The Review recommends a thorough overhaul of the system.

The findings of the Cambridge Review are endorsed by a report, *How Fair is Britain* (Equality and Human Rights Commission 2010), which found that children with a disability face shocking levels of bullying and that there are significant inequalities based on gender, poverty and race.

Summary

This chapter has discussed the controversial aspects of what might at first appear a fairly simple question: how can we have inclusive classrooms, which allow equal educational opportunities for all children? The reason why there are tensions between the ideal and its implementation was discussed. The chapter considered definitions of and provision for children with special educational needs and for inclusion. It has set out the relevant legislation and the implications of this for teachers. It concluded with a consideration of how other countries address special educational needs.

Participation in the suggested reflective activities aimed to actively involve readers in developing their own philosophies and in making the judgements and decisions they will be required to make as teachers in implementing the legislation which aims to promote equal opportunities.

The website related to this book gives additional references to books on English as an Additional Language, on Gifted and Talented Children, Travellers and Children with Special Educational Needs. It also gives the addresses of useful websites.

Questions for discussion

- What is the relevance for us of the report, *How Fair is Britain* (EHRC 2010)?
- Are there tensions between economic development and equality?
- Is it ever possible to justify utilitarianism? (That good is whatever brings the greatest happiness to the greatest number of people.)
- If so, what are the implications for inclusion/SEN in the UK?

(Suggestions for further reading follow, but are only an indication of the wealth of information in the area.)

Further reading

Cigman, R. (ed.) (2007) *Included or Excluded: The Challenge of the Mainstream for some SEN Children*. London: Routledge.
An excellent book in which key authors in the field of Inclusion address many of the most important debates and information in the area. It includes chapters on autism, children with emotional difficulties, the inclusion debate and the views of parents, written by some of the best known authors in the field of Inclusion/SEN.

Hodkinson, A. and Vickerman, P. (2009) *Key Issues in Special Educational Needs and Inclusion*. London: Sage.
This book gives a good overview of the major themes in Inclusion, both internationally and historically. It includes many relevant and interesting case studies for discussion in an accessible way.

Jones, G. (2002) *Educational Provision for Children with Autism and Asperger Syndrome*. London: David Fulton.
This is a key text by an author who is a lecturer in autism and an educational psychologist. It covers the major theories in autistic spectrum disorder (ASD), its identification and the most common intervention strategies used. These include TEACCH. PECS and Makaton, and also the importance of working in collaboration with others including other staff and parents. The book gives a good starting point for the study of ASD.

Pavey, B. (2007) *The Dyslexia-Friendly Primary School*. London: Paul Chapman Publishing.
The book is an accessible and reader-friendly introduction to dyslexia. It includes clear definitions of dyslexia, without distorting the complexities of the subject. It includes practical activities and approaches, many of which could not only benefit a child with dyslexia, but all children in a primary classroom.

References

Ainscow, M., Booth, T. and Dyson, A. (2006) *Improving Schools, Developing Inclusion*. London: Routledge.

Alexander, R. (ed.) (2010) *Children, Their World, Their Education: Final Report and Recommendations of the Cambridge Primary Review*. London: Routledge.

Armstrong, A., Armstrong, D. and Spandagou, I. (2010) *Inclusive Education: International Policy and Practice.* London: Sage.

Centre for Studies in Inclusion in Education (CSIE) (2002) *The Inclusion Charter*. Bristol: CSIE

Clough, P. and Corbett, J. (2000) *Theories of Inclusive Education*. London: Sage.

Department for Education and Science (DfES) (2001) *Code of Practice on the Identification and Assessment of Children with Special Educational Needs*. London: DES.

DfES (2005) *Every Child Matters: Change for Children*. London: HMSO.

Dyson, A. (2001) 'Special Needs in the Twenty-first Century: Where We've Been and Where We're Going', *British Journal of Special Education* 28(1). pp. 24–9.

Equality and Human Rights Commission (2010) *How Fair is Britain? Equality, Human Rights and Good Relations in 2010. The First Triennnial Review*. Scotland: HMSO.

Florian, L. (2008) 'Special or Inclusive Education: Future Trends', *British Journal of Special Education* 35(4). p. 202.

Graber, D. (2002) *The Power of Communication: Managing Information in Public Organizations*. Washington, DC: CQ Press.

Gulliford, R. (1971) *Special Educational Needs.* London: Routledge and Kegan Paul.

Kellett, M. (2008) 'Special Educational Needs and Inclusion in Education', in D. Matheson (ed.) *An Introduction to the Study on Education*, 3rd edn. London: Routledge.

Haralambos, M. and Holborn, M. (2000) *Sociology Themes and Perspectives*, 5th edn. London: Collins.

Lindsay, G. (2003) 'Inclusive Education: A Critical Perspective', *British Journal of Special Education* 30(1). p. 5.

McKay, G. (2002) 'The Disappearance of Disability? Thoughts on a Changing Culture', *British Journal of Special Education* 29(4). p. 162.

NASEN (2009) *Special Educational Needs has Outlived its Usefulness: A Debate*. Series 6, Policy Paper 4, 6th Series, March.

Norwich, B. (2008) 'What Future for Special Schools and Inclusion? Conceptual and Professional Perspectives', *British Journal of Special Education* 35(3): p. 200.

QCA (1999) *The National Curriculum: Handbook for Primary Teachers in England*. London: QCA.

Warnock, M. (1978) *Special Educational Needs: Report of the Committee of Enquiry into the Education of Handicapped Children and Young People*. London: HMSO.

Weddel, K. (2008) 'Confusion about Inclusion: Patching up or System Change?', *Journal of Special Education* 35(3): pp. 127–36.

CHAPTER 8

BEHAVIOUR MANAGEMENT

Deborah Seward

By the end of this chapter, you will:

- understand the powers and rights teachers and schools have in terms of managing pupil discipline

- understand the theories, beliefs and values systems which underpin approaches to managing pupil behaviour

- be able to identify suitable approaches/techniques for managing classroom behaviour successfully.

Introduction

The purpose of this chapter is to provide an introduction to some of the issues surrounding behaviour management in the primary classroom. It will consider why behaviour management is important, teachers' rights, what teachers, parents and pupils need to know. It will also outline a case study in which one school used a social constructivist process to establish a framework for behaviour in school. The activities outlined are intended to extend and develop thinking about the issues for beginning teachers.

Reflective task

- Why do you believe behaviour management is important?
- Make a list of the rights and powers you believe teachers have to discipline pupils.
- Note down your experiences of behaviour management, either as a pupil and/ or as an adult in a primary classroom.

Is behaviour management important?

To answer the question above, we need to consider the rights we have as teachers as well as the rights pupils have. Teachers have a right to teach, indeed as Steer (2009 p. 18) notes: 'Teachers have a right to work in an environment that allows them to use their skills to the full for the benefit of all their pupils.' All children have a right to learn. Children have a right to attend school in safety and to learn without disruption from others' (Steer 2009 p. 18). This clearly identifies the necessity for a safe, calm learning environment where teachers can make decisions about pedagogy based on the context and the needs of their pupils in order to ensure that effective learning occurs. Behaviour management is a key factor in creating a positive learning environment where children feel safe to take risks in learning and where their views and feelings are valued and respected. The teacher's job is to enable and promote successful learning; for this to occur there needs to be effective behaviour management measures in place.

Additionally, pupil misbehaviour has consistently been reported as a source of teacher stress (Borg 1990; Dunham and Varma 1998) and whilst teachers may highlight extreme behaviour, such as physical or verbal assault, as a notable concern it is the lower-level disruptive behaviours which are more common. The child who constantly talks out of turn, fiddles with things, gets up out of their seat – these are the most familiar, everyday challenges for teachers (Elton Report 1989), which can make life very stressful. For some members of the teaching profession, poor behaviour becomes so difficult to manage that they may change careers and as the *Teacher Voice Omnibus, June 2008 Survey* found: 64 per cent of primary teachers questioned believed that 'negative pupil behaviour is driving teachers out of the profession' (NFER 2008 p. 10).

So, behaviour affects the pupil learning experience, in terms of cognitive, social and emotional development as well as the teacher's teaching experience and personal well-being. Indeed, everyone's whole experience of being at school and part of the school community can be affected by both their behaviour and that of other members of the school community.

Establishing a clear framework for classroom management

What do I, the teacher, need to know?

In order to establish a clear framework for discipline in your classroom, you first need to accept that there is no one way of managing behaviour; you need to recognise that what works in one context with one group of children will not necessarily work in the same context with a different group. Challenging behaviours may be a result of a range of contextual issues related to the community, family, school, classroom, peer group and teacher as well as the individual pupil themselves. This is what makes behaviour management so complex. The challenge is to find something which works for you and your children.

In order to do this, you need to be very clear about three areas, namely:

- your powers, rights and responsibilities
- your beliefs and values about learning and teaching, as this will undoubtedly affect how you deal with behaviour
- your understanding of the school's behaviour management policy.

The Education and Inspections Act 2006 (HMSO 2006 pp. 88–95) gave much clearer and broader powers to schools to discipline pupils, and teachers ought to feel confident and knowledgeable enough to apply these in order to ensure good standards of behaviour. These are under constant revision and teachers should keep up to date by accessing the information available via www.teachernet.gov.uk. The following is a list of powers and rights teachers should know are available to them.

Teachers have the right to

- discipline pupils – for breaking a school rule, failure to follow instructions or other unacceptable behaviour
- discipline pupils for misbehaviour outside the school gates should the behaviour and discipline policy allow
- encourage good and punish poor behaviour as outlined in their behaviour policy
- impose detention, if it is part of the school's behaviour policy, giving parents 24 hours' notice
- confiscate items

- use reasonable force to control or restrain pupils where it is necessary to avoid the breakdown of good order or discipline
- search pupils and their possessions if there is reason to do so
- be consulted by governing bodies, along with parents and pupils, about the school behaviour policy
- have respect shown for their professional role as a teacher
- a safe working environment.

Additionally, head teachers have the right to exclude pupils.

 Reflective task: reflections on beliefs and values

How did your initial reflections at the beginning of the chapter match up with the points above? Is there anything which surprised you?

It is extremely important that as a professional you have a clear set of beliefs and values which underpin your teaching, as these will drive how you operate in the classroom and will be reflected in your interactions with pupils and those around you. Consider your own beliefs and values about education, for example do you value pupils' opinions and ideas? Do you aim to empower pupils? Do you value authority? Consider how these values and beliefs may translate into ways of managing behaviour. For example, if you value empowerment, you may encourage pupils to set classroom rules and encourage them to reflect and judge behaviours against these.

As behaviour is learnt, whether this is in school, home or the wider community, it is an area we, as teachers, need to teach and it is our beliefs about learning theory which will affect how we go about teaching this. If, for example, you believe in behaviourist theory, then you will adopt a rewards and sanctions approach to managing behaviour, rewarding appropriate behaviour and punishing inappropriate behaviour – for example using charts, stickers, house points, certificates or excluding a child from playtime for inappropriate behaviour. If, however, you value social constructivism as an approach to learning, then you are more likely to adopt a culture in which children are encouraged to discuss and identify classroom rules which are then used and talked about when dealing with behaviour issues.

This notion that children should be encouraged to talk about potentially contentious issues would reflect Cooper's views (1993 p. 129) as he argues that teachers have a 'moral obligation to enable pupils to articulate their views as effectively as possible'. It can be argued that a key aspect of education is the moral development of the child and, as Piaget argued, morality is actively constructed through 'peer interaction'. This allows children to develop ideas around the notion of fairness, allowing them to actively develop their own moral reasoning and appreciation of others' views. Kohlberg further developed Piaget's ideas (Gross 2004; Moshman 2005; Sheehy 2004) outlining three levels and six stages of moral maturity (Kohlberg et al. 1983). It is clear from the case study that can be found in the web materials related to this chapter that children's ideas and thinking around issues of behaviour were being challenged and they were beginning to operate at the level of 'conventional morality' – making choices about behaviour which was based on the will of the whole school community.

The case study describes a process in which behaviour management has been openly negotiated with pupils in a 'partnership' approach (Ingram and Worral 1993) in which both adults and pupils are working together to influence an important aspect of school culture.

It is clear from this case study that the staff strongly believed in the importance of involving the pupils and listening to pupil views and had incorporated a social constructivist approach to involving pupils in the creation and management of behaviour. Pupils were seen as partners in the education enterprise and as such had a right for their voice to be recognised and respected just as much as the adults in the context did. As can be seen, the values expressed, such as respect, valuing each other, responsibility and fairness, were clearly enacted through the whole-school approach to managing behaviour.

The importance of a whole-school approach cannot be underestimated in successful behaviour management, and as a teacher one of the first policies you need to familiarise yourself with is the behaviour management policy.

Reflective task

Find a copy of your school's behaviour management policy.

How does it help you, the class teacher, to manage behaviour?

Is there anything you need to do in your classroom with regards to creating or reiterating rules?

What are the underpinning values or beliefs about children and behaviour?

On placement, observe how the class teacher manages behaviour – what works successfully? Consider how you can implement the strategies he/she employs.

A whole-school approach ensures consistency and fairness for pupils, so they feel they are being treated equally. This notion of fairness was found to be of importance to children in terms of successful learning with trainee teachers, as outlined by Cooper and Hyland (2002 p. 14): 'Once the ground rules were clear and perceived to be fair, children accepted them. Then it became possible to establish more subtle rules for relating to each other over time.' Children identified 'firmness, fairness, quietness, good humour' (p. 14) as crucial in establishing a successful learning environment.

As part of this relational aspect of the learning environment and in order to manage behaviour successfully, you need to be aware of your own feelings and emotions and how and why you react in different ways. This level of personal emotional intelligence is critical if we are to teach children how to handle their emotions and subsequently manage their own behaviour. There are times when we all, no matter how experienced, feel angry and frustrated when dealing with a difficult class or individual. This is normal. The challenge is to learn how to deal with these emotional responses in a way that provides self-control and results in you establishing and remaining in control. Basic advice would be to take a deep breath, count to 10 and consider your options before reacting. Offer the child a choice – for example, you can choose to finish this now or at playtime. Avoid direct confrontation and remain calm as how you behave will affect the child's reaction.

What do pupils need to know in order to successfully manage their own behaviour?

From day one, you need to show the pupils who is in charge, namely *you*, the adult in the classroom. They need to be aware of your expectations of them and the consequences of pushing the boundaries and how this dovetails with whole-school policies and expectations.

Sharing expectations can be done through dialogue and discussion, as the case study shows, and frequently classroom rules are established and displayed during the first days of teaching. However, what is crucial is how these classroom rules are subsequently used. Pupils quickly learn whether you have valued their ideas and input into the rules through how you use them in the everyday context. If you are serious about listening to pupils' opinions, then you will use the classroom rules, collaboratively created, in your discussions and dealings with behaviour, constantly referring to them. This will contribute positively to the developing relationship you establish with your class. If, however, you allow children to create and then display classroom rules and never use them, then children will learn that you do not value their input, and, because they will be unsure of expectations and boundaries, there will be a temptation, on their part, to constantly test and judge you, especially in terms of what is acceptable behaviour, fairness and equality.

If you are not going to consult pupils about behaviour, then you need to clearly set out what you expect and what the rewards and sanctions will be and how this fits in with whole-school expectations. They will test you out – you can be assured of that – so it is important to remember to be consistent.

Pupils need to know you value good behaviour and what it is like, so praise it! This helps illustrate what you expect of them and provides concrete role models for those children who may not see much good behaviour in other aspects of their life.

You, yourself, are a powerful role model and as such the children will watch and observe how you behave in and around school and this will affect how they behave. You set the standards of politeness, punctuality, dress and being. If they see you speak to the teaching assistant or midday supervisor politely, then they are more likely to do so. The choices adults make in terms of their own behaviour are crucial in influencing children's choices as to how they will behave.

Additionally, pupils need to know how to manage their own behaviour and feelings; this needs to be taught and developed. Ultimately, you are aiming for them to have self-control over and regulation of their own behaviour. They need to know you value them as individuals and that you are interested in their well-being and see them managing their own behaviour as an integral aspect of personal well-being. In order to encourage this aspect, many schools have introduced the SEAL (Social and Emotional Aspects of Learning) materials (DfES 2005), which gives a framework for teachers to address a number of issues around relationships, bullying and feelings. Schools may also use a circle time approach for discussing issues associated with behaviour. This involves sitting in a circle, taking turns in discussion and listening to pupils. It can be used to discuss a variety of issues in an open atmosphere where the teacher becomes a facilitator (DfES 2005 p. 51), one of the group and part of the discussion. If relationships are secure, it is a good vehicle for exploring children's views and addressing issues, and teachers need to show the value they place on pupil opinion – it requires good listening skills from the adult involved. These approaches need to be regularly incorporated into your teaching repertoire so they become a natural vehicle and opportunity for pupils to discuss issues in a safe, secure environment. They are valuable for you to show how you value pupils' personal development as well as often giving you an insight into what makes individuals behave as they do. This insight can then offer you suggestions for reasons for behaviour and allow you the opportunity to consider suitable approaches for dealing with issues.

Reflective task

Identify how you would plan to engage children in a circle time discussion around creating a set of classroom rules. Consider how you would manage this session. What teacher skills are necessary to enable this to happen?

What do parents need to know?

The support from parents in dealing with behaviour is crucial – if there are issues, they need to be aware of them and what you are doing to overcome them so that they can further support your work at home if necessary. Initially, parents need to be aware of school expectations, the behaviour policy and how the school goes about managing behaviour on a daily basis. If a home/school agreement exists, it may well include details of expectations. Parents will also be aware of how you manage behaviour from observing staff at school events, for example at assemblies and performances. However, you may need to be more explicit and talk them through what you do to manage specific behaviours.

In your classroom setting, parents need to know what class rules exist. You may want to write and tell them at the beginning of the year what rules and expectations have been discussed with the children as well as ensuring that these are displayed for all to see.

Daily contact with parents provides a good opportunity to mention good behaviour as well as any concerns you may have and parents' evenings also present an opportunity for a more in-depth discussion about specific individual issues. You will need to be clear about the problem behaviours and what you are doing/intend to do to overcome these. You may also want to discuss details of how you are going to communicate with parents about issues, whether this is a home/school diary or a regular short meeting. By discussing issues with parents, you often find they are having similar problems at home so approaches and ideas can be shared. This process illustrates to parents that you value their input and helps build relationships around the child, ensuring consistency. Very often, once you have established good relationships with parents/carers, they will ask you for advice and this may be an opportunity for you all to source additional support as necessary, as well as involve others such as the school SENCO and specialist teams.

How do I do it? How do I manage behaviour?

Ultimately, in your classroom, it is your responsibility to provide a safe, secure environment where successful learning can take place. Your classroom needs to be well organised and presented, with materials for the lessons accessible, resources ready and stimulating, interesting, engaging lessons well planned. Clear routines and good organisation reduce opportunities for children to disrupt lessons by implying they cannot find materials or because you have to leave to photocopy a worksheet. In order to do this, you need to establish yourself and have presence. Be proactive – don't wait for unacceptable behaviour to occur – set out and establish expectations early on and be consistent with these.

Setting expectations

The pupils will test you out but as long as you are clear and consistent then in the longer term they will respect you. As Sammons et al. (2008 p. 16) note: 'a proactive approach to classroom management may help promote better learning and assist children to become better at managing their own learning behaviour.'

Having a presence means being in the classroom at the start of the lesson, welcoming children and establishing a purposeful start – show you are ready to teach and they should be ready to learn. Have strategies which indicate that the lesson is about to start, counting down from 10, with a timer displayed on the interactive whiteboard, a clapping rhyme or whatever suits you and your children, but ensure everyone is ready to listen, wait and be patient. Be omnipresent – have that ability to know what is happening around you – as all teachers have eyes in the back of their heads! Be aware of what all pupils are doing – position yourself so you can see and observe everyone. Sometimes a look, a tap on the desk, a hand on the shoulder is enough to signal you know what is happening. These quiet approaches do not break the flow of learning but are enough to signal to individuals and groups that you are tuned into their engagement with learning. Often a quiet word also helps to stop behaviour escalating into something more disruptive. Being proactive and dealing with little incidents means you don't allow things to escalate to the point of having to shout or apply more intrusive methods which disrupt the whole group. Consider your organisation and grouping of pupils – who will work well together? Seating plans mean you control the interaction taking place and this can limit opportunities for inappropriate behaviour.

While these less intrusive methods may help with low-level behaviour, there are frequently times when more needs to be done. These steps should always be taken in the light of school and classroom rules, so expectations are consistent; the school in the case study was very clear about this.

In many cases, behaviour can be a reaction to something in school and, for some children, if there is a pattern of inappropriate behaviour, it is well worth analysing any antecedents to the behaviour exhibited. For example, if a child regularly has issues in the playground at lunchtimes, they may exhibit inappropriate behaviour during the afternoon session or there may be a particular grouping of pupils which causes problems. These may only come to light in discussions with pupils about why they behaved inappropriately which is why opportunities for dialogue with individuals is important. If you can work out triggers for inappropriate behaviour, you can avoid the situation occurring or at least support the child in making suitable choices for their actions.

For some children, the exhibition of inappropriate behaviour can be a signal that their learning needs are not being met; perhaps work is too easy or too challenging, or they may need instructions or to have explanations given in a different way. This is why it is important to establish meaningful relationships so you know each individual and can match the learning to their needs. There may be a case for seeking additional support both for the child and for you as the teacher in meeting their individual learning needs.

It should be noted that behaviour can be a reaction to something you, as the teacher, have little control over, for example a family breakdown or bereavement. This is why it is important to have good relationships with both parents and pupils so that these (often short-term issues) can be addressed and the child supported through a difficult situation.

Summary

This chapter has dealt with some of the basic areas you need to consider when dealing with behaviour management. You should have developed a greater understanding of the powers and rights you have as a teacher and realised that these need to be regularly reviewed as they are subject to change. Through review of the case study, you should now be aware of how a social constructivist approach to establishing expectations about behaviour can be achieved. Through reflecting on your own values and beliefs, you should have a clearer idea about how you will approach behaviour in your own classroom, as well as being in a position to now consider some of the issues for parents and pupils. You should also be beginning to consider techniques you will use in the classroom to manage and teach behaviour. In summary, in order to teach behaviour:

- Teach children the behaviours which allow children to reach the shared and stated expectations.
- Make your teaching of behaviour explicit.
- Make this a priority in your teaching time.
- Use a range of approaches to teach behaviour: pictures, photos, role play, circle time.
- Help children understand that behaviour can be learned.
- Ensure you plan for regular reinforcement.

 Questions for discussion

- Consider the implications for your own learning.
- What will your next steps be?
- What will you do in your own classroom to develop effective practice?
- Consider any classroom rules you are aware of.
- Are the rules clear and phrased in a positive manner?
- Are they understood by children?
- Were children involved in creating these rules?
- Do they work, do they promote learning?

Further reading 📖

More details about your powers and rights can be found in the leaflet, *School Discipline: Your Powers and Rights as a Teacher* (2009), available from www.teachernet.gov.uk and a must read for all teachers. The leaflet *Use of Force Guidance* is also available via www.teachernet.gov.uk

Leaflets

DCSF (2009) *Working Together for Good Behaviour in Schools.* Available from: www.teachernet.gov.uk

DCSF (2010) *Use of Force Guidance: Short Summary.* Available from: www.teachernet.gov.uk

NASUWT and DCSF (2009) *School Discipline: Your Powers and Rights as a Teacher.* Available from: www.teachernet.gov.uk

Approaches to dealing with behaviour can be further developed through engagement with scenarios on the behaviour4learning website: www.behaviour4learning.ac.uk – see the web pages for more details of specific programmes.

Behaviour Management (Canterbury Christ Church University College) Review Group (2004) *A Systematic Review of How Theories Explain Learning Behaviour in School Contexts.* London: EPPI Centre, Institute of Education, University of London. (Section 5 is particularly useful.)

Cowley, S. (2006) *Getting the Buggers to Behave.* London: Continuum.

DCSF (2006) *Learning Behaviour. Principles and Practice: What Works in Schools. Section 2 of the Report of the Practitioners on School Behaviour and Discipline Chaired by Alan Steer.* Nottingham: DCSF Publications.

DCSF (2010) *The Use of Force to Control or Restrain Pupils: Guidance for Schools in England.* Available from www.teachernet.gov.uk

Rogers, B. (2007) *Behaviour Management – A Whole–School Approach.* London: Paul Chapman Publishing.

Rogers, B. (2008) *Behaviour Management with Young Children: Crucial First Steps with Children 3–7 Years.* London: Sage.

References

Borg, M.G. (1990) 'Occupational Stress in British Educational Settings: A Review', *Education Research* 10: 103–26.

Cooper, H. and Hyland, R. (2002) *Children's Perceptions of Learning with Trainee Teachers.* London: Routledge.

Cooper, P. (1993) 'Learning from Pupils' Perspectives', *British Journal of Special Education* 20(4): 129–33.

DfES (2005) *Excellence and Enjoyment: Social and Emotional Aspects of Learning*. London: DfES.

Dunham, J. and Varma, V. (1998) *Stress in Teachers: Past Present and Future*. London: Whurr Publishers.

Elton Report (1989) *Discipline in Schools*. London: HMSO.

Gross, M.U.M. (2004) *Exceptionally Gifted Children*. London and New York: Taylor and Francis.

HMSO (2006) *Education and Inspections Act 2006*. London: The Stationery Office.

Ingram, J. and Worral, N. (1993) *Teacher–Child Partnership: The Negotiating Classroom*. London: David Fulton.

Kohlberg, I., Levine, C. and Hewer, A. (eds) (1983) *Moral Stages: A Current Formulation and Response to Critics*. Basel and New York: Karger.

Moshman, D. (2005) *Adolescent Psychological Development: Rationality, Morality and Identity*, 2nd edn. Mahwah, NJ: Lawrence Erlbaum.

NFER (2008) *Teacher Voice Omnibus, June 2008 Survey: Pupil Behaviour*. Nottingham: DCSF.

Sammons, P., Sylva, K., Melhuish, E., Siraj-Blatchford, I., Taggart, B., Barreau, S. and Grabbe, Y. (2008) *Effective Pre-school and Primary Education 3–11 Project (EPPE 3–11): The Influence of School and Teaching Quality on Children's Progress in Primary School*. London: Institute of Education, University of London.

Sheehy, N. (2004) *Fifty Key Thinkers in Psychology*. London: Taylor & Francis Routledge.

Steer, A. (2009) *Learning Behaviour: Lessons Learned. A Review of Behaviour Standards and Practices in our Schools*. Nottingham: DCSF.

CHAPTER 9

PERSONAL AND SOCIAL DEVELOPMENT

Kären Mills and Verna Kilburn

By the end of this chapter, you should be able to:

- consider fundamental questions concerning Personal and Social Education (PSE) as a complex concept

- develop an awareness of your own values and how these can influence the teaching of PSE

- construct and sustain a reasoned argument about the relevance of PSE, in a lucid and coherent manner

- demonstrate a clear understanding of the importance of acknowledging PSE in the curriculum.

Introduction

In a world where societal structures are changing on a regular basis and it could be suggested that in some cases children are 'hot housed' to look and behave like little adults, being a child may well be regarded as very complicated. For most children, growth spurts and adolescence are all part of the physical experience which requires a healthy and nutritional diet. Alongside this physical development, which includes the developing social and emotional aspects in the 'affective domain' of the brain, is the challenge to develop a moral sense of rights and responsibility (Marzano and Kendall 2007). From birth to KS1 and KS2, children experience significant periods in their life. These might include going to nursery and to school, coming to terms with family relationships and making friends. These require a sense of developing maturity and cognisance of, for example, right and wrong, what it is to share and be happy.

This chapter seeks to explore the contentious relationship between the non-statutory guidance and recent legislation, reflecting in particular the teaching of sex education in schools across the key stages. The breadth of the current Personal, Social and Health Education and Citizenship at Key Stages 1 and 2 (PSHEC) Guidance (DfEE/QCA 1999) should prepare children for the complex issues of relationships and their own personal growth and awareness. However, it could be argued that a notional, target-driven curriculum does not fully support the principles embedded within the curriculum, most noticeably in the area of children's emotional health and well-being. The tensions between differing purposes of education, the values-based faith perspective and state-based secular education will be explored.

Rhetoric and practice

            Reflective task

Individually or with others, reflect on the following questions:

1 Define and describe what you believe are the characteristics of personal and social education.
2 Can you reflect upon a lesson that you were taught at primary school which you considered to be a lesson addressing some or all of these characteristics?

This activity may well identify one significant detail, even before we consider approaches to teaching PSE. This is the issue that defining PSE at both a conceptual and political level can be challenging. The words 'personal' and 'social' could be considered to be value laden, 'used as a vehicle for values stemming from different ideologies' (Ryder and Campbell 1988 p. 13) and this tension is not a recent challenge. Since the 1970s, the development of PSE has attracted attention, both at a societal and at a political level, principally through public opinions concerning sex education and through a range of official government publications, most notably the HMI series *Curriculum from 5–16* in the mid-1980s (DES 1989) and more recent legislation related to the Every Child Matters agenda (DCSF 2004).

It is clear that in the National Curriculum (NC) (DfEE/QCA 1999) a sense of values underpins the curriculum, and this is explicitly stated in both the introduction and the non-statutory guidelines for Personal, Social and Health Education (pp. 136–41). A key consideration here is the use of the words 'values'. Rice (2005) proposes that 'values are socially constructed, adopted and adapted in the contexts in which we grow up' (p. 57). So are these values embedded both explicitly and implicitly, open to personal interpretation?

Statutory versus non-statutory

The key here is the status of PSE in schools. Anecdotally, many schools considered two levels of the National Curriculum, the statutory and non-statutory guidance. In the statutory requirements, the written syllabus was clearly conveyed to teachers through detailed programmes of study. While this may, in itself, be contentious, it does give a clear indication of what must be taught. However, it could be suggested that teachers may not feel as 'secure' about the non-statutory guidance, of which PSE, sex and relationship education (SRE) and citizenship education were a significant part. The emphasis on meeting targets and delivering standards often conflicts with the concept of inclusion which underpins other aspects of the curriculum. A study by Mead (2004 p. 22) suggested that student teachers were struggling to observe lessons reflecting the characteristics of PSE:

> PSHE wasn't explicitly taught within the school and there was no timetabled slot. Therefore I was unable to observe any teaching.

> PSHE was often taken off the timetable to make room for other activities to happen. In seven weeks there was only one opportunity to observe and one opportunity to teach.

This may well reflect your own experience of the inclusion, or otherwise, of PSE in your own school and practice. This can be compounded further by considering the aims of education set out in statutory and non-statutory guidance. As we have just discussed, while the statutory element has Programmes of Study (PoS) the non-statutory element of the NC is not set out as a cohesive and tangible set of statements and descriptors. Although PSHE-type activities had always been implicit in primary education, the Every

Child Matters (ECM) agenda became the opportunity for the Department of Education and Science to promote structure and focus in teaching PSHE. The latest thinking is that PSHE should become statutory (Macdonald 2009).

Given these factors, a major concern (for the authors) is that until this becomes a statutory requirement, the differing practice may well result in a tentative and unstructured approach to teaching what is considered to be a key part of children's education.

Standards driven?

Leaving this conflict between statutory and non-statutory teaching behind, it seems that the logical next step would be to reflect on what should be taught. The aims of education have been fiercely debated over the years and it is not the purpose of this chapter to focus on this. However, it would be unwise not to reflect briefly on some aspects of this debate in relation to the content and delivery of personal and social development education.

Historically, the standards and value for money ethos of the draft Education (Schools) Act 1992 sharply contrasted with the emerging parental opinion of the early 1990s which recognised that the ethos and values of a school and society were important. An amendment to the bill required evidence through inspection of schools that schools were promoting 'the Spiritual, Moral, Social and Cultural (SMSC) development of pupils at schools' (Education [Schools] Act 1992, Section 2). The accountability issue now demanded that inspectors look for evidence of developing SMSC and the challenge emerged of defining what this would look like in practice. What resulted was a reductionist approach to the processes and observable outcomes, a set of content and skills that could be measured and therefore assessed. In effect, this became a reflection on what the schools did to promote SMSC development, confusion between the moral and social and a bias towards a religious interpretation of the spiritual (Trainor 2005).

Developments to redress the balance included guidance notes, training courses and amendments to the 'package' of SMSC to widen the brief and incorporate attitudes, behaviour and personal development. The introduction of the Primary Framework *Excellence and Enjoyment* (DfES 2003) addressed the content further and many schools embraced the wealth of materials, using non-statutory guidance, published resources and access to training courses to enrich their understanding. In terms of delivery, some schools chose to make separate provision for personal and social development as opposed to embedding it in a themed approach to teaching and learning.

What is important here is that the challenge of teaching and assessing values cannot be underestimated in this context. For example, what exactly is meant by 'values'? Are these the values of a homogenous society that can be identified and agreed upon or, given that the UK population is rich in diversity and culture, is there freedom for families and cultures to make choices? Can we have a shared vision of what values we want to share and teach our children? This is clearly problematic and the situation is compounded further when we consider the legislative nature of a National Curriculum. Perhaps this is why personal and social education remains outside the statutory requirement. It is evident that this is an evolving process towards a consensus about personal and social development which continues to the present day.

What do we teach and how?

Having established that the teaching and delivery of personal and social education is a complex area, it is important to make some decisions about how and what we teach.

Case study

Mrs J has been a Year 1 class teacher for 3 years. She has developed her practice to include aspects of PSHE in her teaching. She organises her pupils in a mixture of ability and friendship groups according to the task and pays attention to the giving of positive praise for all aspects of classroom practice. Mrs J has signs around the classroom to promote healthy well-being, for example 'Now wash your hands' and 'Let's share' over the toy area. She encourages the children to use positive language about each other and acts as a role model for this at all times. If there are specific challenges that arise from pupil conflict, she uses a mixture of positive behaviour management to deal with the incident and circle time to tease out the general issues, specifically dealing with bullying and the feelings involved. She is developing a process of evaluation and review with her class of 28 4–5-year-olds, where children begin to set their own learning goals and identify where there may be barriers to their learning.

In reflecting on this case study, it is worth considering whether Mrs J explicitly sets out a cohesive plan for her children, developing the necessary hierarchy of concepts and skills that will result in her class developing social, emotional and behavioural skills. It is clear that Mrs J *has* a plan, but given the tensions explored earlier in this chapter, it is not enough to set out a series of arbitrary 'one-off' activities, which may or may not reflect the values of the individual, school or community. Given these issues, it could be suggested that something more systematic and less susceptible to reflecting individual values is required.

Children need to develop key skills, knowledge and understanding in systematic, developmental ways. These are:

- *awareness of themselves and others*, by exploring how they think and feel and how they relate to others. This helps them to understand themselves and plan for their own successful learning
- *management of their feelings*, by recognising and accepting their feelings and seeing this as a way to manage the range of behaviours which may affect their learning, for example anger and anxiety
- *intrinsic motivation*, so that they can set their own goals, and take an active part in their learning
- *empathising with others*, by being able to view and understand things from another child's perspective, taking into account their feelings and then to modify their own responses to meet that need
- *social skills*, especially the skills to communicate with a range of audiences, to negotiate and resolve differences so that they can take part in a group.

The Social and Emotional Aspects of Learning (SEAL) resources (DfE 2005) provided an excellent example of how these skills are clearly linked to PSHE and Citizenship/ NHSS and other whole-school or setting initiatives, suggested learning opportunities and lesson plans for developing children's social, emotional and behavioural skills with intended learning outcomes for children at each of the four colour-coded levels embedded within each theme.

There are some planned differentiated learning opportunities intended for small-group work with children who need additional help in developing their social, emotional and behavioural skills in a supplementary 'Silver' set. In addition, there is a whole-school assembly/Foundation Stage group time script and questions with six ideas for varying it each year: these ideas are intended to launch a series of classroom-based activities on the theme. Reflecting the educational merits and requirements of extending children's achievements by the setting of homework, there are some suggested activities for families to do together at home.

While such a resource may seem prescriptive and an 'off the peg' solution to the challenges of teaching PSHE, teachers/practitioners are clearly expected to use their professional judgement to decide which activities are developmentally appropriate for their children, and how to 'mix and match' when working in mixed-age classes.

Using such a resource, the case study of Mrs J can now be cross-referenced against a generally developmental set of resources to establish if Mrs J was teaching PSHE in a systematic way, explicitly defining a progressive series of activities which contribute to her children's personal and social development. If you access the Blue set, you will see that there are key ideas which Mrs J explores. For example, her process of 'evaluation and review' is supported by the activity on page 6 ('Setting our goals') and can be cross-referenced with learning outcomes which reflect both PSHE and speaking and listening (p. 2). Her use of circle time is acknowledged good practice by another advocate of PSHE who has published extensively – Jenny Moseley (2005). She outlines the deployment of specific strategies to explore issues relating to PSHE which include 'circle time' and 'golden' rules and rewards.

What we are intending to establish here is that, despite the tensions outlined, there are opportunities to explicitly develop PSHE through the use of specific resources. What this provides is a recommended approach which supports teachers in planning and delivery of this core aspect. However, the themes do not solely represent or address all the aspects which need to be covered in the PSE curriculum.

Further research from the Good Childhood enquiry (The Children's Society, 2006) called for the assessment of personal and social development. This may seem quite straightforward as there are clearly some attributes which can be identified. These may include making judgements and decisions, cooperation and independence (Lyseight-Jones 2005). However, the difficulty arises in that many of these attributes depend on our own perception of what it means to be independent. It is clearly subjective, unlike assessing tacit knowledge of, for example, combining numbers. In PSE, there is no clear tangible outcome, whereas in other subject areas it could be argued that the child either knows the answer to for example, 2 + 2 = 4, or not.

Sex and relationship education

One particular aspect which lends itself to exploring the tensions of values and knowledge is that of sex and relationship education (SRE).

Reflective task

With a friend ...

- What do you understand by the term SRE?
- What should schools teach?
- What do schools teach?

> SRE aims to inform children and young people about relationships, emotions, sex, sexuality and sexual health. It enables them to develop personal and social skills and a positive attitude to sexual health and well-being. (National Children's Bureau 2010)

This seems quite straightforward on the surface and there is clear guidance about what should be taught for all teachers to access. However, reflect on your own answers to the activity above. Does this take into account the age of the children and the appropriateness of the setting? Does your answer consider parental rights and wishes and possibly the conflicting cultural and religious perspectives that might well be implicit in your school?

It is clear that this is more complicated than teaching children a set of technical facts of life and answering random questions that may be asked about relationships. It is also not about parents abdicating their responsibility in favour of the schools taking the lead in teaching their child the facts of life! The roles of the parent and the school are not mutually exclusive and there needs to be a carefully structured and coordinated approach in place by the school which is transparent to the parents.

This is widely accepted and acknowledged, with both legislation and guidance which must be referred to in the teaching of sex and relationship education, and it is this which reflects the issues discussed so far about values, choices and legislation.

Legislation and guidance

The 1996 Education Act stated that the SRE elements in the National Curriculum Science Order across all key stages are mandatory for all pupils of primary and secondary age. Parents cannot withdraw their children from any science lessons which will address SRE through those elements of the PoS which teach about life processes, health and reproduction. Furthermore, all schools must have an up-to-date policy which is available for parents to refer to. This must describe the content and organisation of SRE provided beyond the statutory Science component of the National Curriculum. Schools have the right not to teach SRE beyond the Science orders in the NC and therefore their policy must include a statement which reflects what is or is not provided in SRE.

In short, the SRE Guidance (DfEE, 2000, p. 7) builds on these legal requirements and states that: 'all schools must have an up to date SRE policy which:

- defines SRE
- describes how SRE is provided and who is responsible for providing it
- says how SRE is monitored and evaluated
- includes information about parents' right to withdrawal
- is reviewed regularly
- is available for inspection and to parents.'

SRE is planned and delivered as part of PSHE and Citizenship. Schools are expected to have an overall policy on PSHE and Citizenship, which includes SRE. Governing bodies are expected to involve parents, children and young people, and health and other professionals to ensure that SRE addresses the needs of the community, education and health priorities, and the needs of children and young people.

Case study

Mr S teachers a mixed Year 5 class in an urban faith school. In PSE he is teaching a cross-curricula theme of families and he has been asked by the head teacher to produce a large entrance hall display for parents evening. To appeal to the children in his class, he has decided to ask them to bring photographs of media personalities in family settings. One pupil brings in a picture of a civil partnership ceremony between a world-famous pop star and his male partner. As the child hands this over to Mr S, she asks, 'Sir, what is a civil partnership?' She goes on to tell Mr S in great detail about how this is her mum's favourite singer but that her dad frequently ignores the conversation or says 'it's wrong'.

There are clear challenges here about the potential tensions between the school culture and the societal culture in the first instance, and school and diocese, school and parents in the second instance. In relation to the former, many religions and faiths embed rules of 'morality' as an important part of the doctrine and in many cases these can become prescriptive. However, there are also moral codes which could be seen as guides for personal conduct: in this case the individual has a point of reference for their behaviour. This could be exemplified by the following example of 'you must be married before having sex' (prescribed) or the understanding 'that it is better to be in a trusting and committed relationship'. Given the scenario above, the factors of teaching in a church-affiliated school which requires upholding the moral values inherent in that faith could pose a state of unacknowledged tension where the teacher holds two contradictory opinions without feeling any discomfort, let alone dissonance. This state can be identified and is known as cognitive polyphasia. Furthermore, any delay by the teacher in addressing this moral code, either by acknowledging this issue or not taking a 'moral stance', could bring the school and the parent into conflict.

Questions for discussion

Is this only a religious conflict? Are you aware of any other cultural attitudes which
   may make the teaching of SRE problematic?

Proactive or reactive sex education?

Recent headlines in the tabloid press outline the government agenda for making sex education compulsory (Times Educational Supplement). This would appear to be a common-sense response to combat the perceived increase in teenage pregnancies and the growth of sexually transmitted diseases. Recent research by John Moores University (Downing and Bellis 2009) states that children are going through puberty earlier and that they need to understand the implications of this sooner. The research goes on to claim that unprotected sex could be avoided if this gap between children developing and adulthood and consequently when adult information is given is addressed. However, what is becoming clear is that education and more formal sex education in schools may now be straying into an area where many parents have clearly defined views of what should and should not be taught outside of the parental sphere of influence. The issue of age appropriateness – what should be taught to children at what age – cannot be ignored but finding a balance between what should be taught at home and at school and at what age is demanding.

Questions for discussion

What do you feel parents want from SRE?
What should you take into account when responding to contingent questions about sex-related issues from children in school?

The way forward

In April 2010, the then Labour Government accepted the recommendations of an independent review led by Sir Alasdair Macdonald into making the teaching of PSHE statutory in both primary and secondary phases. However, this legislation has subsequently been shelved. The stance on SRE is still an interesting one and worth considering further in line with the recommendations:

> The existing right of parental withdrawal from SRE should be maintained. Where parents do choose to withdraw, schools should make it clear to them that in doing so they are taking responsibility for ensuring that their child receives their entitlement to SRE through alternative means. This right of withdrawal does not extend to the existing statutory elements of the National Curriculum requirements regarding sex education in Science at Key Stages 1 to 4 and we recommend that this should continue to be the case. (Macdonald 2009 p. 4)

Emotional health: an unnecessary extra?

The focus of this discussion has primarily been about the PSE curriculum and the explicit nature of specific themes and topics. However, the importance of addressing issues cannot be underestimated when faced with the following statistics:

- One in 10 children between the ages of 1 and 15 has a mental health disorder. Estimates vary, but research suggests that 20 per cent of children have a mental health problem in any given year, and about 10 per cent at any one time.
- Rates of mental health problems among children increase as they reach adolescence. Disorders affect 10.4 per cent of boys aged 5–10, rising to 12.8 per cent of boys aged 11–15, and 5.9 per cent of girls aged 5–10, rising to 9.65 per cent of girls aged 11–15. (Mental Health Foundation 2010)

The Cambridge Review (Alexander 2010) suggests that physical and emotional health should be taken together and become mandatory components of the primary curriculum. It comments that well-being is not just about physical and emotional welfare. It is also about raising aspirations through educational engagement. It recommends that this 'domain' should explore the interface between emotional and physical development and health and their contribution to well-being and attainment.

Questions for discussion

- What are your experiences of children with issues of emotional health that you have observed in schools?
- What responses to these issues have you seen from the school?

Why is attention to emotional health important?

'Health is the basis for a good quality of life and mental health is of overriding importance in this' (Article 24 of the United Nations' Convention on the Rights of the Child cited in Smith 2002). Indeed, this notion of emotional health is embedded in the Every Child Matters agenda in its first aim of being healthy:

> Positive emotional health and well-being helps pupils understand and express their feelings, builds their confidence and emotional resilience and therefore enhances their capacity to learn. (Kent Trust 2010)

A substantial minority of children are likely to experience moderate or severe psychological problems at some point in their childhood or more commonly in early adulthood. These range from emotional and behavioural problems and are most commonly anxiety issues and phobias. Children can be and are affected by a range of family issues, for example divorce and bereavement, and are obviously not equipped emotionally with the resources or the life experiences to deal with these in the way that most adults can do. The issue of child poverty is also heavily publicised by today's society. Statistics from the 2008/9 'Homes Below Average Income' survey show that 13.4 million people in the

UK (22 per cent) are income poor. Of those 13.4 million people, 53 per cent are in households which include at least one child (Child Poverty Action Group).

Combine this with the resultant material peer pressure to keep up with children who have 'sophisticated toys', mobile phones, laptops for example, and there is an increase in some children's perception of happiness reflecting material wealth.

Research commissioned by Bernardos (Smith 2002) concluded that there were some general factors which should be considered by schools to promote resilience in the middle years. These included positive school experiences, trusting relationships with teachers and good home–school liaison links.

 Summary

This chapter has discussed the controversial issues related to the teaching of PSE. Issues of assessment, legislation and teaching approaches which initially may seem straightforward have been critiqued and reviewed: this has resulted in a picture that is both debatable and subjective, based on our own personal values system. By identifying more specifically the teaching of sex and relationship education (SRE), the legislative issues become even more debatable. In this area, the curriculum offered in schools has been cited as inadequate based on current headlines and societal comments. However, the overlap between school and parental responsibility is a difficult concept and getting the balance right has been discussed as challenging and controversial. In short, the legislative issues and status of PSE to include SRE could be a paradox. By participating in the suggested reflective activities and related web material, readers will develop their own awareness of these issues and in doing so will be challenged to scrutinise their own approaches to the teaching of PSE. These judgements and decisions will be an important aspect of their own developing knowledge and skills as a teacher.

 Questions for discussion

Consider how this chapter has challenged your awareness of your own values and how these can influence the teaching of PSE.

In your view, should PSE be a statutory part of the National Curriculum? What are the complexities of this issue?

Further reading

Buck, M., Inman, S. and Tandy, M. (2003) *Enhancing Personal, Social and Health Education: A Framework for Learning (School Concerns)*. London: Routledge.
This text develops the teaching of personal, social, health education and citizenship (PSHEC) in primary and secondary classrooms. There is an interesting discussion about challenging policy through looking at effective practice and the purpose of schools in developing this aspect of the curriculum. Case study material presents these ideas in an accessible and meaningful way and develops class and whole-school-based issues.

Haralambos, M. and Holborn, M. (2000) *Sociology Themes and Perspectives*. London: HarperCollins.
This key text sets out definitions of culture and society which are a useful basis for exploring the moral issues and societal values referred to in this chapter. Key themes including religion, sociological perspectives and education underpin the discussions of moral values and establish further evidence about the difficulty of legislating for some aspects of teaching PSE.

References

Alexander, R. (ed.) (2010) *Children, their World, their Education: Final Report and Recommendations of the Cambridge Primary Review*. London: Routledge.
DES (1989) *Personal and Social Education From 5–16*. London: HMSO.
DfE (2005) *Social and Emotional Aspects of Learning (SEAL)*. Nottingham: DfE.
DfEE/QCA (1999) *The National Curriculum for England at Key Stages 1 and 2: A Handbook for Teachers*. London: HMSO.
DfEE (2000) *Sex and Relationship Education Guidance*. Nottingham: DfEE.
DfES (2003) *Excellence and Enjoyment: A Strategy for Primary Schools*. Nottingham: DfES.
Downing, J. and Bellis, M.A. (2009) 'Early Pubertal Onset and its Relation with Sexual Risk Taking, Substance Use and Anti-social Behaviour: A Preliminary Cross-sectional Study', *BMC Public Health* 9: 446.
Lyseight-Jones, P. (2005) 'Assessing Issues within Personal and Social Development', in M. Buck, H. Burke and S. Inman (eds) *Assessing Personal and Social Development: Measuring the Unmeasurable*, 2nd edn. London: Falmer Press, pp. 33–48.
Macdonald, A. (2009) *Independent Review of Making Personal, Social, Health and Economic (PSHE) Education Statutory*. Nottingham: DCSF.
Marzano, R. and Kendall, J. (eds) (2007) *The New Taxonomy of Educational Objectives*, 2nd edn. London: Sage.

Mead, N. (2004) 'The Provision for Personal, Social, Health Education (PSHE) and Citizenship in School-based Elements of Primary Initial Teacher Education', *Pastoral Care* June: 19–26.

Mental Health Foundation (2010) www.mental-health.org.uk/information/mental-health-overview/statistics

Moseley, J. (2005) *Circle Time for Young Children*. Oxon: Routledge.

National Children's Bureau (2010) *Sex and Relationships*, Sex Education Forum. London: National Children's Bureau.

Rice, L. (2005) 'Promoting Positive Values', in M. Cole (ed.) *Professional Values and Practice*. London: Fulton.

Ryder, J. and Campbell, L. (1988) *Balancing Acts in Personal, Social and Health Education*. Bristol: Routledge.

Smith, R. (2002) *Promoting Children's Emotional Health*. Available at: www.barnardos.org.uk/promoting_children_s_emotional_health_a_research_review.pdf (accessed 18/10/10)

The Children's Society (2006) *Good Childhood: A Question for Our Times*. London: The Children's Society.

Trainor, D. (2005) 'Personal and Social Development Within the National Context: A Review of Recent and Current Initiatives', in M. Dowling (ed.) *Assessing Children's Personal and Social Development: Measuring the Unmeasurable?* 2nd edn. London: Falmer Press.

Websites

Child Poverty Action Group: www.cpag.org.uk/povertyfacts/index.htm

DCSF (2004) *Every Child Matters*. Available at: www.dcsf.gov.uk/everychildmatters/

Education (Schools) Act 1992, Section 2 www.legislation.gov.uk/ukpga/1992/38/contents/enacted

Kent Trust: www.kenttrustweb.org.uk/Children/hs_ehwb.cfm

Mental Health Foundation: www.mentalhealth.org.uk/information/mental-health-overview/statistics/

The National Children's Bureau: www.ncb.org.uk/

The Children's Society: www.childrenssociety.org.uk/all_about_us/how_we_do_it/the_good_childhood_inquiry/1818.html

CHAPTER 10

DIALOGICAL, ENQUIRY AND PARTICIPATORY APPROACHES TO LEARNING

Donna Hurford and Chris Rowley

By the end of this chapter, you should be able to:

- make connections between dialogue, enquiry and participatory approaches to learning

- discuss, in an informed way, how dialogue and participatory approaches can contribute to learning

- plan for a variety of enquiry and participatory approaches in the primary classroom.

Introduction

Dialogical enquiry and participatory approaches

This chapter is concerned with approaches to leading children into active participation and enquiry, through involvement in their own learning. The terms 'enquiry', 'learning' and 'active participation' are closely related. We link these approaches to dialogue and discussion because these aspects of learning are often dealt with separately in the literature and yet clearly they are a form of enquiry and participatory learning. We draw upon a range of literature and research in order to justify these approaches and we offer some examples of how they might be put into practice in the primary curriculum.

A rationale for dialogical, enquiry and participatory approaches

Theories

In many ways, it seems strange to need to articulate a rationale for using enquiry and participatory approaches in a primary classroom. Why would we not want children to enquire, participate, be involved with learning and to work with each other? To affirm the place of participatory approaches to learning, we can draw on a variety of literature. Dewey (1902) provides a rationale for child-centred education. Pollard gives a summary of constructivist and social constructivist models of learning in school classrooms (2008, p. 182). Freire (1970) argues for transformative and emancipatory education for communities which are otherwise unheard of and oppressed. Emergent theories of creative approaches (Craft 2000, 2005) and global education (DfID 2005; Hicks and Holden 2007; Oxfam 2006) emphasise the importance of talk and interaction.

Policies

Assessment for Learning (Assessment Reform Group 2002) focuses on learner participation. The commitment to inclusion of our current education system (QCDA 2010), and policies such as Every Child Matters (DfES 2003a), aim to ensure that no children are oppressed by their education. Furthermore, the value accorded to 'pupil voice' is evident through school councils and Personal, Social and Health Education (PSHE) and in initiatives such as Social Emotional Affective Learning (SEAL 2005). However, to further develop children's participation in their learning, we should also consider the potential transferability of such methodologies as 'Participatory Learning and Action'

(PLA) which seeks to enable '... full participation of people in the processes of learning about their needs and opportunities, and in the action required to address them' (multi-stakeholder processes). If we look to current policies on approaches to teaching and learning we can be encouraged that 'a central message of this document [*Excellence and Enjoyment*] is that teachers have the power to decide how to teach' (DfES, 2003b p.16).

Theory and policy in practice

Research also provides us with approaches to teaching and learning and by critically reviewing these from practitioner perspectives we can explore ways to enhance learning. You may wish to consider how the statements in Table 10.1 reflect your own practice. In many ways, these are challenging lists, setting high expectations of teachers and facilitators to keep learners engaged, motivated and challenged. Elements of the lists suggest that the teacher or facilitator needs to be a risk-taker and innovator. It could be argued that the very notion of learner participation requires an element in which the teacher 'lets go' of some element of control to the learners. This requires, however, a strong grasp of both the subject matter and the pedagogy on the part of the teacher, who must adopt practices which are well illustrated by the FACTS (Feedback, Application, Challenge, Thinking, Self-esteem) model from Nottingham (2010), summarised in the table on p. 152.

Defining enquiry

The starting point for enquiry is curiosity, so perhaps we should really be considering first how we stimulate curiosity in the classroom. What do we understand by curiosity? To what extent can we rely on children's innate sense of curiosity and what role does the teacher have in ensuring that this can flourish? Is the curriculum that we have planned one which encourages curiosity? Is such a curriculum compatible with a target-driven curriculum and, if so, how? These fundamental questions have to drive our approach to enquiry for, while enquiring might be a fundamental aspect of human development, it is easily forgotten in a crowded curriculum.

The basis of curiosity is often experience and in the primary school this can take many forms. Experience can be a visit, a visitor, an activity, a story, an image or indeed anything which has an impact and which raises possibilities for questioning. An experience is generally shared and teacher mediated. In other words, the experience alone is not the only component of a process of developing enquiry. It must be rich, yes, but children must often be helped by the teacher, in shifting the peripheral to the meaningful. One of the great early exponents of the fundamental importance of experience in learning was Dewey, and, though some of his critics saw his proposed curriculum as one which left learning to the child with little teacher guidance or reference to well-established subject methodologies, careful reading of Dewey suggests otherwise. *The Child and the*

Table 10.1 Analysis of the characteristics of enquiry learning and participation

Nottingham (2010 p. 6) 'Challenging Learning' (FACTS model)	DfES (2003b p. 29) 'Excellence and Enjoyment' 'Principles of learning and teaching'	Barnes (2007 p. 134) 'Cross-curricular Learning 3–14' 'How teachers can help children learn creatively'	Chambers (2002 pp. 8–9) 'Participatory Approaches' 'Do's for facilitating participatory approaches'
Feedback Provide information related to the task, which helps move pupils towards their learning objectives.	Build on what learners already know. See Table 10.2 Promote assessment for learning.	Show respect for the child's background. Identify the areas of strength in each child.	Empower and support, be confident ('they can do it'); watch, listen, learn.
Application Apply activity to a learning goal related to value and expectation.	Make learning vivid and real.	Give plentiful opportunities for holistic, contextualised and meaningful learning. See Table 10.2	Innovate and invent – try new things, be bold, take risks; be optimally unprepared and flexible.
Challenge Make a situation more demanding or stimulating to encourage learning.	Make learning an enjoyable and challenging experience.	Learn the arts of pedagogy. Give attention to subject knowledge.	Embrace error, learn from mistakes.
Thinking Develop the skills to reason and to reflect upon the ideas and concepts that you meet. *See Activity 2*, Table 10.3	Enrich the learning experience.		Be self-aware and self-critical; improvise; have fun, joke, enjoy.
Self-esteem	Ensure every child succeeds.	Work at engaging each child.	Establish rapport; respect and be nice to people; unlearn/abandon preconceptions.

Curriculum (Dewey 1902) shows that Dewey conceived a curriculum in which the child's experience works alongside the subject curriculum.

> Nothing can be developed from nothing, nothing but the crude can be developed out of the crude and that is surely what happens when we throw the child back upon his achieved self as finality, and invite him to spin new truths of nature or of conduct out of that. (Dewey 1956 p. 18)

In other words, Dewey recognised that the child's experiences needed mediating through the subject knowledge and expertise offered by the teacher.

Enquiry, values and dialogue

Dewey goes on to identify the importance of selecting appropriate stimuli for gaining new experience. After that, he saw what he called the 'logical' (relating to subject matter) and the 'psychological' (relating to experience *and values*) as being mutually dependent, like the dependency between 'notes an explorer makes and the finished map that is constructed' (Dewey 1956 p. 19).

Based on our understanding of this interdependence of subject matter and values, we designed the activities below which give equal importance to the values children bring to their learning and subject knowledge. Alexander (2006 p. 32) discusses the complex relationship between 'talking' and 'knowing' as a way of testing evidence, analysing ideas and exploring values. He outlines the views of cynics to these approaches but concludes that dialogue still remains a key way by which teachers can move children's understanding forwards.

Dewey did not just see education as a balance between the subject and experience either. He recognised that in a world of massive and rapid change the child's social skills were equally important. (In Dewey's time, this was the continued growth of industrial society. Today it is the shift to an information society and probably in the future there will be even more radical shifts to an ecologically sustainable society.) Dewey saw the development of values as essentially part of a process which is integral to the psychological and cognitive development of the child.

> When the school introduces and trains each child into membership of society within such a little community, saturating him with the instruments of service, and providing him with the instruments of self-direction, we shall have the deepest and best guarantee of a larger society which is worthy, lovely and harmonious. (Dewey 1956 p. 29)

Dewey, then, saw the way in which we select the material that we teach as well as how we teach as intimately connected and influential, not only on how we manage an enquiry but also on the values that are embedded in it. He saw an ability to enquire as one of the essential tasks which a school should be developing. Dewey's vision of the curriculum is different from, but not necessarily incompatible with, many aspects of the curriculum that we have today, in terms of both values and enquiry learning.

Enquiry, rigour and subjects

Participation and enquiry, then, cannot be separated from values education. What is more, these methods can all be related to subject knowledge. We would also draw attention to recent research which indicates that participation and enquiry are closely related to dialogue in learning. Alexander (2006), for example, refers to 'constructive dialogue' as more than just conversing, and this is very much the basis of the Philosophy for Children programme developed in the 1980s by Lipman (1993) and others since. Alexander (2010 p. 283) refers to the submission to the primary review by SAPERE (The Society to Advance Philosophical Enquiry and Reflection in Education), suggesting that 'teachers should be given more encouragement and preparation in stimulating and managing classroom dialogue', along with 'more opportunity in the curriculum for "open enquiry"' (see Activity 3 Table 10.3 for an example of this approach).

Examples of planning a curriculum through participation, enquiry and values education

We shall now consider how we might manage this type of participation and enquiry in the classroom in ways which are both practical and yet rigorous in the contexts of today. The three short examples attempt to illustrate some of the theoretical ideas above, and in particular:

- They encourage participation where children have opportunities to make choices under guidance from the teacher.
- They encourage enquiry methods.
- They embed subject knowledge in a variety of ways ranging from specific skills to exploring concepts.
- They make use of dialogue in the classroom and encourage the development of values.

The context for the examples in Table 10.2 and 10.3 is a short topic on 'Where did my breakfast come from and how did it get here?' The context for the example in Table 10.4

Table 10.2   Where did my breakfast come from and how did it get here? A people map

Resources	Open space indoors or outdoors; locality map or world map; signs of local places.
Learning Outcome	To develop map skills through an experiential people map.
Success Criteria	To show awareness of relative positions of localities or countries.
Assessment	Peer review questions and group feedback. What have we learnt from this activity? What did we have to think hard about? How would we do this next time?
Organising the Activity	Depending on the children's awareness of the world map, choose either to focus on the immediate locality with the school as the central point or a world map with the country where the school is located as the central point. If the children know or are ready to learn compass points, ask them to make labels for the four main compass points and to identify where they need to go. Once the compass references are in the right places, bring all children to the map's central point all facing in the same direction (one of the four compass points). If you are standing in a large open or outdoor space, you may need to set parameters for the 'people map' so that everyone is clear about how far they can go and begin to understand relative distances.
	If you are making a school locality map, you may want to provide the children with signs or symbols representing features in the local area with which they are familiar. Working either in pairs or groups, the children have to take a sign and discuss where they think the place is in relation to the school. Wait until all groups have discussed and decided where they will go and decide how they will move: all together or a group at a time. Groups will probably have to review their location once others move into their places.
	As children's travel experiences will vary, you may want to explore this first in class and extend it to where family members have travelled, have lived or live and then use these experiences for the map. Consider if all children need to have personal or vicarious travel experiences to be included in this activity. Alternatively, you could either give out signs for a selection of countries or ask the children to choose a country. Arrange pair or group work as explained above.

Table 10.3   A journey map

Resources	A class of pupils; open space indoors or outdoors; locality map or world map; signs of local places.
Learning Outcome	I will be able to work well with my group.
	I will find out what I already know about our breakfast food's journey, including the transport and the jobs that were needed to bring it to my table.
Success Criteria	I will listen carefully to others, share my own ideas and help the group members work together on the activity. I will be able to talk about what I knew about my breakfast food's journey and I will be able to say what I want to find out next.
Assessment	Self/peer/teacher review of posters' fitness for purpose; teacher observation; teacher questioning; self/peer/teacher review of presentations and what has been learnt during the topic.
Organising the Activity	The whole class will discuss and agree on what would make effective group work and agree to adopt the agreed criteria. The group needs to decide how to share out the group tasks. Each group has a different breakfast food (each food will need to have a country of origin indicated on the label), a sheet of flip chart paper and marker pens. The teacher will explain that the purpose of the activity is to find out what we already know about the breakfast food's journey and what we will need to find out or check. The groups need to know that the outcome of the activity is to have a poster from each group. The poster must be a map of their food's journey with pictures or symbols showing the means of transport and jobs that were needed to bring the food from its source to the classroom. Re-assure the children that it is OK not to know everything about the food's journey, encourage them to think about what they know about other foods and to share their ideas. Allow 15 to 20 minutes for the posters to be completed.
	Each group now reviews other groups' posters by walking around the room to view them. Alternatively, groups could present their posters to the rest of the class. This could be an opportunity to consider and develop presentation skills. Through the poster review, the pupils can begin to identify what they know and need to know about their food; how well they worked as a group and what they want from their posters.

is a short topic on our water supply. The plan in Table 10.2 focuses on learning-specific learning map skills through physical participation and questioning.

Reflecting on the activity

How does this approach to identifying and developing map skills differ from more traditional map work? Possibly the most striking difference is the children's physical involvement in the creation of the map. As Pollard reminds us, 'we now know that the most effective deep, long-term learning is meaningful and conceptual' (2008 p. 201). Tanner (2007), like Pollard, recognises the value of participatory approaches and notes how they can 'motivate pupils, engage their interest and provide memorable experiences which encourage deeper learning' (p. 154). It is this pursuit of deeper learning that seems so well aligned with participatory approaches. However, it is not sufficient to dot the curriculum with more participatory experiential learning experiences. While Barnes (2007) recommends that 'experiences' are interpreted through the relevant skills and subject knowledge, curricular integration would also apply to participatory approaches. Making learning deep, meaningful and conceptual requires an open-minded and flexible approach to how we enable children to engage with the curriculum.

Reflective task

As a group or individually, using the format in Table 10.2 as a model, plan an activity for another subject (or based on a combination of two subjects), colour-coding opportunities where pupils can: participate by making choices under the guidance of the teacher; use enquiry methods; see where skills and concepts central to the subject are embedded in the activity; encourage discussion involving values.

The plan in Table 10.3 focuses on learning about the international transport of food, in ways which involve interactive group work and discussion of values.

Reflecting on the activity

Consider which areas of learning you think this activity would cover. Once you have captured your own thoughts, consider the findings in Table 10.4 which show student teachers' evaluation of the mapping activity. The headings used to evaluate the activity are taken from Oxfam's (2006 p. 4) model for Global Citizenship. According to Oxfam (2006), participatory approaches to learning can '[give] children the opportunity to develop critical thinking about complex global issues in the safe space of the classroom' (p. 2). The Oxfam scheme of work for Global Citizenship illustrates how values and attitudes can be integrated into the participatory learning activities. As teachers, we are expected to plan and assess learning in terms of understanding, knowledge and skills' development and maybe we consider the impact of learning on values and attitudes less frequently. We may assign these aspects of learning to RE and increasingly to PSHE – however, what if we deeply embed engagement with values and attitudes into our teaching and learning practices? What difference do we think this would make? Barnes talks about how schools seek to accommodate the 'all-encompassing sphere of shared values' (2007 p. 146) and notes the importance of values arising from 'genuine and sustained conversations'. Arguably, classroom practice provides regular and meaningful opportunities for these conversations which can in turn be facilitated through participatory activities.

The plan shown in Table 10.5 focuses on deepening understanding of a complex concept through dialogue. This plan uses as its stimulus a story by Raymond Briggs (*The Man* 1992). The approach for KS1 would be essentially similar though the stimulus

Table 10.4   Evaluating potential and actual learning from the participatory activity: 'mapping the journey of a breakfast food'

Knowledge and Understanding	Skills	Values and Attitudes
Geography: map skills; relative distances; climate; landscapes; means of transport	Creating a meaningful map; demonstrating awareness of relative distances; transferring information from a globe or world map to own group map	Developing respectful awareness of similarities and differences between home and other places
Science: properties of materials (food and packaging); preserving foods; processing foods		Valuing food
Maths: understanding estimation and how to improve accuracy; knowing measures of distance and how they relate (metres/kilometres); knowing how to calculate	Estimating and calculating distances	Developing awareness of globalisation and how it affects us all
Literacy: understanding text has meaning; understanding how symbols can convey meaning	Reading labels for information; designing and using symbols; speaking and listening	Having an inclusive approach to sharing information through visual literacy
Group work: understanding how to contribute effectively to a group	Turn-taking; listening; critical thinking; negotiating; presenting own views; sharing ideas	Empathy; respect; cooperation
PSHE/AfL: developing self-awareness of what I already know and don't know	Identifying what I need to find out; listening to feedback	Self-awareness; being self-critical and receptive to critically constructive feedback
PSHE/Global Citizenship: understanding the contribution others make to my well-being; developing understanding of the work needed so I have food		Respect; empathy; self-awareness

choice would need to be more suitable. (See the final reflective task in this chapter which links to web pages supporting the choice of stimulus.)

Reflecting on the activity

In this case study, the children chose the question 'Who owns water?' It would be easy for a teacher to look at this question and see it as one which has an answer. It is, however, a rich question with lots of potential for dialogical enquiry.

The key concept chosen by the children was ownership, emerging presumably from the notion that water is owned by the utilities company from which we buy it. In

Table 10. 5   A Year 3 group studying where their water comes from

Learning Outcome	The ability to reflect more deeply on the meaning of a key concept, in this case that of ownership.
Success Criteria	I will be able to ask thoughtful questions and, in talking about one of those, I will begin to see how we might challenge each other's ideas.
Assessment	Self-assessment of my contribution to the discussion. Teacher assessment of responses to exercises carried out after the discussion.
Organising the Activity	A visit to the local water treatment works provided an excellent stimulus, but since the intention was to develop more philosophical questions we moved the children into the role of a group of 'little people' living on a fictional island. To do this, a story *The Man* by Raymond Briggs was used (1992). This story is particularly appropriate because it has embedded in it many questions. It involves a small man (he could stand on your hand) who arrives in a boy's bedroom. As the book progresses, various dilemmas become evident. Should the boy treat him in the same way that he would treat any man? Is it fair to treat him differently because of his size? After reading this book, the children were led into the fictional island where these small people depended upon the mainland for their water supply. The role of the book at this point had been both to introduce a fictional element which would distance the children a little from their own place and also to encourage a deeper level of questioning from them, modelled by the issues raised in the book. Gradually, these discussions were developed into a series of questions. At this stage, it is essential that the teacher understands the nature of a 'philosophical question', one which we could talk about together based upon our own experiences of similar yet different aspects of life. Such questions invariably encompass a range of concepts and it is these concepts (big ideas with rather fuzzy boundaries) that we want to develop different understandings of. Support in identifying and supporting children in creating this type of question can be found in numerous books on philosophy for children. Increasingly, I use the 'questions quadrant' developed in *20 Thinking Tools: Collaborative Enquiry in the Classroom* (Cam 2008). Once the question is chosen, the teacher manages a whole-class enquiry exploring the meanings using philosophy for children techniques.

practice, however, this dilemma offers an excellent way into a dialogue which raises many sub-questions. Is it really the water that the company owns or is it the cost of collecting, purifying and transporting it that we are paying for? Do I own the water that falls upon my roof? If so, do I have responsibility for either storing it or paying someone else (another utilities company) to take ownership of it in removing it?

Children will often show remarkable creativity if encouraged to discuss in this way, providing the teacher understands the nature of the discussion. To do this, training in the nature of philosophical enquiry with children is needed and this can be found via the Society for Advancing Philosophical and Reflective Learning in Education (SAPERE).

There are many ways of developing further children's thinking on the concept of ownership. Our aim is not to write exercises which lead to an answer so much as exercises which promote deeper thinking around the nature of the concept.

In this example, there were certain moments in the dialogue which could be seen as 'critical events' in that they had a significant impact on the dialogue. (For more information on critical events, see Woods [1993] and further examples in Rowley and Cooper [2009 pp. 132–3]). Amy, for example, suggested that water 'belongs to the earth'. This was later challenged by Stuart who said that 'The Earth can't own something if I can't pick it up'. Stephanie then challenged Stuart with an example: 'But a tree can own water because it takes it up from the ground'. This shows how one statement (in this case by Amy) is often critical in dialogue and whether that is picked up and developed by other children can depend a lot on the teacher's handling of it.

These examples suggest that both participatory approaches and dialogue can, handled well, develop deeper learning through actively engaging the learner in a real enquiry.

Reflective task

We learn a great deal by trying out the activities we plan with children first: the advantages and pitfalls. In a group, at your own level, list key philosophical questions related to ownership. Decide on the question to be explored. One person records the ensuing discussion as a concept map. Following the discussion, consider what the concept map shows: ideas which led to further ideas; ideas which were contested; how through discussion the group has arrived at a deeper understanding of the concept of ownership than any individual had previously. Write individual self-assessments based on the learning objectives and success criteria of the lesson plan. (See also the web material for this chapter and consider this task alongside the discussion questions below.)

Summary

In this chapter, we have attempted to justify participation and enquiry methods as key elements of primary learning. We have argued that enquiry methods are often closely related to participation and that the method that we adopt has important implications for both the knowledge and value aspects of learning. We have further investigated dialogue as an essential aspect of enquiry and participation in primary classrooms, both potentially leading to deeper learning.

Questions for discussion

- How could you integrate participatory approaches to learning into a cross-curricular theme you would like to explore with your class?
- How would you define participatory approaches to learning? What would you say are its fundamental features?
- Do methods of enquiry differ in different subjects or in 'domains of knowledge' (as defined by Alexander 2008)?
- How important is dialogue as a method of whole-class enquiry?
- To what extent are primary children able to ask philosophical questions?
- What is the significance of the stimulus that you use to motivate children's enquiry? (See additional web materials (pp. 29–38) to help develop both this question and the reflective task on page 159)

Further reading

Chambers, R. (2002) *Participatory Workshops*. London: Earthscan.
This guide is written for facilitators of participatory workshops. It provides thorough and clear explanations of ways to engage participants in learning. Many of the activities are directly transferable to a classroom setting and others have the potential to be easily adapted for classroom and school use.

Global Dimension (available at: www.globaldimension.org.uk/) provides easy access to a wide range of websites, activities and resources to support participatory and interactive engagement with thematic approaches to global education and other learning contexts.

Oxfam Education (available at: www.oxfam.org.uk/education/) provides a wide range of online and downloadable participatory activities and resources designed for Global Citizenship and are easily transferable to other learning contexts.

References

Alexander, R. (2006) *Education as Dialogue: Moral and Pedagogical Choices for a Runaway World*. Hong Kong: Hong Kong Institute of Education and Dialogas. p. 43.
Alexander, R.J. (2008) *Towards Dialogic Teaching: Rethinking Classroom Talk*, 4th edn. York: Dialogos.
Alexander, R. (ed.) (2010) *Children, Their World, Their Education: Final Report and Recommendations of the Cambridge Primary Review*. London: Routledge.
Assessment Reform Group (2002) *Assessment for Learning: 10 Principles*. London: Assessment Reform Group. Available at: www.assessment-reform-group.org/CIE3.PDF

Barnes, J. (2007) *Cross-Curricular Learning* 3–14. London: Sage.

Briggs, R. (1992) *The Man*. London: Random House.

Cam, P. (2008) *20 Thinking Tools: Collaborative Enquiry in the Classroom*. Camberwell: ACER.

Chambers, R. (2002) *Participatory Workshops*. London: Earthscan.

Craft, A. (2000) *Creativity Across the Primary Curriculum: Framing and Developing Practice*. London: Routledge.

Craft, A.R. (2005) *Creativity in Schools: Tensions and Dilemmas*. London: Routledge/ Falmer.

DfES (2003a) *Every Child Matters*. Available at: www.dcsf.gov.uk/everychildmatters/

DfES (2003b) *Excellence and Enjoyment: A Strategy for Primary Schools*. Available at: http://nationalstrategies.standards.dcsf.gov.uk/node/88755

DfID (2005) *Developing the Global Dimension in the School Curriculum*. London: DfID/DfES.

Dewey, J. (1902) *The Child and the Curriculum*. Chicago: University of Chicago Press.

Dewey, J. (1956) *The Child and the Curriculum*. Chicago: University of Chicago Press.

Freire, P. (1970) *Pedagogy of the Oppressed*. Harmondsworth: Penguin.

Hicks, D. and Holden, C. (eds) (2007) *Teaching the Global Dimension*. London: Routledge.

Lipman, M. (1993) *Thinking Children and Education*. Dubuque, IA: Kendall/Hunt.

Nottingham, J. (2010) *Challenging Learning*. Berwick upon Tweed: JN Publishing.

Oxfam (2006) *Education for Global Citizenship: A Guide for Schools*. Oxford: Oxfam.

Pollard, A. (2008) *Reflective Teaching*, 3rd edn. London: Continuum. Available at: www. rtweb.info

QCDA (2010) *The National Curriculum*. Available at: http://curriculum.qcda.gov.uk/ key-stages-1-and-2/

Rowley, C. and Cooper, H. (2009) *Cross-curricular Approaches to Teaching and Learning*. London: Sage.

Tanner, J. (2007) 'Global citizenship', in D. Hicks and C. Holden (eds) *Teaching the Global Dimension*. London: Routledge, pp. 150–60.

Woods, P. (1993) *Critical Events in Teaching and Learning*. London: Falmer.

Websites

SEAL (2005). Available at http://nationalstrategies.standards.dcsf.gov.uk/primary/ publications/banda/seal

Society for Advancing Philosophical Enquiry and Reflection in Education SAPERE: www. sapere.org.uk/

Multi-stakeholder processes – Participatory Learning and Action (PLA). Available at: http://portals.wi.wur.nl/msp/?page=1275

CHAPTER 11

RACE, CULTURE AND ETHNICITY

Diane Warner and Sally Elton-Chalcraft

By the end of this chapter, you should be able to:

- comply with (and seek to go beyond) the legal requirements that concern diversity and promote social cohesion

- understand the impact of your own ethnicity and attitudes towards diversity on your role as a teacher

- reflect on research which investigates cultural awareness among primary children and student teachers

- develop teaching and learning approaches which challenge intolerance and promote equality.

Introduction

This chapter will outline the current picture of racial and ethnic diversity in the UK for new and upcoming classroom practitioners, including statutory requirements and non-statutory guidance. Through consideration of your ethnicity and recent research into children's and student teachers' attitudes towards cultural diversity, you will be able to critically appreciate the importance of developing pedagogic approaches which are culturally responsive and challenging for you, your learners and the school community.

We are all racial and cultural beings, whether we belong to the majority or minority cultures and this affects the way we think, act and interact with one another. Culturally responsive teaching understands this and also recognises that racial and ethnic groups are vibrant and to be valued and cherished. This type of teaching also recognises that such groups are diverse within themselves, rather than being homogenous units. Therefore, recognising children as both individuals and inheritors of a particular cultural dynamic will promote positive self-esteem, racial equity and social justice.

UK classroom statutory requirements and national guidance for teachers

The UK has been an ethnically diverse group of countries for centuries but it is in the last few decades that large groups of peoples, from the Caribbean, Asia, the African countries and more recently those from the European Union, have arrived. Varying reasons for this demographic range from economic change to military and political unrest abroad, leading to the need for employment, refuge or asylum. The 2001 Census identified a Black and Minority Ethnic (BME) population of 8 per cent which it mainly categorised into: Mixed, Asian, Black and Chinese.

In maintained primary schools, 12 per cent are from BME groups (see www. education.gov.uk/ and look at 2007), their spread reflecting the concentration of BME populations in urban areas. Some schools in these areas have 100 per cent of minority ethnic children, while some in rural or suburban areas will have none. Most schools lie on the spectrum somewhere between.

Characterising this diversity of cultures in the UK are: religion, language, customs and values, and often a strong sense of community. However, the 2001 Census alerts us to the fact that minority ethnic groups are varied:

> different groups share some characteristics but there are often greater differences between the individual ethnic groups than between the minority ethnic population as a whole and the White British people. (www.ons.gov.uk/census/index.html)

These differences reflect their histories as well as current social phenomena. Pakistani Muslims in Lancashire, for example, may share many values and practices with

Somali Muslims in West London, but there will be cultural and religious differences too, based on their past and how and where they live now. Alternatively, those whose heritage combines two or more racial backgrounds, for example, a Caribbean-English or Irish-Chinese child, will be of both cultures and represent a new culture, which will develop as they develop and express themselves.

Race Relations Amendment Act (2000)

Teachers have to abide by legislation. The Race Relations Amendment Act states that a body, like a school, must have 'due regard' to:

- eliminate unlawful racial discrimination
- promote equality of opportunity and good relations between people of different racial groups.

In addition, it places specific responsibilities on schools to help them meet the general duty and improve the educational experience for all children, in particular those belonging to minority ethnic groups. It should not be a bureaucratic exercise. These specific duties are to:

- prepare a written statement of the school's policy for promoting race equality, and to act upon it
- assess the impact of school policies on pupils, staff and parents of different racial groups, including, in particular, the impact of attainment levels of these pupils
- monitor the operation of all the school's policies, including, in particular, their impact on the attainment levels of pupils from different racial groups
- take reasonable steps to make available the results of its monitoring.

Schools have a duty to eliminate unlawful racial discrimination and to promote equality of opportunity and good relations between people of different groups.

Community cohesion

From September 2007, schools have been under a duty to promote community cohesion in three main areas:

- **Teaching, learning and curriculum** – to teach pupils to understand others, to promote common values and to value diversity, to promote awareness of human rights and of the responsibility to uphold and defend them, and to develop the skills of participation and responsible action.

- **Equity and excellence** – to ensure equal opportunities for all to succeed at the highest level possible, removing barriers to access and participation in learning and wider activities and eliminating variations in outcomes for different groups.
- **Engagement and ethos** – to provide a means for children, young people and their families to interact with people from different backgrounds and build positive relations, including links with different schools and communities locally, across the country and internationally.

(DCSF 2007)

The community cohesion agenda aims to eliminate racial discrimination and promote positive race, cultural and faith relations in society, including schools. This involves developing understanding, reflection and challenges for teachers and learners to share common experiences and values, build identity and self-esteem and rightfully assume responsibilities for positive diversity. This agenda relates to all schools, from those with mid to high racially diverse populations or mainly white schools. The Teacher Net website is a good source of information and supporting material (www.teachernet.gov. uk/wholeschool/communitycohesion/).

Reflective task

Use the interactive map on the Multiverse website to find out the ethnicity of primary school children in the area where you grew up, where you now study or work, and another part of the UK where you might have another personal or professional link (www.multiverse.ac.uk/attachments//PrimaryPupilEthnicity/index.html).

1 Examine your own attitudes to the communities in these areas. Why do you think this?
2 How does this relate to legal requirements, your geographical position and your future plans?

Teachers and children: attitudes and approaches

Having considered the legal requirements and begun to think about cultural identity, we now invite you to consider the approaches to multicultural education you have seen in schools and begin to recognise good practice. We also ask you to consider your own mindset and evaluate how you can make a positive contribution to schools in the area of diversity. In this section, we draw on our own research to highlight how race, ethnicity and attitudes towards these, can impact on teachers' and children's world views and behaviour. As you read, consider your own culture, those whom you might teach and the dominant cultural perspective expressed in the curriculum in primary schools today.

Children's awareness of race

Research in both predominantly white and also diverse schools found that the majority of 10-year-old children displayed anti-racist attitudes but nevertheless had internalised the prevailing Western white privilege mindset, whatever their own ethnicity (Elton-Chalcraft 2009). While recognising that the sample was comparatively small (about 80 children from four schools), it became apparent that most children in the multi-ethnic schools who were reasonably knowledgeable about their own culture and other cultures displayed anti-racist behaviour and attitudes (Figure 11.1, Quadrant A). Many children from all four schools were anti-racist even though they displayed limited knowledge (Quadrant B). A handful of children, mainly white boys from a low socio-economic background and in the low sets for maths and literacy, expressed racist comments. In this example, Bart, a white boy, and Kurt, a boy whose mother is white and whose father is of Jamaican heritage, discuss people of different cultures:

Kurt: They're ugly. [giggles]
Sally: They're ugly – so you think people who aren't the same culture as you are ugly?
Kurt: Yeah.
Sally: Why do you say that?
Kurt: Because they've got funny eyes and different to ours – ours are like that, theirs are bozeyed. [making facial gestures]
Bart: Yeah but Heidi [Kurt's girlfriend] is a different culture to you and everyone else in, and some people in, this thing, in this school, has [a] different culture to you but you like 'em – you're friends with 'em. So I don't know what you're pointing that for – ugly … And so if Heidi's got a different culture to you are you gonna dump her?
Kurt: [embarrassed giggle] Nnooo.
           (Elton-Chalcraft 2009 p. 114)

This interchange is interesting because Bart, who had himself expressed racist sentiments, was criticising Kurt's remarks. Thus, Bart and Kurt display racist attitudes towards a particular group but anti-racist attitudes towards a particular individual whom they dissociated from that group (Elton-Chalcraft 2009 p. 114; Troyna and Hatcher 1992). As a beginning teacher, are you aware of the stances towards different cultures held by the children in your placement schools? Is there an ethos of mutual respect or white Western privilege?

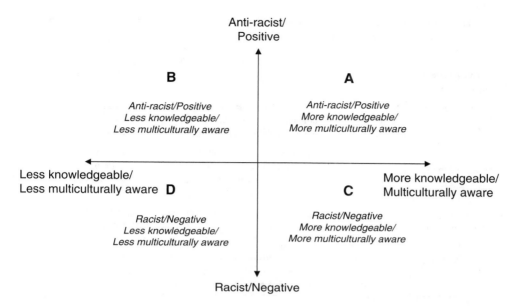

Figure 11.1   The range of children's attitudes and knowledge (Quadrants A, B, C and D)
Source: Elton-Chalcraft 2009

A small number of children in the research were deemed to be knowledgeable about their own and other cultures but still displayed racist viewpoints (Quadrant C). These children were either expressing disgust at an unfamiliar culture, while in the main expressing anti-racist sentiments towards numerous cultures, or they exhibited racist behaviour which they almost instantly regretted. Rachel, a girl of Caribbean heritage, also made a gesture with her eyes but instantly said, 'I shouldn't have done that', possibly because I asked her why she was making a gesture with the corner of her eyes. Many children from one of the multi-ethnic schools described one Muslim boy's racist name calling. However, Roy was described as a bully who dominated both Muslims like himself and other children (Elton-Chalcraft 2009 pp. 110–11).

Schools may attempt to be inclusive, refrain from stereotyping and promote community cohesion and anti-racism. Yet there may still exist within schools a white Western privilege outlook which assumes that the dominant culture of white Western mindset is superior (Dadzie 2000; Elton-Chalcraft 2009; Gaine 2005).

Multicultural stances in schools

The previous section invites you to consider the children's awareness of race but there is a need to understand the school's 'institutional body language' too (Dadzie 2000).

Table 11.1   Types of multiculturalism (Elton-Chalcraft 2009 p. 82, adapted from Kincheloe and Steinberg 1997)

1	Conservative multiculturalists (mono culturalism)	are 'tokenist'. They attempt to address multicultural issues but, deep down, they believe in the superiority of Western (white) patriarchal culture.
2	Liberal multiculturalists	are dedicated towards working to 'one race'. They attempt to gloss over differences in an attempt to make everyone equal and the 'same' ('they' are the 'same' as 'us' – they just happen to be a different colour).
3	Pluralist multiculturalists	believe pluralism is a supreme social virtue, where diversity is pursued and exoticised. There is cultural 'tourism' where 'they' (as opposed to 'us') live in an exotic parallel world. For example, Hanukkah is the Jewish Christmas (an example of neo-colonialism).
4	Left essentialist multiculturalists	are extreme in promoting the minority culture, to the extent that the dominant culture is seen as 'bad' and the marginalised as 'good'.
5	Critical multiculturalists	believe in the promotion of an individual's consciousness as a social being. They promote an awareness (self-reflection) of how and why his/her opinions and roles are shaped by dominant perspectives. They appreciate that there are differences within, as well as between, cultures.

The table above offers a rudimentary tool to consider how well a school (or class) approaches issues of diversity, ranging from tokenistic to critically multicultural. Where would you place yourself, schools you have visited or individual teachers?

The aim is for schools to adopt a 'critical multicultural' stance; however in their journey to this goal, many schools may still find themselves at the starting line – with a commitment to merely adhere to legislation. In practice, this could be use of a limited range of multicultural resources such as a welcome poster in different languages, an annual Hindu dance event or a Caribbean storyteller. The lesson ideas at the end of the chapter provide examples of anti-racist approaches which fulfil the critical multicultural stance.

Teachers seeing and understanding race and culture in the classroom

Recent research among 40 student teachers showed both a deep desire to meet all children's needs alongside a lack of racial and cultural awareness (Warner 2010). This lack of awareness, in their thinking and attitudes, caused them to make automatic responses and assumptions that were based on their own cultural heritage. Reasons for this cannot be easily pinned down and neither would it be right to simplify what is a complex area, but the research identified factors which could be seen as useful starting points for everyone, whatever your cultural background. These were family, schooling and community and the social context of one's upbringing. Such factors can be seen as highly influential aspects of our identity formation and affect, in some way, how we see others.

Nearly all of the students in the study were of the majority ethnic group of the UK, i.e. White British. One had a part-European heritage. All had been educated and lived in white communities, and were currently studying at a mainly white university. It is pertinent to consider what values and assumptions they might have already formed about cultures, resulting from this mono-cultural focus of their backgrounds, and think about how much this applies to all of us. Townsend (2002) describes this as a 'chain of entrenching, white-privilege practices', while Ambe (2006) speaks of 'deep-rooted patterns' which are part of our unconscious being.

Cultural starting points

The students acknowledged their mono-cultural backgrounds, with one stating, 'you simply draw on what you know'; while another, who had lived in the countryside as a child, explained:

> I'd never seen anybody of a different colour; you just knew people in the village. You didn't even think there was an outside world.

Commenting on the use of multicultural children's literature in the classroom, one stated:

> I understand why we have multicultural books because we have a multicultural society, so obviously we need to but I do feel sometimes that by making a book specifically for reading that is on an Asian subject matter, I think that can also make it more of an issue than it actually is.

Other students were worried about appearing ignorant of other cultures and religions, particularly while on placements in racially diverse schools. One commented:

> In 100% Asian school I might see it as more of a challenge because you are not as aware of the culture and beliefs; you're more of an outsider in some ways. Because you're not fully aware of their culture or beliefs I think I'd be more worried that I'd do something that'd offend them or be seen as wrong.

King (2004) suggests that a wariness of approaching cultural differences can result in following known attitudes and approaches, which only affirm the high status of the prevailing cultural majority, and the lower status of minority cultures. This 'avoidance' approach allows the side-stepping of the issue of how far we see minority cultures as subsidiary and unimportant, and therefore raises questions over teaching for equality of opportunity. Anti-racist legislation, community cohesion and school policies and curricula are important markers in this.

In contrast, the student teachers in the research displayed and discussed areas of their lives which resisted a white privilege mindset and displayed a deep desire to teach with equity and understanding. Recognising his own cultural position and the desire to teach with equity, Will, part Ukrainian and part English, articulated his difference:

> My granddad was dark skinned and my mother was a single teenage mum, so although I did not know it at the time, I grew up understanding what it meant to be different.

His later employment in a firm which employed many Black and Asian peoples, also affected his outlook:

> You want school to reflect what's life. The reality is that you might grow up in a white area … but that's not how the world is … As educators we have the opportunity to make sure that children experience as many opportunities as they can and as diverse [sic] as they can.

Helena became more aware of societal attitudes towards difference and disadvantage because of her mother's job as a care worker with learning-disadvantaged people. As a teenager, seeking to become a teacher herself, Jessica often visited the school of her aunt, head teacher of a multiracial West Midlands primary school, noting that the multi-cultural displays and signs in other languages provided important modelling of other cultures to the children. Lou, who lives in the white part of a racially segregated Northern town, has been able to hold on to her existing positive beliefs about racial diversity. While on placement at a white school, an incident, involving the negative reaction of some parents about a new Asian child, jarred against Lou's sensibilities and understanding about teaching children equitably.

> We need to reduce ignorance and provide models to help children know they are important and reduce feelings of isolation. Some say 'teaching's teaching', but I think it's [racially-aware teaching] important … It brings a different experience and that's important.

Becoming a culturally responsive teacher

The openness of these comments reveals that alongside personal cultural histories, the potential to re-shape attitudes is present. Participants in this research had begun to recognise that they did not exist in a cultural vacuum but that they were coming from the cultural majority and white privileged position. As both of these influence the way we teach, educators should aim for the 'critical-multiculturist' position, stated earlier, by questioning the underlying cultural assumptions of the curriculum and developing anti-discriminatory, inclusive pedagogies.

Initial teacher training and ongoing CPD are important catalysts in replacing entrenched ideologies and self-satisfied thinking and actions with challenging and trans-forming practices which reflect the complex and shifting nature of our multicultural society. Embracing more multi-faceted understandings, and encouraging this with chil-dren, dismantles blind simplicity and makes difference positive. Teachers need to present opportunities to replace unquestioned attitudes with informed, intellectual, reflexive and ultimately transformative beliefs and principles.

Reflective task

Consider a critical incident in school which presents a challenge with reference to issues of diversity, e.g. racist name calling in the playground.

1 Situate yourself in that position. What is the most appropriate response and why?
2 Consider why the incident took place – what is the 'institutional body language' of the school? Is this an isolated incident or a typical occurrence? What steps could a school take to ensure a critical multicultural approach?

Further scenarios can be found on the Multiverse website at www.multiverse.ac.uk/ViewArticle2.aspx?contentType=2&menu=29795&ContentId=15658

Teaching and learning for cultural and ethnic diversity

Being aware of ourselves as racial and cultural beings is an important position and enables an authentic and viable teacher–pupil relationship. This is a valuable attitude to foster in all schools to avoid a 'colour-blind' approach, an approach which comes from a failure to acknowledge race and ethnicity, or an uncertainty about how to notice it and then avoidance of the issue (Gaine 2005; Pearce 2005). Jones (1999) also suggests that there can be an attitude of professional indifference and lack of interest in the subject. This type of stance can lead to the formation of negative racist attitudes in children because, according to Pearce, 'unthinking racist insults and unintentional stereotypical racial references' are not linked to racism and therefore not challenged (p. 35).

The following two examples of classroom practice will provide ideas and stimulate thinking for further teaching and learning in the area of valuing and raising awareness of racial and ethnic diversity.

Using Persona Dolls: an early years foundation and KS1 approach

Brown (2001, 2008) gives practical advice on how to use Persona Dolls in the early years to combat discrimination. Her ideas can be extended for KS1 and KS2 children, particularly within RE lessons. Used alongside other approaches, Persona Dolls can provide a rich resource for learning 'about' and learning 'from' a particular religion/culture/way of life which is a requirement of many RE syllabi (QCA 2004).

Introducing Jeetinder   Introduce the Persona Doll and encourage your class to enthusiastically engage with the doll by asking lots of questions.

Name: My name is Jeetinder Singh. I am a Sikh which means ... *What's your name?*
Language: I speak Punjabi and English. *Do you speak other languages?*
Family: My sister's called Manjit Kaur. Girls often have Kaur after their name and boys often have Singh. But in this country that is sometimes a problem because of the use of first names and surnames so sometimes girls use Singh as a family name. Manjit is 14 and goes to secondary school. She is doing a GCSE in Punjabi (it's the language of many Sikhs who live in the Punjab – north-west India and south-east Pakistan where my grandparents came from). Manjit and Tejpreet, my brother, go to Punjabi school on Sundays; I'm going to go when I'm a bit older. *What are your brothers and sisters like?*

My family came to Britain in 1970, when my Dad was 10. (Show children where the Punjab is on the map). Manjit and my elder brother, Tejpreet, who's 11 and I, were all born in this country. *Where were you born?*

Food: I like eating vegetable curry and dahl made from lentils. I also like fish and chips, especially from the chip shop round the corner from where we live. *What is your favourite food?*
Morning routine: In the mornings, I get up, wash, have breakfast and get ready for school. My mum used to help me tie my jurra (top knot) but I can do it myself now. (Children may ask *Why do you have a top knot?*) In the Sikh religion, we believe it is important to keep our hair long. But actually my cousin Jagdeep and his dad have cut hair but they are still Sikh. In my family, the men have long hair and my dad wears a turban which takes him a while to put on! *How do you get ready in the mornings?*
Playground: On my way here, I went on the slide and swings at the playground just down the road from your school – my favourite is the slide. *What's yours?*
Religion: I sometimes get teased by older children for wearing a top knot. I don't get teased in the infants. *Have any of you been teased? What did it feel like? What did you do? What can I do?*

 A problem, like the one above, would be introduced at the end of the first lesson or in the second, with use of the Persona Doll to demonstrate the problem-solving technique. For this and further ideas, visit the Sage website: www.uk.sagepub.com/cooper

The Island *by Armin Greder (2007): a KS2 approach*

This picture book provides an unusual and challenging resource and stimulus for teachers to enable children to engage with issues of cultural diversity and difference. The story follows a lost and desperate man, washed up on an island where he is confronted by forbidding walls and hostile islanders. He is allowed to stay but because he is different he is treated as an outcast. He is finally set adrift in his burning raft and the islanders return to their heavily fortified, narrow existence. It includes themes of:

* racial and cultural difference
* racism

- effects of immigration, including refugees and asylum-seekers
- human responses and the role of community.

The suggested teaching plan (full details on the adjoining Sage website) covers five sessions, although it could easily be extended to cover a two-week period. This length of time allows for a development of understanding of diversity through the effect and appreciation of the narrative and linked activities designed to draw learners towards greater awareness and knowledge of how we should live together. It uses a cross-curricular approach, which includes Literacy and PSHE, particularly providing significant time for children to share ideas and views and to know how to listen to and accommodate one another. When using the plan, teachers should also think about the cultural, linguistic and ability needs of their pupil groups so that it can be suitably adapted.

1. Preparatory activity   Ask children to think of between two and four aspects of their lives at home, school and in their communities that they really like and wouldn't want to be changed by anyone new coming in. Provide them with 'bricks' made from brown sugar paper to write their ideas on. Stick the bricks on a large display board, or hang them from a line suspended across the room, to symbolise a wall. This 'wall' will later be dismantled as the children discuss and discover positive ways of embracing change and difference.

2. Introducing the book   The book contains powerful black and white images which will elicit thoughtful discussion, so a good way of sharing it is to scan each page into a computer program to project onto a whiteboard. Look at the front cover; ask for predictions and responses. Read the first part of the story and talk about the children's initial feelings. In pairs, children should discuss the man and his feelings. Write these on one side of the wall.

3. Beginning to explore the story and its messages   Use drama activities to explore the actions and motives of the villagers. These could include:

- freeze frames – the children adopt the pose and view of a villager
- hot-seating – the teacher adopts the role of the man, taking questions from the 'villagers'. Give children time to work in groups to think of questions which reflect how their village might feel. Encourage thoughtful questions and ensure there are no racially negative or inappropriate questions through giving some examples and by appointing a group leader to guide and monitor the others.

4. Reflecting so far   Link the children's responses back to the wall, emphasising that although these are natural responses, they may not be helpful and supportive. Discuss and take predictions about the ending of the story.

The complete plan continues the children's journey of understanding and can be found at: www.uk.sagepub.com/cooper

Summary

In this chapter, we have enabled you to begin to appreciate and understand what it means to be a racially aware and anti-discriminatory teacher. This includes the suggested ways in which you can adhere to, but also go beyond, the legal requirements for promoting community cohesion, tackling racism and discrimination and valuing and celebrating children's cultural and racial heritages. You have been challenged to consider the impact of your own ethnicity and attitudes towards diversity on your role as a teacher and have been offered the opportunity to engage with current research which discusses white privilege, colour blindness and teacher mindset.

Teachers are always on a journey of discovery where constant re-evaluation of attitudes and ways of seeing the world becomes a key characteristic of learning for themselves and their pupils. This involves questioning, observation, engagement in dialogue and examination of one's thoughts and actions and the effect on other people. It also involves understanding your school's interaction with its community and intersecting with the pupils' different cultural and social identities, through home–school events, visits and meetings with parents and carers.

Even if the pupils appear to be of a similar cultural position, it is important for teachers to dismantle notions of perceived social norms of race and class, which may characterise children as 'cultural others', who don't quite 'fit in'. Teaching instead should centre on a more accurate picture of the existing pluralistic society of the UK and enable what Townsend (2002) calls 'culturally-responsive pedagogy', whereby behaviours, paradigms and judgements are altered. Teachers therefore need to draw on culturally plural modes of teaching which recognise, celebrate and raise the status of minority cultures; and on anti-racist modes which challenge the power imbalance experienced by minority-ethnic pupils by engaging in teaching which builds identity and gives pupils a sense of playing an equal part in building and sustaining their school and community. These attitudes and practices, alongside a critical multicultural approach, should be adopted by teachers in both multi-racial and white schools, so that our pedagogies are transformed.

Questions for discussion

- Look at school policies on anti-racism, community cohesion, cultural diversity: how is policy demonstrated in practice? What could your contribution be at a whole-school level?
- Within your own classroom, what changes would need to be made to reflect a positive 'institutional body language'?
- What steps would you introduce to challenge children's thinking (through planning, cross-curricular activities, through a story or poem) in adhering to a critical multicultural approach?

References

Ambe, B. (2006) 'Fostering multicultural appreciation in pre-service teachers through multicultural curricular transformation', *Teaching and Teacher Education* 22(6): 690–9.

Brown, B. (2001) *Unlearning Discrimination: Persona Dolls in Action*. Stoke-on-Trent: Trentham Books.

Brown, B. (2008) *Equality in Action: A Way Forward with Persona Dolls*. Stoke-on-Trent: Trentham Books.

Elton-Chalcraft, S. (2009) *It's Not Just About Black and White Miss: Children's Awareness of Race*. Stoke-on-Trent: Trentham Books.

Dadzie, S. (2000) *Toolkit for Tackling Racism*. Stoke-on-Trent: Trentham Books.

DCSF (2007) *Duty to Promote Community Cohesion: Draft Guidance*. Available at www.dcsf.gov.uk/consultations/downloadableDocs/Duty%20to%20Promote%20Community%20Cohesion%20Guidance%20FINAL.doc

Gaine, C. (2005) *We're All White, Thanks: The Persisting Myth about White Schools*. Stoke-on-Trent: Trentham Books.

Greder, A. (2007) *The Island*. Crows Nest, NSW: Allen & Unwin.

This publisher's web page will provide further details on *The Island* and more teaching ideas: www.allenandunwin.com/default.aspx?page=94&book=9781741752663

Jones, R. (1999) *Teaching Racism or Tackling It: Multicultural Stories from White Beginning Teachers*. Stoke-on-Trent: Trentham Books.

King, J.E. (2004) 'Dysconscious Racism: Ideology, Identity and the Miseducation of Teachers', in G. Ladson-Billings and D. Gillborn (eds) *The Routledge Falmer Reader in Multicultural Education*. Abingdon: Routledge Falmer. pp. 71–83.

Kincheloe, J.L. and Steinberg, S.R. (1997) *Changing Multiculturalism*. Changing Education Series. Buckingham: Open University Press.

Pearce, S. (2005) *You Wouldn't Understand: White Teachers in the Multi-ethnic Classroom*. Stoke-on-Trent: Trentham Books.

QCA (2004) *Religious Education: The Non-statutory National Framework*. London: QCA.

Townsend, B. (2002) 'Leave No Teacher Behind', *Qualitative Studies in Education* 15(6): 727–38.

Troyna, B. and Hatcher, R. (1992) *Racism in Children's Lives*. London: Routledge.

Warner, D. (2010) 'Moving into the Unknown', *Race Equality Teaching* 28(3): 39–43.

Part 3

FROM TRAINEE TO TEACHER

In reading Parts 1 and 2 of this book, you will have realised that complex, professional judgements are required in all aspects of teaching. You should have become increasingly aware of the kinds of questions to ask and evidence to consider in making them. There is rarely a single correct answer because there are so many variables to consider. By now, you should have developed, discussed and examined your personal educational philosophy which informs these judgements. In Part 3, Chapters 12, 13 and 14 aim to show you, in practical contexts, how to take your professional thinking further, in reflecting on and thinking critically about educational issues. Chapter 15 reminds you of the statutory professional responsibilities you need to take into account in doing so. The final chapter gives an overview of the wide range of Standards for Qualified Teacher Status that have been addressed at increasingly advanced levels, through the book, and suggests the ways in which you should now be in a position, not just to become a qualified teacher, but also to take responsibility for your own continuing professional development and perhaps look towards taking a Masters degree in Education in the future.

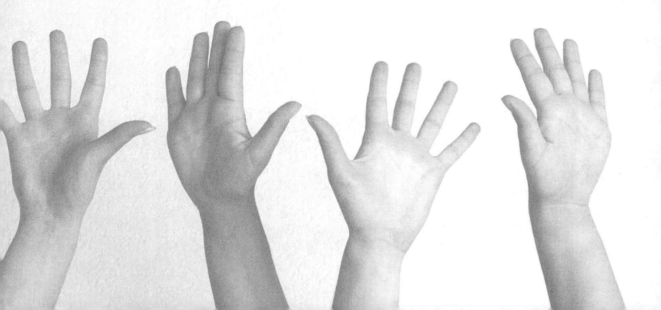

CHAPTER 12

REFLECTIVE PRACTICE

Andrew Read

By the end of this chapter, you should be able to:

- reflect on descriptive accounts of your own practice

- plan for and provide evidence of your own reflective practice

- begin to establish an overview of your own developing reflective practice.

Introduction

Chapters and books on reflection and reflective practice tend to open with a section describing various theories and frameworks. But theory can distance us from the process of reflection itself: it is the *application* that makes the difference, to your own primary practice and to your written accounts of this. So this chapter begins with an example of a trainee's descriptive lesson evaluation and identifies some potential starting points for reflection (including dealing with *unforeseen situations*, and recognising *theories in use*), putting these in a theoretical context. Questions to ask when looking back at lesson evaluations and observations are suggested: these may energise the beginning of the reflective process.

An example of a discussion between a trainee and a mentor serves as a basis for thinking about reflecting on values. Opportunities to consider the *cognitive dissonance* between *theories in use* and *espoused theory* are identified, leading to *critical reflection-on-practice*.

Drawing on an individual trainee's experience, an example of what the *reflective process* might look like is provided. Ways of organising evidence in order to demonstrate meeting the Professional Standards for QTS, and a model for viewing this reflective process from a *meta-reflective* perspective, are suggested.

Starting points for reflection

Put simply, reflection involves thinking about something. But we think about things in different ways: we recall (for example, what we were told about behaviour management in a lecture), we consider (for example, what the lecturer meant by the phrase 'assertive discipline'), we interpret (for example, we settle, perhaps temporarily, on what 'assertive discipline' means). The characteristic of reflection, the element that makes it different from other ways of thinking, is that it is thinking that leads to a 'useful outcome' (Moon 1999 p. 4). In the context of the classroom, this is thinking that leads 'towards higher-quality standards of teaching' (Pollard 2005 p. 17). The case study below shows how Anna thought about her lesson early in her first placement.

Case study

Anna, Placement A, Day 7. Year 2 class. 28 pupils. Written lesson evaluation

Today I read the text we will be using this week to the class. I made sure all the children were listening before I started by reminding them of my rules. I gave J and R a sticker each because they had their arms and legs crossed first and I

(Continued)

wanted to see good listening. I asked G to sit on the carpet by my feet so I could keep an eye on him. I read the story with a clear voice and all the children were engaged because they were looking at me. I had to stop once because B started talking to his neighbour. I wrote B's name on the board and drew a sad face next to it. B said he couldn't see the pictures. I told him to put his hand up next time he had something to say. B remained quiet for the rest of the story. When I had finished reading the story I asked the children to put their thumbs up if they had enjoyed the story. All the children put their thumbs up so this was a successful lesson.

This is the beginning in two senses for Anna: it is the beginning of her experience in school within the context of her course; this is also, potentially, the beginning of a process of reflection. Her evaluation is descriptive: the term *descriptive* sometimes implies a need for further analysis – this is the case when the phrase 'too descriptive' is written by tutors on student essays. However, description can be a positive starting point, providing context and a basis for exploration (Ghaye and Ghaye, 1998). In addition, the evaluation is the result of an experience: Kolb argues that 'immediate personal experience is the focal point of learning' (1984 p. 21). But something is missing from Anna's evaluation, at least on the surface, preventing it from leading into a reflective process: it is a recollection, an account of something that happened. What sets reflection apart is that it leads to a *useful outcome*. In a sense, Anna's evaluation is complete in itself.

Having said this, there are several aspects within this piece of descriptive writing that suggest opportunities for reflection. For a start, it is packed with theory. Brookfield argues that 'most workers ... are theorists': 'they are constantly testing out hunches, intuitions, and guesses about what will work against their own reality' (1987 p. 152). When one of these approaches is effective in one particular context, it is put aside to be used again when a similar situation arises. Brookfield argues that these effective approaches are similar to Schön's *theories in use* (1987): an effective approach is identified, some explanation is provided for why the approach is effective, and the theorist demonstrates an openness to change in the light of shifting circumstances (Schön 1987). Such *theories in use* may also evolve from what we observe or from what we understand to be the accepted model in the particular situation. *Theories in use* may stem from our own prior experience as pupils: we think back to our favourite teachers, or perhaps to those with the strategies we feel in retrospect were the most effective: these strategies may form the basis of our theories. These theories form what we know about 'good practice': we might talk about 'what works well with these pupils'.

Reflective task

Look at Anna's lesson evaluation.

What theories does Anna bring to her lesson? What effective approaches does she identify? What does she see as 'good practice'?

What explanations for these approaches does Anna provide?

What evidence for the effectiveness of these approaches is there in Anna's evaluation?

Anna's lesson evaluation also indicates that parts of the lesson presented her with responses from the pupils that she had not anticipated. Schön talks about the element of surprise, where 'something fails to meet our expectations' (1987 p. 26). Brookfield suggests that these 'unforeseen situations' trigger the need for us to 'question our habitual ways of working' (1987 p. 151). As Tripp states, when introducing the idea of critical incidents, 'we have to ask both what happened and what allowed or caused it to happen' (1993 p. 9). Schön uses the notion of *surprise* as the basis for a discussion of 'reflection-in-action' (1987). Schön argues that reflection-in-action occurs when we are in the middle of doing something (for example, in the middle of reading a story) and 'our thinking serves to reshape what we are doing while we are doing it' (1987 p. 26). Anna's evaluation suggests that surprise, reflection-in-action and some reshaping took place: 'I had to stop once because B started talking to his neighbour. I asked him to share what he had to say with the rest of the class.' This is complicated, however, because Anna's lesson evaluation is written *after* the event – it would, of course, be very difficult to write it at the time – and in part is a recount of her reflection-in-action. She may, indeed, be unaware of her reflection-in-action. A next step could be for Anna to explore the ways in which she responded to the unexpected within the lesson, or, as Schön puts it, to 'reflect *on* our reflection-in-action' (Schön 1987 p. 31).

Reflecting on reflection-in-action

One of the difficulties of this is that it may be difficult to see where and when something unexpected has happened. When we write a lesson evaluation after the event, we are already filtering and editing the experience, summarising what happened and quite possibly missing important details. Descriptive writing in this context can be very useful: a detailed statement of what happened during the course of the lesson, without any interpretation or analysis, can support the writer in identifying key moments. A lesson observation by a peer or mentor can provide this descriptive detail; an audio recording might

Table 12.1   Anna, Placement A, Day 7. Year 2 class. 28 pupils. Lesson observation by mentor

3.15 – Anna has all pupils on carpet – some quiet talking from pupils; Anna waits for 10 seconds, folds her arms; gives stickers to J and R – says, 'Well done, good sitting'. Anna continues to wait – looks at G, raises her eyebrows, puts finger to her lips – G continues to talk to his neighbour. Anna says, 'G, come and sit next to me – I want to be sure you're listening'. G moves. Anna raises her eyebrow at other pupils, says, 'I can't see anyone else who deserves a sticker' – the talking stops. Anna shows the front cover of a picture book – *Not Now Bernard*.

3.18 – Anna asks, 'Does anyone know this story?' Most of the pupils raise their hands. B says, 'I like the bit when ...' Anna says, 'B – you must remember to put up your hand.'

3.20 – Anna reads the story – holding the book to her right, the pages are open towards the pupils, Anna looking around the book to see the text. Most pupils are engaged – M and N are playing with something on the carpet; B is whispering to his neighbour – M, N and B are sitting to Anna's left.

3.22 – Anna notices B, stops reading. Anna writes 'B' on board and draws a sad face. B says, 'But I can't see the pictures.' Anna says, 'I've already told you – you must put up your hand.'

provide a useful and more manageable alternative. Table 12.1 shows a lesson observation by Anna's mentor.

Even where the details of the lesson are recounted in detail, it can still be hard to spot where reflection-in-action has taken place. It can be harder still to know what to do with the reflection-in-action once you have spotted it. However, spotting it can be the start of a reflective process. There are lots of models of reflective processes. When reflecting, people 'recapture their experience, think about it, mull it over and evaluate it' (Boud et al. 1985 p. 19). The *recapturing* might be a descriptive account recorded in a journal, or part of a lesson evaluation or a lesson observation; the *thinking/mulling* is where the process becomes potentially reflective. *Evaluating* involves making some kind of judgement. When we judge something, we compare it, often subconsciously, with a set or sets of criteria. These criteria are external (for example, the Professional Standards for Qualified Teacher Status) or internal (i.e. our own set of values and beliefs, our own personal philosophy). It could be argued that Boud et al. (1985) miss the crucial next step in their simplified definition: when reflecting, people evaluate then *respond* in some way that moves the process towards a *useful outcome* (Moon 1999). Table 12.2 shows an example of how Anna might move from the descriptive to the reflective.

The questions in *questioning my response* could be generalised and applied to any descriptive account of practice in order to step into a reflective process: Why did I act in this way? What led me to this approach? What did I aim to achieve by acting in this way? How was I feeling when I did this? How did this approach relate to the needs of the pupil/s? What impact did my action have?

The *evaluation* column also specifically addresses the trainee's own values. Closer thinking about how our practice in the classroom relates to our values provides a further opportunity to enter a reflective process.

Table 12.2   Shows how Anna might move from describing her practice to reflecting on it

Descriptive		Reflective (reflecting on reflection-in-action)	
Recapturing experience		Thinking about it/mulling it over	Evaluating
Unforeseen situations	My response/ reflection-in-action	Questioning my response	Identifying an aspect to develop – leading to an outcome
B is whispering to his neighbour.	Anna writes 'B' on board and draws a sad face.	Why did I draw a sad face on the board?	How does my response fit with my values?
		Where does this approach come from? What was my aim?	To what extent did I achieve what I wanted to (short term/long term)?
		How did B's whispering make me feel?	To what extent did I understand and address the needs of the pupil/s?
		What was my aim in writing B's name and drawing the sad face?	How else could I have handled this unforeseen situation?
		To what extent was my response a reflection of my needs?	
		What impact did drawing the sad face on the board have on B's behaviour?	
B says, 'But I can't see the pictures.'	Anna says, 'I've already told you – you must put up your hand.'	Why did I repeat the rule?	
		Where does this approach come from? What was my aim? How did B's objection make me feel?	
		To what extent was my response a reflection of my needs?	
		What impact did the repetition of the rule have on B?	

Reflecting on values

Table 12.3 shows an excerpt from a dialogue between a trainee, Khadija, and her mentor.

Khadija has a rationale for how she has organised the groups. This is her *theory in use*. The discussion with the mentor begins to challenge this. Khadija hesitantly suggests an alternative arrangement but comes up against a barrier: 'we put the pupils in literacy groups for history'. This is in line with Ghaye and Ghaye's notion of *critical reflection-on-practice* (1998 p. 33) in which the status quo, in this case the 'accepted routine' of children working in literacy groups for history, is challenged. By bringing it closer to the surface Khadija has an opportunity to clarify her understanding and to question 'assumptions made about effective teaching'. It is important to recognise that 'critical' here, as Ghaye and Ghaye make clear, is *not* a synonym for cynical, destructive or negative: *critical reflection-on-practice* is not an invitation to Khadija to lay into practice at the school; it 'has the intention of being creative and constructive' (Ghaye and Ghaye 1998 p. 34).

Table 12.3   Khadija, Placement A, Day 9. Year 4 class. 27 pupils. Lesson focus: History. Discussion with mentor

Mentor: Tell me about how you organised the pupils today.

Khadija: They were in their ability groups with the less able group at the table at the back where the TA can work with them – they were labelling the pictures – they needed something simple to keep them on task. The most able group were with me – I wanted to challenge them, get them to think about how they could use the artefacts to build up a picture of what life was like during the War. The middle-ability groups had the worksheets – I wanted them to work in silence so that the noise level in the classroom was kept down.

Mentor: What information was the ability grouping based on?

Khadija: I had the pupils in their literacy groups. The most able group are all working at Level 4c in reading and writing.

Mentor: How did their reading and writing skills support them during the discussion work with the artefacts?

Khadija: Well, one of them needed to scribe down the ideas they came up with on the paper. But ... I suppose it was really more about the discussion ... asking questions ... suggesting what the objects could have been used for.

Mentor: How might you have organised the groups differently?

Khadija: I guess more of the pupils could have been involved in this kind of activity. The TA could have supported the less able group – she was doing that anyway. The middle groups would struggle though: they're not very good at collaborating or getting their ideas down on paper and I couldn't scribe for them all. I could have put them into mixed-ability groups but that would be tricky to manage because we put the pupils in literacy groups for history.

However, the challenge to accepted routine is only implicit in the mentor's questions. The mentor could suggest to Khadija that she puts the pupils in mixed ability groups for the next history lesson. But, as Dewey (1926) argues, the student 'can't see just by being "told", although the right kind of telling may guide his seeing' (in Boydston 1984 p. 57). Reflection is significantly about ownership, and it is important that Khadija works through this and understands for herself that a shift in her idea of 'good practice' could be beneficial for the pupils.

Within this discussion, Khadija's *theory in use* clearly implies a set of values that underpin her practice. But these values are not necessarily the values she shares publically. We may all do this at various points: we tell our friends or colleagues that we live by one set of values but in practice we may be less consistent. For example, we may tell our friends that we are committed to re-using plastic carrier bags at the supermarket but then find ourselves taking fresh plastic carrier bags at the checkout because we have forgotten to bring the ones we have at home. This is linked closely to the idea of *theory in use* (what we do in practice) and *espoused theory*, which Brookfield describes as 'the theories that people claim to follow, even when their own actions contradict this claim' (1987 pp. 152–3). Before starting this placement, Khadija shared her theories with her peers; these *espoused theories*, shown in Table 12.4, imply a set of underlying values.

Brookfield describes the friction 'between what we say we believe and what we privately suspect to be true' as *cognitive dissonance* (1987 p. 153). While it can be uncomfortable to recognise that our thinking may be inconsistent and that *cognitive*

Table 12.4   Khadija's *espoused theories*

Pupils need to discuss their ideas in order to construct new knowledge and understanding.

All pupils need to be challenged in order to achieve to the best of their ability.

It is important to support pupils in their development of independence and autonomy.

dissonance is present in our own dealings with theory and practice, this does provide a springboard to reflection. Dissonance demands resolution, and this resolution represents the *useful outcome* that is central to reflection. However, it would be misleading to suggest that the reflective practice model, *in practice*, is a simple one.

Reflective task

Look at the discussion between Khadija and her mentor and the list of Khadija's *espoused theories*.

What values underpin Khadija's *espoused theories*?

What *theories in use* are evident in Khadija's comments? What values do these suggest?

What *cognitive dissonance* might there be between Khadija's theories in use and her espoused theories?

The reflective process in action

Table 12.5 shows how Khadija's practice in history lessons developed over several weeks.

Khadija adapts her practice emerging with an alternative *theory in use*. She tries out a number of strategies: the 'discussion time', the mixed-ability grouping, the distribution of roles. The strategies she experiments with are not new to the world of teaching and learning, but this is not a problem. Pollard (2005) makes it clear that *reviewing* work published in the area of practice concerning us and *gathering* models of 'good practice' from other teachers are key elements in the reflective process (2005 pp. 17–23). Indeed, it could be argued that there is nothing new in education: it has all been tried out before. However, the strategies Khadija introduces during her placement are *innovatory* because they are *new to Khadija's practice* and may also be *new to the pupils* or *the learning context* (i.e. that classroom, that subject, that time of day). As she adjusts her approach, she begins to demonstrate the 'creative and

Table 12.5   Shows how Khadija's practice in history lessons developed over several weeks

Khadija's practice (i.e. what she does in class)	Khadija's rationale	Khadija's evaluation (sometimes after mentor observation and discussion)	The reflective process
Day 9: All pupils work in 'ability groups' Some pupils work in silence	'We put the pupils in literacy groups for history' Manages noise level	'The lesson worked well because the pupils who find collaboration difficult did the worksheets and the noise level was kept down'	*Descriptive reflection-on-practice* (Ghaye and Ghaye 1998) in Khadija's account of lesson to mentor Opportunity for *critical reflection-on-practice* (Ghaye and Ghaye 1998) with possible challenge to routine identified *Cognitive dissonance* between Khadija's *espoused values* and *theories in use* recognised (Brookfield 1987; Schön, 1987)
Day 14: Introduces 5-minute 'discussion time' at the start of group work	'... to help pupils clarify with each other what they have to do'	'The most able group seemed to use "discussion time" most effectively'	*Collecting/analysing evidence* (Pollard 2005) *Perceptive reflection-on-practice* (Ghaye and Ghaye 1998), drawing links between descriptions and Khadija's 'personal feelings' (Ghaye and Ghaye 1998 p. 29)
Day 19: Introduces mixed-ability grouping in history lesson	'I thought the more able pupils could model discussion'	'Some of the less able pupils were just sitting there – not taking part at all – it was frustrating' (*reflecting on reflection-in-action*, Schön, 1987)	A new *theory in use* emerging. Khadija hypothesising and 'deducing new implications for action' (Kolb 1984 p. 21)
Day 19: Stops the lesson – gives each group six roles (manager, scribe, time-keeper, etc.) to distribute	'I needed to do something to get them all joining in' (*reflecting on reflection-in-action*, Schön 1987)	'It worked quite well. There was more participation although the more able pupils tended to dominate – they often took the manager role'	
Day 24: Introduces group activity where outcome is collaborative – focus in lesson introduction on different roles	'They knew they had to talk about what their own role was'	'It was all about talking – some of the less able pupils had quite a lot to say – they were quite articulate in front of the class. We still need to do some work on collaboration, though'	*Cognitive dissonance* resolved to some extent – discussion of ideas integrated into practice *Useful outcome* (Moon 1999) achieved *Higher-quality standards of teaching?* (Pollard 2005)

Table 12.6   Professional attributes recommended for the award of Qualified Teacher Status, which relate to the process of reflection on practice

Those recommended for the award of QTS should:

Q7 (a) Reflect on and improve their practice, and take responsibility for identifying and meeting their developing professional needs.
    (b) Identify priorities for their early professional development in the context of induction.

Q8 Have a creative and constructively critical approach towards innovation, being prepared to adapt their practice where benefits and improvements are identified.

Q9 Act upon advice and feedback and be open to coaching and mentoring.

constructively critical approach towards innovation' required by the Professional Standards (Q8).

However, when we try something new in the class, it may often initially 'fail' because of our own uncertainty and the pupils' unfamiliarity with the novelty. It is important, however, to use this 'failure' to move forward. In order to improve practice, we need to refine and try again, rather than return to the safe ground of the status quo. Reflective practitioners are, essentially, learners. The experience of trying something out and finding that it does not quite work involves risk: this parallels the experience of pupils. By participating in the reflective process, practitioners can become a role model 'to support and guide learners to reflect on their learning' (Professional Standards, Q28).

Providing evidence of your own reflective practice

As part of your teacher training course, induction year or further professional development, you may be required to assemble a portfolio of evidence demonstrating that you have met or are in the process of meeting the Professional Standards at different levels. But how might you provide evidence of reflectiveness (Q7), of your ability to adapt (Q8), and of your constructive openness to advice from mentors and tutors (Q9)? Table 12.6 shows relevant Professional Attributes recommended for the award of Qualified Teacher Status (QTS).

One way of demonstrating reflective practice in a portfolio is through *organisation*: evidence needs to be organised in a way which implies the reflective process that has taken place. Returning to the example of Khadija's developing practice (p. 187), evidence could be provided through an appropriately sequenced selection of lesson plans, lesson observations, lesson evaluations and reflective journal entries, as suggested in Table 12.7.

Table 12.7   Suggests ways in which evidence of reflection on practice can be provided

Day 9	Lesson plan: *ability groups*
	Lesson evaluation: 'the lesson worked well'
	Reflective journal: recognition of *cognitive dissonance* following discussion with mentor
Day 14	Lesson plan: *discussion time*
	Reflective journal: *rationale* ('to help pupils clarify ...')
	Lesson evaluation: *discussion time* worked for *some* pupils

Published work may also have had an impact on Khadija's thinking. She may have read some articles or chapters on encouraging pupils to work collaboratively, or on enabling participation in group work. However, when constructing your portfolio, a photocopied chapter, article or excerpt from either of these, only demonstrates that you are able to photocopy. The links between theory and practice, between what you have seen or read and what you do, need to be explicit.

This reflective process can be made more explicit through *annotation*. However, annotation needs to be brief. The word implies 'notes' rather than an essay. If these notes become lengthy, the annotation may become too descriptive. Overly descriptive annotations may suggest that the examples you provide do not provide sufficient evidence. A simple set of conclusions to draw from this is that you need to *welcome* observation and discussion, retain *all the evidence*, *keep it organised* in a way that is easy for you to explain, and *maintain a reflective journal*.

Maintaining a reflective journal

A reflective journal may be a requirement or a recommendation. What it can do is remind you about how you used to think and how and why this thinking has shifted. However, writing 'Reflective Journal' on the cover of an exercise book will not ensure that the contents are reflective. By interrogating *yourself* about the source or location of the evidence you are drawing upon, opportunities to evaluate and analyse evidence (Pollard 2005) emerge, leading to thinking about *innovatory* ways of doing things, active experimentation (Kolb 1984) and useful outcomes (Moon 1999). Table 12.8 gives examples of questions you could use as a starting point for interrogating your own thinking.

You can also interrogate your thinking about the reflective journal itself:

Reflective journal	Why is this passage particularly descriptive?
	Why did I choose to write about this particular event?
	What incident/s caused me to reflect on my reflections-in-action or on my values? (Q7)

Table 12.8 Examples of starting points for interrogating your own thinking

Location/source	Interrogating yourself
My thinking	What experience leads me to think this?
	What other philosophies are there?
	What barriers are preventing me from thinking differently?
Plans	To what extent does this represent what actually happens/happened?
	To what extent did this lesson meet the objectives I sought? (Q7)
	To what extent did *all pupils* develop understanding/skills/knowledge/values? (Q7, Q8)
	How effective were the different elements of the lesson: differentiation, assessment, resources, etc.? (Q7, Q8)
Lesson evaluations	How effectively did I teach? How appropriate were my approaches in the context of this lesson? (Q7, Q8)
	What did pupils learn? How do I feel about this? (Q7, Q8)
	How could I have done this differently ... in a way that reflects my developing personal philosophy? (Q7, Q8)
Written lesson observations	To what extent does this reflect my own thinking about the lesson?
	How clear am I about my strengths and the areas I need to develop? (Q7)
	What questions does this raise about my practice? (Q7)
Annotated examples of pupils' work	What does this show about pupil learning?
	What does this show about *my understanding* of pupil learning? (Q7)
	To what extent does this work provide evidence that my practice echoes my developing philosophy? (Q8)
Records of discussions with mentors and tutors	What was the purpose of this discussion?
	To what extent was my own learning enhanced by this discussion? (Q7, Q8, Q9)
	What do I need to do now? (Q7, Q9)

The process of reflecting on reflection has already been touched upon in relation to reflecting on reflection-in-action. However, by extending this, taking it from the micro to the macro, opportunities to engage in meta-reflection emerge. These can form the core of thinking and writing about reflective practice and can be supportive when working at Masters level.

Meta-reflection

At its simplest level, reflection is about finding a solution: you identify a concern, think about it, try something out, and, when it works, refine your practice accordingly. Khadija's reflective experience sees just such a change in practice. Once this outcome is achieved, you start again: a new reflective cycle kicks off when a new concern is identified.

However, there are problems with this model. One is that, as a trainee or as a teacher, you will encounter several concerns, simultaneously or on successive days, all of which require some kind of resolution. As a reflective practitioner, several reflective cycles will be running at the same time.

The other, more complex, issue is that the reflective process is not really circular, although the simplified visual models (Kolb 1984; Pollard 2005) may suggest this, and it is not an 'evenly progressive sequence' (Illeris 2006 p. 151). Once a solution has been found, you will not, as a reflective practitioner, re-enter the process at the same starting point. You will have acquired a new set of reflective skills, new understanding around the role of the teacher, and have refined the values that underpin your thinking; you will be drawing on a broader range of experience. Your re-entry into the reflective process will be deeper than your previous entry. So rather than a cycle, the process is a *reflective spiral*. This, in essence, is similar to Bruner's spiral curriculum model (1960): Bruner argues that 'any subject can be taught effectively in some intellectually honest form to any child at any stage of development' (1960 p. 33). If we consider reflection to be a spiral process, then the reflective practitioner might return repeatedly to the same element of practice (for example, behaviour management) but each visit would involve a deeper response acknowledging the practitioner's *stage of development*.

When looking at this spiral in a meta-reflective way, you need to step back. You can create your own analogy for this stepping-back. *Helicoptering* is one that serves as an example: as you rise above the reflective process, the details of the reflective landscape (e.g. what you said to the class, how the pupil responded, how well you thought the lesson went) become less clear; the overall geography (e.g. the way your values shifted from the beginning to the end of a placement, the kinds of concerns that occupied your thoughts) becomes clearer. Meta-reflection is about reflecting on the whole reflective process, identifying themes and patterns, recognising changes in depth and breadth.

Take Anna, for example. Her initial concerns focused on pupils following the rules and ensuring that pupils were quiet. By the end of Placement A, she had developed *a range of teaching, learning and behaviour management strategies* and was using them effectively (Q10). She became much more aware that different pupils had different requirements, so by the beginning of Placement B her focus was on *how to make effective personalised provision* for the pupils in her class (Q19), particularly those with English as an additional language. This in turn led her into developing her knowledge of approaches to assessment (Q12). Her confidence in using formative assessment strategies developed but she became conscious that she tended always to initiate opportunities for self- and peer-assessment. By the beginning of Placement C, Anna's focus was on supporting and guiding learners *to reflect on their learning* (Q28).

Looking at this from a meta-reflective perspective, Anna might argue that her initial reflections were about getting the pupils to do what she told them. She was focused on establishing her authority, but was less aware of (or concerned about) the pupils as individuals. As her confidence in her presence in the classroom increased, she began to acknowledge pupils' individual needs, adapting her practice accordingly. In her final placement, her attention shifted to enabling pupils to operate independently. Anna could think about this process as a meta-reflective continuum:

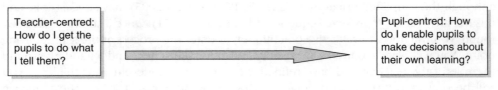

Teacher-centred: How do I get the pupils to do what I tell them?

Pupil-centred: How do I enable pupils to make decisions about their own learning?

Figure 12.1

 Summary

Descriptive accounts of your practice such as lesson evaluations and observations form a practical starting point for the reflective process. By questioning these accounts, concerns related to practice may emerge. Sometimes these concerns will relate to the cognitive dissonance between what you say you believe and what you do in practice. Resolution of this dissonance, in which *critical reflection-on-practice* (Ghaye and Ghaye 1998) plays a part, is at the heart of the reflective process. As you gain experience and confidence, your engagement with reflection will become deeper and broader: a reflective spiral. By retaining a broad bank of evidence, and by organising and questioning this appropriately, you demonstrate reflective development. By stepping back from the evidence, a broader perspective emerges and opportunities to reflect on your own reflective development emerge.

 Questions for discussion

- How do you respond to unforeseen situations in the classroom? Why do you respond in this way?
- What are your *espoused theories* and what *cognitive dissonance* is there between these and your *theories in use*?

(Continued)

- What were your key concerns about practice at the start of your programme? To what extent have these shifted as your experience has broadened?
- Where do you stand on the teacher-centred to pupil-centred continuum?
- What would a continuum which more effectively represented your own reflective development look like?
- What are the obstacles to your engagement with reflective practice? How might you overcome these?

Further reading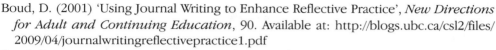

Boud, D. (2001) 'Using Journal Writing to Enhance Reflective Practice', *New Directions for Adult and Continuing Education*, 90. Available at: http://blogs.ubc.ca/csl2/files/2009/04/journalwritingreflectivepractice1.pdf

Boud discusses *occasions of reflection*, the ways that journal writing can be used, and identifies some of the barriers to journal writing.

Illeris, K. (2006) *How We Learn: Learning and Non-learning in School and Beyond*, 2nd edn. Abingdon: Routledge.

Illeris discusses models of learning and suggests versions which might better reflect reality.

Moon, J. (2001) *Reflection in Higher Education Learning: PDP Working Paper 4*. Learning and Teaching Support Network: Generic Centre. Available at: www.york.ac.uk/admin/hr/training/gtu/students/resources/pgwt/reflectivepractice.pdf

Moon summarises some key theoretical approaches to reflection and discusses the relationship between reflection and learning.

References

Boud, D., Keogh, R. and Walker, D. (eds) (1985) *Reflection Turning Experience into Learning*. Abingdon: RoutledgeFalmer.

Boydston, J. (ed.) (1984) *John Dewey: The Later Works Volume 2: 1925–1927*. Southern Illinois: SIU Press.

Brookfield, S. (1987) *Developing Critical Thinkers: Challenging Adults to Explore Alternative Ways of Thinking and Acting*. Milton Keynes: Open University Press.

Bruner, J. (1960) *The Process of Education*. Harvard: Harvard University Press.

Ghaye, A. and Ghaye, K. (1998) *Teaching and Learning through Critical Reflective Practice*. London: David Fulton.

Illeris, K. (2006) *How We Learn: Learning and Non-learning in School and Beyond*, 2nd edn. Abingdon: Routledge.

Kolb, D. (1984) *Experiential Learning: Experience as the Source of Learning and Development*. Englewood Cliffs, NJ: Prentice-Hall.

Moon, J. (1999) *Reflection in Learning and Professional Development*. Abingdon: RoutledgeFalmer.

Pollard, A. (2005) *Reflective Teaching*, 2nd edn. London: Continuum.

Schön, D. (1987) *Educating the Reflective Practitioner: Toward a New Design for Teaching and Learning in the Professions*. San Francisco: Jossey-Bass.

Tripp, D. (1993) *Critical Incidents in Teaching: Developing Professional Judgement*. Abingdon: Routledge.

CHAPTER 13

ENQUIRY AND CRITICAL THINKING

Diane Vaukins

By the end of this chapter, you should be able to:

- understand what is meant by enquiry and critical thinking
- understand why it is an essential skill for both teachers and pupils to learn
- understand the personal disposition you need to develop, in order to become a critical thinker
- develop a personal philosophy, in order to manage your own professional development and communicate your thinking to other professionals and stakeholders in education.

Reflective task

Using the previous chapter and your developing philosophy of education, reflect on what you have learnt so far.

What kind of teacher do you think you will be?

Have you changed your mind as you have studied different modules and completed school-based placements?

Are you starting to question why things are as they are in the primary classroom?

Introduction

The first section of this chapter begins by considering what is meant by critical thinking and why it is an essential skill for both teachers and pupils to learn. Next, the personal disposition you need to develop in order to become a critical thinker is discussed. Then the processes involved in thinking critically are explained. The second section considers contexts in which teachers need to apply critical thinking skills. The third section discusses ways in which teachers can develop critical thinking skills in children throughout the primary school.

What is meant by critical thinking?

Thinking is something we all do subconsciously, but there are times when it is necessary to focus our thoughts in order to deal with specific situations. Moore and Parker (2009) refer to this as 'thinking about thinking'. They refer to truth and the application of reason while Cottrell (2005) suggests that it involves the use of skills and attitudes. Dewey (1909) offers the idea that it involves active participation and often creates further thought as a result of conclusions reached.

Before you can begin to offer opportunities for children to become critical thinkers in the classroom, you must first decide what your own interpretation is and if indeed you are a critical thinker. For many people, it is a natural process. Chaffee (2009), a key writer on critical thinking in education, claims that it is his philosophy of life and how he defines himself, and that what we believe in has to stand the test of evaluation.

However, for many, it is a completely new idea, something that needs to be learned and practised. Critical thinking essentially means reasoned, disciplined thinking, which informs your decisions about what to think and how to behave. Reading, writing, speaking, observing and listening can all be done critically – or uncritically. There is no single definition of critical thinking. Paul (1988) calls it the ability to reach sound conclusions based on observation and information. Beyer (1983) describes it as assessing the authenticity, accuracy and worth of claims about knowledge, beliefs or arguments. Norris (1985) says that critical thinking enables you to apply everything you know and feel, to evaluate your own thinking and especially to change your ideas or behaviour. It is a skill which everyone can improve but it does not necessarily develop with maturity. Therefore, it should be learned at all ages (Lipman et al. 1980).

Reflective task

Consider what has been discussed regarding the definitions of critical thinking.
   Do you consider yourself to be a critical thinker?
   If you do – how will you begin to transfer these skills to the teaching profession?
   If not – what will you need to do in order to develop these skills ready to enter the teaching profession?

Why is critical thinking essential for teachers and pupils?

Qualifying as a primary teacher is just the beginning. Like driving a car, once you gain your licence, then you really begin to understand how to drive, adapting your style to suit the needs of the vehicle that you are driving. This is just so once you qualify to teach. You need to adapt all that you have learned in your training to the needs of the school, the curriculum, but most importantly the children in your class. As you do this, you will be developing and forming a personal philosophy of education and establishing the kind of teacher you will ultimately become.

One purpose of critical thinking is to ensure that delivery of the curriculum is as effective as possible. Many factors can help you to become a critical thinker. Amongst these is the desire to want to learn and delve deeper into the learning of others, creating independent learners with enquiring minds ready to become effective members of the community in which they live.

Another is to enable the process of reason and justification of ideas once discussion has taken place and all viewpoints have been considered. This can then lead to effective and significant change reflecting new ideas.

It should be clear by now that teachers, and we hope their pupils, are constantly asking questions, making judgements and decisions, often about issues involving values and contradictory viewpoints. Therefore, critical thinking is not an isolated skill unrelated to other skills in education. It is a seminal skill that permeates everything teachers do. It is essential to playing a responsible part in a democratic society. This theme runs throughout this book, particularly in Chapter 1 which describes constant changes in educational legislation, Chapter 2 on educational philosophy and learning theories, Chapter 6 on reflective practice in the early years, Chapter 9 on dialogical enquiry and philosophy for children,

Chapter 12 on reflective practice and in the following chapter which explores educational issues. However, this chapter looks systematically at what the process of critical thinking involves and how you can practise and develop it in a variety of school contexts.

What personal disposition is necessary to develop critical thinking skills?

Critical thinking requires intellectual empathy and intellectual humility. First, it is important to want to ask questions and to recognise and be prepared to engage with problems. In order to be well informed, it is important to seriously consider other people's points of view, to listen to other people's reasons and to be reflectively aware of your own beliefs. Look for alternative hypotheses, explanations, sources and plans and be open to them and only take up a position if this is justified by the information available. For critical thinking to be a valuable process, it is important to communicate well with others, not to intimidate or confuse others, taking into account their level of understanding and also their feelings. Critical thinking requires a willingness to be clear, precise and accurate and to think in terms of breadth and depth and to be fair. It is also essential to be honestly willing to criticise yourself, for example to admit that you do not have all the information or it cannot be known or that your inferences are unjustified. A lack of these dispositions can lead to self-deception and closed-mindedness. It is helpful in developing these qualities to sometimes argue in support of a case for which you have no real sympathy, and to identify your own ignorance about a subject, admitting that you 'thought you knew but merely believed'. It takes time, practice and commitment to learn to become less biased and more broad-minded, through intellectual empathy and humility. This involves personal and intellectual development. The basis for critical thinking then is that you are rational rather than emotional, that you are self-aware and able to recognise your own motives, bias and assumptions, are honest and not deceiving yourself, open-minded and disciplined.

How to learn to think critically

Although contexts for critical thinking in education are numerous, the underlying processes are the same. They need to be learned and practised, for developing sound, critical judgement is an ongoing goal. Throughout your study at university, you have been challenged in your assignments to be critically analytical using research and theory to support your developing views. This thought process should not end once you qualify. Rather, it should be the basis on which you build and develop your. professionalism. However, alongside the views of research and theory, when you are in post as a teacher you now need to take into account wider issues that affect the school you are in.

Reading critically

A lot of information you will want to use as evidence to support or criticise an argument will be from your reading of newspaper articles, professional and academic books and journals. It is important to be aware of the hidden techniques which writers (or speakers) may use to try to persuade you. It is still possible, even in a free and open society, to try to indoctrinate by only presenting one side of a case or omitting prejudicial material.

Reflective task

Read the Secretary of State for Education, Michael Gove's response to a question about his free schools policy, in the House of Commons (21.06.10) on the companion website (www.uk.sagepub.com/cooper). Then consider the following points:

- Does he try to persuade you of the rightness of his policy through appeals to your emotions or through offering sound evidence?
- Does he appear to set out the case for free schools in a rigorous fashion without actually doing so?
- Does he imply that one point follows logically from another when this is not the case?
- Does he give any good evidence to support his free schools policy?
- Does he confuse fact and opinion?
- Does he use emotive language, make assertions posing as arguments, make rash generalisations?
- Does he use 'persuader words' to persuade you of what is being said?
- Are the statistics reliable?
- Does he suggest that 'everyone knows that'?
- Does he make assertions which are not supported by arguments?

Try this interrogation of some other texts and avoid using these hidden techniques yourself!

Analysing competing perspectives

There is growing interest in the concept of 'community cohesion' and also in faith schools. In discussing the following question, you will develop your ability to analyse competing perspectives and develop your own informed perspective. You will need to read the following articles:

Grace, G. (2003) 'Education Studies and Faith-based Schooling: Moving From Prejudice to Evidence-based Argument', *British Journal of Educational Studies* 51(2): 149–242.
Short, G. (2002) 'Faith-based Schooling: A Threat to Social Cohesion', *Journal of Philosophy of Education* 36(4): 559–72.

Reflective task

As you read the articles above make notes on the following questions:

- What were the key claims advanced?
- Were the key claims supported by reference to research evidence?
- Could the key claims be counteracted by reference to any research evidence?
- Did the articles support or counteract the claim that faith schools enhance community cohesion?

Then, if possible, work in two groups, one in favour of the emergence of growing numbers of faith schools and one opposed to this development. Each group should identify and present some key arguments to support the allocated position, followed by a debate of the issues.

You may wish to deepen your understanding by visiting the websites of the Citizenship Foundation, Multiverse, or Runnymede Trust.

There is no single definition of critical thinking processes but the following sequence is a basic guide or checklist for evaluating your developing critical thinking. Do you:

- recognise the problem then identify and formulate a question, about which there are different points of view to explore?
- gather the information from different perspectives (what you have read, heard, seen, done)?
- analyse the evidence from different perspectives? Develop arguments from different viewpoints?

Here are some of the questions you may want to ask: How valid is the evidence? Is it justified by the proponent's expertise? Do people have conflicting interests? Do the sources agree? Are the reasons given sound? Were hypotheses justified? How? Was minimal inference involved? Is the report based on the proponent's experience or that reported by someone else? Are there any records? Is data reliable? Is there a breadth of evidence? Are claims made about people's beliefs and attitudes reliable? Are claims that certain things happened valid? Is that the author's intended meaning? Is there evidence and counter evidence? Are there any other explanations? Are there unstated assumptions and values? Balance, weigh and decide if any value judgements made are acceptable:

- Compare similarities and differences between arguments from different perspectives.
- Then identify different conclusions reached, the reasons given for reaching them and unstated reasons for reaching them. Dispose of anything which is irrelevant.

- Ask and answer questions clarifying or challenging each viewpoint (e.g. Why? What do you mean by …? Give me an example. But what if …? What are the facts? Is this what you are saying? Can you say a bit more about that?) Look at the structure of the argument from different perspectives and summarise it.
- Synthesise the argument from different perspectives.
- Reach a personal conclusion. (It may not be possible to reach a group consensus.) Reconstruct your own thinking on the basis of wider experience. Is the proposed conclusion consistent with all the known facts?

Contexts in which teachers apply critical thinking skills

Classroom management and organisation

Once you have established what critical thinking is, the next thing to consider is how to facilitate and develop this in your classroom. At first, you will be experimenting with all sorts of different teaching styles to find what best suits both yourself and the children in your class. Your placement experience should have given you an insight into the type of teacher you are and your targets for your induction year will help to focus on areas of pedagogy that you need to develop further. How should your classroom be set up? What resources will you need if you are going to facilitate the type of learning that involves critical thinking? If learners are to be able to weigh up the pros and cons of any situation, they will need access to all the relevant information to allow for a balanced judgement to be made. This might involve the use of books, the internet, interviewing different people, time to discuss, mull things over, ask questions and much more.

 Reflective task

Read the descriptions below and decide which best describes the kind of teacher you are at present:

Didactic

Teachers with this approach generally see themselves as deliverers of information, informing children of the knowledge that they need through instruction and expecting them to remember it. There is little room, if any, for children to explore ideas for themselves or offer any ideas of their own.

(Continued)

(Continued)

Facilitator

Teachers with this approach focus on activity-based learning. They expect children to use their initiative and learn in an active rather than a passive way. Collaboration forms part of this style of teaching.

Learner

Teachers with this approach see themselves as part of the learning process, working together with the children to discover answers and solutions to problems.

Consider your response to this task and decide whether you may need to begin to adapt the way you teach in order to be able to achieve a classroom where children are inspired to want to learn, encouraged to make enquiries and ask questions. It may be that you need to be a combination of all three styles or use a different style for different areas of the curriculum.

Curriculum planning

You might wonder why it is necessary for a teacher to think critically about issues regarding the curriculum when it has been compiled and written by experts. Surely a great amount of time, expertise and money have been spent on constructing a curriculum suitable for primary school children. If this is the case, then would it not be better to simply take the prescribed curriculum and deliver it to learners? This would, after all, ensure that all children in all classrooms were receiving the identical experience and content and would seem to be what the National Curriculum was designed to do.

However, if you think back to Chapter 1 and the history of the current primary curriculum, then it should be clear that there are many influences on the content of the curriculum of the day, not least the government that happens to be in power at the time. A result of this is that the content and level of expectation of achievement for children aged between 5 and 11 years is ever-changing.

How then do you make sense of all this?

Professionals and stakeholders in education

Having begun to establish your own philosophy, you may discover that this does not always sit well within the constraints of the primary education system you are working in. However, as a qualified teacher, you are working within the constraints of a given curriculum and primary school system that involves being accountable to other professionals and stakeholders. Important among these are parents and governors.

Parents

Toady more than ever, parents are expected to be involved in the education of their children. As a class teacher, you are responsible for reporting on the progress of children both throughout the year, at parent evenings and at the end of each year when a full written report is required. You will be required to make complex judgements about pupils' attitudes, relationships, attainment and progress based on evidence and to convey this in appropriate ways through discussion with parents. What sort of evidence do you collect? How? How do the different kinds of evidence connect? How does it relate to what parents tell you? How can you work in partnership with them to support their child's learning? Children and families are different and this needs to be taken into account in considering these questions.

Governors

Although the head teacher is ultimately responsible for managing a school, it is the governing body that sets the strategic framework that is to be implemented. Within this framework will be objectives, targets, policies and strategies for monitoring and evaluating progress across the school. The governing body also acts as a critical friend to the head teacher, in order to ensure that the children are receiving the most effective education.

As a class teacher and subject manager, it will be necessary for you on occasion to write reports about the attainment and progress of the children in your class ready to deliver to the governors. This will involve careful analysis of results and justification of your actions. As previously mentioned in this chapter, you will need to have thought critically about your teaching methods and future development in order for this report to play an effective part in school development.

Developing children's critical thinking skills

Enquiry

When children begin school, they are natural enquirers, full of imagination and brimming with questions. The introduction of the Creative Curriculum and the increased importance of the role of play in KS1 strived to nurture and develop this natural enquiry and channel it towards the prescribed levels of achievement set down in the National Curriculum.

This type of enquiring mind is not exclusive to children in early years settings and KS1 but can become lost or repressed as children move through the primary years. As a newly qualified teacher, it is all too easy to become so involved in the everyday running of your classroom and ensuring that you are delivering the required content of all subjects, that you begin to forget the importance of taking time to consider questions such as: Why I am doing this? What is the purpose of …? How can I improve this? Is there another way to approach this? Is this relevant to the children in my class? If you are not an enquirer or critical thinker, how can you facilitate, develop and encourage this in your classroom?

Teaching for thinking

Is it really possible to teach children to think and what does teaching for thinking really mean? As previously mentioned, in order to develop enquiring minds, children need to be encouraged both to ask and answer questions. The type of questions that are asked and the follow-up to the answers are paramount to the success and effectiveness of this pedagogical style.

There are several types of question to consider when trying to encourage and teach children to be active thinkers. These are typically: closed, open and probing.

- **Closed questions**: usually require a yes or no answer or there is just one answer. For example – What is your name? Would you like a cake?
- **Open questions**: are usually able to be answered in more than one way. For example – What did you think of …? How would you do that?
- **Probing questions**: are usually used to encourage thinking as they require the questioner to listen to the answer and direct their questioning in an investigative way in order to elicit as much information from the child being questioned, and hence ascertain the level of knowledge and understanding. For example – when assessing the ability level of children in your class, it is important that they are able to explain and demonstrate their knowledge in various ways including discussion. Use of probing questions will allow children to develop their thought patterns and ideas.

Reflective task

As a class teacher, it will be your responsibility to assess the level of achievement of children in your class. In some cases, you may have the added task of administering government tests and ensuring that the children in your class are prepared both academically and mentally for such requirements. In order to do this effectively, you will need to think carefully and develop different strategies.

- How will you arrange the children – friendship groups, ability groups?
- How do you question?
- How do you record and act on any assessment outcomes?

Critical thinking across the curriculum

From the beginning, children need to understand the enquiry processes. The National Curriculum suggests that enquiry skills

> enable pupils to ask relevant questions, to pose and define problems, to plan what to do and how to research, to predict outcomes and anticipate consequences, and to test conclusions and improve ideas. (DfEE/QCA 1999 p. 22)

While Owen and Ryan (2001) argue that 'enquiry is taught, not just caught, and needs to be modelled carefully by the teacher', the Cambridge Review (Alexander 2010 p. 24) refers to the need for children to learn how to approach electronic media, including film and television, with the same critical awareness as reading and writing. 'If language unlocks thought', it says, 'then thought is enhanced and challenged when language is pursued with purpose and rigour' (p. 25) and children learn how language is used in different ways in different disciplines.

An example of an activity where children combine these skills might be: creating an account of the past, whether it is written, given in role play or a display or involves asking questions about sources. These may be written, oral, buildings, sites or artefacts. Often there is no single correct answer because sources are incomplete, and for other reasons. It is necessary to make inferences, supported by reasoned arguments, to listen to the arguments of others, and perhaps change your own view. Accounts and interpretations of the past are constructed by selecting, interpreting and combining sources to create a reasoned argument; there may be different but equally valid interpretations.

These skills of reasoning, inference, interpretation and justification are transferable across many curriculum subjects and children need to be encouraged to make the links between the learning in one subject to that in another. In order to do this, the teacher will also need to use similar skills in planning, evaluating and assessing.

Faith and belief

The Cambridge Review (Alexander 2010 p. 24) considers that non-denominational schools should teach about religious beliefs, respect and understanding, but that they should also encourage children to discuss the validity of religion itself.

Citizenship and ethics

The Cambridge Review (p. 24) emphasises the importance of this area of the curriculum, in terms of widespread concern it found about material greed and the aims of education to encourage respect and reciprocity, interdependence, sustainability, celebration of culture and community, exploring, knowing and common sense. The Review sees dialogic teaching as essential in doing this in a 'domain which has global and national components and includes values, moral codes, customs and procedures by which people act'.

Reflective task

Now that you have been introduced to critical thinking, enquiry and reflection, try to outline your personal philosophy of education and learning. You might want to look back over your lesson observation feedback. Note the areas where thinking has been mentioned and consider what you need to do in order to be able to put this advice into practice. For example, it may have been noted that you need to give children more thinking time or that your questioning needs to allow more discussion to take place.

Summary

This chapter has briefly outlined what is meant by enquiry and critical thinking, in order for you to grasp the ideas and begin to develop your own skills in these areas. The use of different methods of enquiry and questioning will help to improve both your own thinking and that of those for whom you will be facilitating learning in the future. Government policies, teaching approaches and philosophies, scholarly literature and educational debates in the media will continue to change and will always have influence over the education of future generations. All these things should enable you to effectively develop a personal philosophy, in order to manage your own professional development and communicate your thinking to other professionals and stakeholders in education. Qualifying to teach should be just the start of a journey of enquiry and thought, both for yourself and for all the children you will share learning with in the future. Perhaps the most important thing of all for you is to encourage and embrace the idea that in order for children to become critical thinkers and enquirers, they will need to challenge *your* ideas and ways of thinking. However, as Rice (1985) points out: 'To really ask is to open the door to the whirlwind. The answer may annihilate the question and the questioner.' How you manage this is something you will need to decide for yourself.

Questions for discussion

- What is my personal philosophy of education and learning? Has it changed since I read Chapter 2? How?
- Am I a critical thinker?
- How am I going to facilitate critical thinking for the learners in my classroom?
- What are my teaching approaches/styles?

Website

Independent Thinking: www.independentthinking.co.uk/default.aspx
This website promotes and offers ideas for developing independent thinkers. It offers interesting ideas to change the way you may have thought about learning in the past and offers new ideas to encourage independent thinking.

References

Alexander, R. (ed.) (2010) *Children, their World, their Education: Final Report and Recommendations of the Cambridge Primary Review*. London: Routledge.

Beyer, B. (1983) 'Common Sense about Teaching Thinking Skills', *Educational Leadership* 41: 4–6.

Chaffee, J. (2009) *Thinking Critically*, 9th edn. Boston, MA: Houghton Mifflin Harcourt.

Cottrell, S. (2005) *Critical Thinking Skills*. Basingstoke: Palgrave MacMillan.

Dewey, J. (1909) *How we Think*. Boston, MA: D.C. Heath and Co.

DfEE/QCA (1999) *The National Curriculum: Handbook for Primary Teachers in England*. London: DfEE and QCA.

Lipman, M., Sharpe, A.M. and Ofskanyoy, F.S. (1980) *Philosophy in the Classroom*. Philadelphia, PA: Temple University Press.

Moore, B. and Parker, R. (2009) *Critical Thinking*. New York: McGraw-Hill.

Norris, S.P. (1985) 'Synthesis of Research on Critical Thinking', *Educational Leadership* 42: 40–5.

Owen, D. and Ryan, A. (2001) *Teaching Geography 3–11: The Essential Guide*. London: Continuum.

Paul, R. (1988) 'Critical Thinking in the Classroom', *Teaching K–8* 18: 49–51.

Rice, A. (1985) *The Vampire Lestat*. New York: Ballantine Books.

CHAPTER 14
EXPLORING ISSUES IN EDUCATION

Andrew Slater

By the end of this chapter, you should be able to:

- understand what is meant by topical educational issues, and their impact on children, schools and society, by using frameworks to explore competing perspectives

- find related, relevant literature, both professional and academic, in journals, books and on the internet

- investigate and evaluate the relationship between your own professional experience and the competing perspectives

- engage in professional debate about contentious issues in education and develop your own argued viewpoint, supported by evidence.

Introduction

This chapter will help you to think more deeply about themes and issues in education. A helpful starting point is *The Shorter Oxford Dictionary* which defines an 'issue' as 'a point or matter in contention' (Little et al. 1959 p. 1051). Where there are issues there is inevitably debate. Some issues are complex. Relevant information may be interpreted in differing ways. Influential research teams or pressure groups with particular interests may offer different perspectives on the best way forward. It is seen as essential that student teachers and teachers are equipped to explore and engage with such debates.

The chapter begins by showing you how to identify different perspectives on an educational issue through analysis of wide reading, linked to your personal experience in schools. Then it helps you to identify the kinds of questions to ask about a variety of current issues. Next, it considers how to explore widely used concepts such as 'social cohesion', and concludes with a framework for systematically analysing the different dimensions of educational issues, for example local, national and global dimensions.

Current issues, competing perspectives, questions and evidence

There is sometimes a risk that broad educational themes (e.g. standards in primary education or accountability in education, 'personalised learning' or 'healthy eating') may be presented in a predominantly descriptive way. Such presentations obscure the underlying issues which demand fuller analysis and discussion. It is here that an informed focus, which creates a platform for deeper and more reflective consideration, is a professional requirement. This will lead to a clearer appreciation of ways to address the identified problems.

Identifying competing perspectives

Reading and research

Exploration of competing perspectives is not easy. It may require consideration of the perspectives of influential organisations or groups with vested interests. The views of organisations may reflect deeply held values or a priori commitments. However, pressure groups also sometimes commission independent research which helps to shape key policy commitments. Teaching associations, for example, often have clearly thought-through stances and policies in relation to a wide range of work-related issues. In practice, a range of factors may shape the policy adopted by teaching associations with regard to specific issues such as the remodelling of the workforce. Formal policy positions may be informed by reference to independent research. But, at the same time, they may also draw upon perceptions relating to the interests of the association's members, evidence gleaned from surveys or evaluations and the underlying value commitments of the association.

One of the main challenges in focusing upon the competing perspectives relating to a current issue is to develop a dynamic appreciation of how arguments are developing, taking into account the subtle ways in which key parties utilise data from research. It is also important to appreciate that sometimes organisations change their policies and approaches in response to changing circumstances.

Where an organisation has a strong commitment, you may feel that there is a need to be prepared to reflect upon the ways in which relevant information is employed to support or reinforce key arguments and claims. It is arguably here that your own independent reading is particularly important.

More generally, it should be noted that the status of research should always be of interest to the reader. In exploring some current issues, it is likely that you will find that you need to engage with relevant research studies prepared by teachers or other independent researchers. The theme of bullying is a case in point. The theme has been explored by many independent researchers, including teachers preparing action research projects located in individual schools. The evidence available from international studies is also of considerable interest (Cowie and Jennifer 2007; Rolande and Munthe 2001; Smith 2003). A balanced coverage of bullying or aggression in school requires some engagement with research of this kind. It also requires careful consideration of major studies and significant government reports which address emerging issues. For example, the theme of cyber bullying has attracted growing attention in recent years. It is important to be aware of recent reports and guidance provided by the DCSF and other key agencies which focus upon this problem (DCSF 2007a).

In exploring research evidence, it is important to ask key questions. How reliable is the research? What is the nature of the link between separate studies? Remember that reference to peer-reviewed journals provides real assurance about quality.

Table 14.1 provides a framework which you may find useful when you begin to develop your own reading focusing upon a selected theme. It is sometimes helpful to keep a concise record of this kind as you develop your reading. The comments made in each column are simply indicative of the kinds of points which may begin to emerge from this process.

Personal experience

Your exploration of research relating to a selected theme will help as you begin to explore an issue in greater depth. However, it is also important to recognise the

Table 14.1   A framework for recording reading about a selected issue

Status of source	Key points and findings	Implications for debate and discussion relating to selected current issue
Recent large-scale research study completed by a team from a major university	A range of recommendations. The key recommendations are: …	This appears to be an important study …
		The scale of this study is one factor which may suggest that there is a need to explore the recommendations carefully. However, there may still be some grounds for caution. Interestingly, this is a point which the research team also appear to recognise
A recent DfE Report Such a report is not a piece of academic research; however, it provides some important insights into significant recent developments which are relevant to my area of interest	Key recommendations are: … Reference to a range of case studies which appear to highlight aspects of best practice	Highlights important recent developments … Provides a timely overview which offers some clear guidance, drawing upon case studies
Action research project completed in one school setting	Detailed suggestions made re. areas for progress in one school setting	Possible implications for other similar contexts. However …

relevance and value of the experience you have gained when in school. It is, after all, in the dynamic context of school-based training that a sharper appreciation of the impact of problems such as bullying and obesity emerges. Moreover, this promotes greater understanding of the impact of such issues upon children, schools and families. It is also when you are in school that you have an opportunity to gain more meaningful insights about effective strategies to address areas of concern.

Formal research studies are not the sole source of meaningful knowledge and understanding. Helpful insights which lead to a more subtle understanding of an issue may emerge from a process of active reflection upon relevant aspects of school-based experience. A capacity to be reflective has consistently featured in the QTS training standards. Through developing the skills of reflection, you begin to challenge your own thinking and so develop a more profound appreciation of the opportunities and challenges which particular current issues present.

Identifying key questions

It is helpful to have some key questions in mind when you begin to focus upon a new issue. An issue which attracts debate is actually likely to be a theme which has important implications for a range of groups:

- What are the implications of this issue for teachers and learners?
- What are the implications of this issue for schools, families and the wider community?
- What are the implications of this issue for the student teacher?

It is particularly important that you are prepared to ask your own questions when focusing upon a current issue. The questions which you feel are most pertinent are likely to reflect the experience that you have gained in school. You will also find that your questions are likely to reflect your reading and any related discussion with other students.

Table 14.2 highlights a number of current themes. It also identifies some of the kinds of questions that it may be helpful to consider when focusing upon each of these issues. But you will see that only three questions are raised in relation to each selected theme. You may feel that this is grossly inadequate. In practice, there are likely to be many more debating points relating to each topic. As you look at each section in Table 14.2, consider whether there are any other questions which are worthy of attention in relation to each of these issues.

Table 14.2   Current issues and related questions

Educational inequality

- Is there evidence that educational inequalities are being reduced?
- Is there any evidence that educational inequalities can be tackled through the redistribution of resources?
- Is there research evidence which shows the best ways to tackle educational inequalities?

Bullying

- Is a consistent whole-school approach the best way to tackle bullying?
- Is there evidence that the problem of bullying is becoming more serious?
- Do some teachers miss warning signs of bullying problems because they have too many commitments?

Testing and standards

- Is there evidence that standards in primary schools are currently rising?
- Is there evidence that the current approach to assessment has resulted in rising standards?
- Which forms of assessment are most closely associated with rising standards?

Education and community cohesion

- Do strong school communities have a wide impact upon a locality?
- Is parental involvement the best way to build strong school communities?
- Does the formal school curriculum or the 'hidden curriculum' have the greater impact upon cohesion at school level?

Creativity and standards: tensions and debates

- Do schools which place an emphasis upon creativity achieve high standards?
- Is there evidence that a lack of creativity leads to low standards of attainment?
- Do children vary in their responses to creative approaches in the classroom?

Questions and resource implications

Some important questions have begun to come into focus as this section has considered current issues in primary education. But, so far, no attention has been given to an important underlying issue: namely, that of fair resource allocation. How adequate then is this approach? On the surface, the issue of resource allocation may seem to be far removed from the experience of the student teacher visiting classroom contexts for limited periods of time. But for the foreseeable future, it is likely that issues relating to resource allocation will assume growing significance. It is arguable that the debate about class sizes is a case in point. Over the years, this debate has attracted considerable attention. The benefits of small classes have been consistently noted (Blatchford and Basset 2003). Yet it is likely that it will be increasingly difficult to sustain meaningful dialogue relating to this theme without significant reference to economic considerations. In short, small teaching groups are particularly expensive. There are significant opportunity costs in teaching small groups. It is arguable that meaningful debate relating to the best way forward has to grapple with this unfortunate reality.

The current educational context is one in which the underlying issue of resource allocation is likely to be a growing pre-occupation. Its relevance for major themes such as inclusive education and curriculum content and delivery is obvious. This raises a further point which is worth consideration. How will key decisions which relate to life chances and equal opportunities be made? In the years to come, important questions will inevitably be raised about policies and priorities. It will be important that such debates are underpinned by a genuine commitment to social justice and fairness (Rawls 1971).

Where the issue of resourcing is raised, other questions inevitably begin to demand attention. Who should exercise control when resources are allocated? Who is entitled to make key decisions? Who ensures that resources are used in responsible and cost-effective ways? Such questions shift attention to an important and related theme: namely, the question of how accountability systems operate to ensure that resources are used effectively.

On the basis of the points highlighted within this section, it may now be possible to identify some further generic questions which it is helpful to raise when focusing upon a current issue. The questions are as follows:

- Are resources currently used well?
- Is it clear that policy changes and innovations are leading to progress?
- Does current research highlight best practice?
- Is there a growing consensus about the best way forward?

What do you feel about this list? Do you feel that these questions take into account the need to be prepared to consider the relevance of resource allocation? Are there questions which you would delete or add to this list? In developing a framework to support exploration of a chosen current issue in primary education, you may find that is helpful to develop your own list of such questions.

Reflective task: research evidence and your own school experience

This task is designed to help you as you continue to think about the process of exploring educational issues. It raises a series of questions relating to the broad theme of behaviour management. The task should remind you of the need to:

(a) read widely, taking into account relevant recent research
(b) reflect upon experience gained in school
(c) focus upon competing perspectives, taking into account key insights and implications.

Assess the following questions:

- Is there research evidence to show that behaviour management is less challenging in classrooms where teaching is good?
- Is there evidence that all children respond well to positive behaviour management strategies?
- Are there ever times when it is appropriate to utilise behaviour management strategies which undermine established whole-school approaches?
- How can an appropriate balance be maintained between provision for the needs of individuals and groups?
- Is high-quality teaching the best way to tackle the problem of poor classroom behaviour?
- Is there research evidence to show that poor short-term memory is a factor which leads to behaviour problems for some children?

Consider the following points as you assess the questions:

(a) How can my own reading help in the process of developing my thinking relating to each of these questions?
(b) How does the experience that I have gained in school influence my responses to these questions?
(c) What other questions would I raise in order to develop a thorough exploration of an issue relating to effective behaviour management?

A generic framework to support exploration and analysis, based on core concepts

Key ideas can also be expressed more clearly when there is a determination to develop an analytical approach. Moreover, this process is assisted where there is a clear grasp of underlying concepts which can support exploration of current issues. Within this section, attention focuses upon some widely used concepts.

Clarifying widely used concepts

'Poverty'

Firstly, it is important to analyse what is meant by concepts which are often employed loosely in ways which create confusion. For example, the concept of 'poverty' is widely used in the social sciences and is an example of a term which often requires further clarification. Hence, a distinction is made between its absolute and relative dimensions. For some analytical purposes, this distinction is particularly helpful: it opens up the possibility of more meaningful analysis of a whole range of issues relating to social inequalities. Indeed, one influential dictionary of sociology suggests that the term 'relative poverty' 'is used to demonstrate the inadequacy of definitions of absolute or primary poverty by referring to the cultural needs of individuals and families within the context of the rest of society' (Jary and Jary 1991 p. 489). Other such concepts include 'social capital', 'social mobility' and 'social class'. It is important to be clear about their core meaning. Equally, it is important that terms are used appropriately when developing an analysis or discussion focusing upon a current issue.

'Community cohesion'

It is certainly likely that there will continue to be lively debate about the real meaning of the term 'community cohesion'. In this context, it is important to note that the recent DCSF guidance (2007b) provides a helpful starting point:

> By community cohesion we mean working towards a society in which there is a common vision and sense of belonging by all communities; a society in which the diversity of people's backgrounds and circumstances is appreciated and valued; a society in which similar life opportunities are available to all; and a society in which strong and positive relationships exist and continue to be developed in the workplace, in schools and in the wider community. (DCSF 2007b)

There are times when a concept gains a particular significance or resonance. It is therefore important to be alert to this tendency. The concept of 'community cohesion' is a relevant example here. The broad question of how schools may play a role in promoting 'community cohesion' is currently receiving a great deal of attention.

'Surveillance'

'Surveillance' is another concept which offers scope to gain intriguing insights relating to some current issues. It is arguable that the theme of surveillance has increasingly featured in social research in recent years (Hier and Greenberg 2007). Its growing significance may reflect the fact that the overt use of techniques for surveillance has been one of the most striking social developments of the modern or, perhaps more accurately, post-modern era. Nowadays in town centres, surveillance cameras keep a watchful and paternal eye upon members of the public. Motorists drive with care because of the presence of hidden cameras on busy roads. Speed cameras act as a constraining mechanism encouraging motorists to be watchful and at the same time reducing accidents.

The processes of surveillance which characterise today's society do not merely operate through obvious monitoring systems such as these. The work of the French thinker Foucault, for example, serves an important reminder that subtle forms of surveillance have actually featured in schools for many years (Foucault 1977). Moreover, it is arguable that reference to the theme of surveillance can offer important insights about the psychological impact of current systems for monitoring and accountability. Sometimes there may be a rather fine line between positive processes designed to support monitoring and accountability and less desirable processes of surveillance.

A wider question is perhaps whether the impact of surveillance is always necessarily negative. Reference to the issue of school violence, for example, provides a timely reminder that sometimes surveillance can have positive as well as negative effects. School-based bullying is perhaps more likely to occur in contexts where monitoring systems are weak. Equally, school-based bullying can all too easily occur in contexts far removed from adult supervision. Adult 'surveillance' may play an important role in preventing such bullying. Yet, somewhat paradoxically, it is also arguable that the concept of surveillance can be employed in making sense of an apparently growing phenomenon: bullying via mobile phones and computers is particularly unpleasant and serious in its consequences, precisely because it employs techniques of surveillance which cause enduring pain (DCSF 2007a).

Basic conceptual dimensions to support analysis of issues

Basic conceptual dimensions which provide a framework for analysis of current issues form relatively straightforward contrasts. These are the *local/global* and *local/central* divisions; the division between *public and private* spheres; and the split between *representation and reality*. The local/central divide is an addition to three pairs of terms which you may have already encountered on some social science courses (Anderson and Ricci 1994; Open University 1996). Each of these divisions will be examined in more detail below. However, before focusing attention on these concepts, it may be helpful to pause to reflect upon the way in which the education system in England and Wales has changed during the last 30 years.

During this era, education has become a major priority for central government and spending on education has risen dramatically. Government priorities have been embedded in a constantly developing legislative framework which has seen the development and revision of a National Curriculum and a constant drive for improvement and effectiveness. New systems for testing, monitoring and accountability have become important during this period (Bartlett and Burton 2007; Chitty 1998; Maclure 1988).

In this era of innovation one constant has remained. It is still the case that it is in local contexts that the policies of central government are implemented. Moreover, the independent, or interconnected, actions of local authorities, governing bodies, head teachers and class teachers all affect the relative success of failure or policies from the centre.

Local/global and local/central

The local/global and local/central conceptual themes are each relevant precisely because they open up the possibility of examining such links. Through attention to the interface between the 'local' and 'central', some sense can be made of the way in which the policies of central government impact in the regions. Interestingly, when developing an analysis of such policies, there is no need to suggest that all power is held in the centre. Nor is there any need to assume that communication simply flows in one direction. Some of the most significant questions to raise and examine may indeed relate to the ways in which the actions of central government reflect and respond to developments and innovations in local contexts.

The issue of 'healthy eating' can serve to illustrate the utility of the local/global and local/central themes. In recent times, and in part as a response to external pressure, central government has pushed for improved standards of diet and nutrition. Yet even though this approach has apparently been in response to public demand, it has run into difficulties in some local contexts. In this case, analysis of the interplay between local and central factors may help to shed some light on the challenges which central government faces when seeking to ensure that a widely supported social policy is implemented effectively. More broadly, it should be noted that research has consistently shown that local factors are of major importance when exploring key issues relating to health education (Mayall et al. 1996).

The division between local and central dimensions is an important conceptual theme which may illuminate a whole range of major or minor issues in relation to which decisions from the centre have impacted in local contexts. Moreover, its relevance is not merely confined to an examination of the ways in which the decisions of central government are implemented at school level. The real area of debate may sometimes be the link between the school and the local authority. For example, a local authority may seek to ensure that secondary schools adopt a particular procedure with regard to the disclosure of examination results. Yet individual schools may seek to implement this policy in differing ways which actually undermine standardised practice.

The notion of a division between the local and the global can also be applied to the link between international bodies and national governments. Once again, the conceptual distinction between the local and the global opens up a potentially rewarding framework to support discussion, debate and analysis.

You will have noticed that in focusing upon the issue of healthy eating, I have tended to focus upon the local/central conceptual division. You may also wish to reflect upon whether there are any local/global dimensions to this debate. For example, issues of sustainable development, food supply and related ethical questions may also require attention within the context of unfolding debate relating to this issue.

Reflective task: local/global and/or local/central?

Is it actually helpful to highlight two separate conceptual divisions here? Or are these two strands actually separate dimensions of an underlying local/global divide?

Public/private

The division between public and private spheres is an important characteristic of our society. It is far from surprising then that the *public/private* divide can be highlighted as a third conceptual dimension which may shed light on some current issues in primary education. For example, the issue of whether or not it is appropriate for some children to be educated at home raises important questions which relate to children's rights and entitlements. There is currently significant interest in the contexts in which children benefit from opportunities to participate in society (Hart 2009). But it is arguable that where education is provided at home, some of these opportunities may be missed. Reference to the public and private divide may help in the formation of questions to enhance debate relating to the issue of whether or not it is appropriate to provide education at home.

An enduring feature of the education system in England and Wales is that there is an influential independent sector which is in significant ways less subject to government control and regulation. The fact that some independent schools are still known as 'public' schools should not obscure the underlying point: schools in the independent sector are private institutions, albeit institutions which are increasingly run by companies and trusts running families of similar schools (Ball 2007).

Attention to the public/private division can help in making some sense of a whole series of underlying questions. The issue of what independent schools contribute to the public good in return for charitable status currently deservedly attracts attention. Somewhat less obviously, the issue of whether children in the private sector are afforded the same protections and privileges as state-sector pupils is worthy of attention now that we live in an era when it is claimed that 'every child matters'. The public/private conceptual theme can underpin exploration of both of these questions.

On the surface, the division between public and private sectors is precise. Yet, reflection upon some of the most significant changes since the 1980s suggests that this is by no means so obviously the case. The creation of grant maintained schools and the subsequent development of colleges and academies under a range of guises have to some extent blurred this distinction, although the position of academies is not quite the same as that of fully independent schools. The Education and Inspections Act (2006) also had significant implications with regard to the role of local authorities. It paved the way for the emergence of a new generation of 'trust schools' (Parker et al. 2007). Such schools – 'liberated' from some aspects of local authority control – could work closely and collaboratively with a range of outside sponsors. This development had significant implications which related to the areas of democratic accountability, finance and public interest.

A further significant policy initiative has seen new opportunities for parent groups to create free schools. Over time, it will be interesting to see whether there are tensions between this development and other policy priorities, including the need to form and maintain cohesive communities. It is arguable that there is scope to raise important questions about this theme, drawing upon the public/private divide. Key areas for consideration may relate to children's rights. In time, questions relating to the participatory entitlements of children who attend free schools may also command attention. Reference to the public/private conceptual theme may well prove rewarding in the process of making some sense of this policy development.

Representation/reality

The relevance of the fourth major conceptual theme – namely, the division between *representation and reality* – is perhaps less immediately obvious, given the underlying nature of many of the core issues in primary education. But attention to wider political debate in recent times highlights the way in which processes of presentation and representation impact upon the 'real' world. The representation/reality divide offers one route to begin to get beneath the surface of debates which concern trust and spin. It opens up a line of analysis which has the potential to contribute to an informed exploration of current issues with a political dimension by focusing attention on the gap between claims and underpinning realities.

This division is helpful for a second reason. It draws attention to the need to explore some of the ways in which stereotypes, images and ideas impact upon social life. Media images may play a key role in shaping perceptions of particular groups. Such images may create tensions and sharpen divisions. Stereotypical images can work to close off opportunities and thereby may contribute to continuing inequalities. An analysis focusing upon the gulf between representations and realities is likely to have a heightened sensitivity to such injustices.

The process of developing an analysis which raises questions about the links between representation and reality is by no means simple. Yet images, stereotypes and perceptions may influence choices, lines of action and an underlying sense of identity.

Of course, media-driven images may not always be passively absorbed. The representation/reality theme is helpful precisely because it opens up the possibility of asking searching questions about responses to images and stereotypes. Further, it opens up the possibility of asking questions about the ways in which a sense of identity may be constituted and re-constituted. Reference to the representation/reality theme may therefore provide a helpful framework to support analysis of some current issues, including perhaps most notably issues which relate in some way to identity.

Table 14.3 returns to the concepts introduced at the beginning of this section. The table highlights some debating points or issues which each pair of concepts may help to analyse. Sometimes, when identifying questions relating to a selected current issue, you may find that one set of pair of concepts is particularly helpful. However, it is also likely that you will find that there are times when it is appropriate to refer to each dimension. For example, there may well be times when reference to the 'public/private' dimension proves helpful when considering issues relating to the fair allocation and use of resources. An illustration would be a debate relating to the issue of whether families should be required to contribute towards the cost of school trips.

Table 14.3   Concept divisions and issues

Divisions and distinctions to prompt the process of asking questions	Examples of possible areas for which the distinction is relevant
Local and central dimensions	Issues which raise questions relating to fair allocation and effective use of resources
	Decision making with regard to curriculum content
	Assessment systems
	Monitoring systems and accountability arrangements
Local and global dimensions	Issues relating to sustainable development and responsible use of resources
	Issues relating to the impact of new technologies
	Issues relating to the role of government in education
	School starting age
Representation and reality	The presentation of information relating to academic performance
	Policies and strategies relating to behaviour management
	Policies and approaches which relate to bullying and associated problems
	Gender stereotypes and academic attainment
Public and private spheres	The role and responsibilities of family units
	The boundary between the responsibilities of families and schools
	Accountability issues relating to independent schools
	School organisation and control

Reflective task: concepts and current issues

This creates an opportunity to reflect more fully upon the utility of the concepts discussed in this section. As you focus upon each of the concepts, you may wish to reflect upon relevant aspects of your own professional experience.

Take a look at each of the concepts highlighted below. Discuss what you feel is the core meaning of the term. Consider whether you feel that the concept is likely to be helpful when discussing a selected current issue. Working with a discussion partner, decide upon three issues which you feel it will help you to analyse. You may also wish to think about whether the concepts create scope to gain fresh insights relating to any new issues *which currently require particular attention.*

Concept	Possible areas of relevance
Inclusion	Exploration of special needs
	Exploration of good practice in the classroom
	Highly relevant concept for debate relating to community cohesion
Surveillance	Possible relevance to aspects of discussion relating to systems for accountability, including ...
	Possible relevance when focusing upon forms of bullying, including ...
Social capital	A concept which will be helpful when exploring ...
	A concept which can be divided into ...
Social mobility	A concept which is vital for discussion focusing upon inequalities, including ...
Social class	A concept which is vital for exploration of many themes, including ...
Equal opportunities	A concept which is vital for discussion of many themes, including ...

There is one further point to note when reflecting upon some of the concepts which may support analysis of selected current issues in primary education. The concepts which assist here can in some respects be seen as family members. The concepts of 'choice' and 'parental power', for example, form part of a network of interconnected concepts relating to the notion of a 'market'. Equally, it is arguable that the concept of 'surveillance' forms part of a wider network which relates to the theme of power and control. You will find that it is rewarding to prepare concept maps of relevant and interconnected terms when you begin to focus upon a new issue. Reference to such terms helps when identifying key questions. Appropriate reference to concepts also helps when preparing a carefully focused analysis of a selected theme.

Preparing written assignments

First, when preparing assignments, it is always important to try to support key claims through reference to your own reading. As you focus upon selected sources, you will no doubt need to develop a constructively critical approach. But it is most important to be critical when focusing upon our own work (Fairbairn and Winch 1996).

Second, it is important to recognise that many issues are highly complex. When preparing assignments which focus upon selected issues, there is a need to be somewhat cautious when offering suggestions about the best way forward. Clearly, carefully considered reference to research evidence is likely to be helpful. But a tentative rather than dogmatic approach may well provide a stronger platform for discussion which notes salient points and provides genuine insight.

Summary

This chapter has emphasised the importance of exploring and evaluating current issues in education. The enhanced understanding which emerges from this process will be informed by your reading. It will also reflect your own experience. The chapter has noted that you will need to make sense of competing perspectives – a process which implies that you can assess the claims and motivation of relevant stakeholders. The chapter has provided frameworks which enable you to do this by reading systematically and critically. It has also recognised the value of reflecting on your professional experience. The importance of identifying key questions to support the exploration of current issues has been stressed. It has also been seen that you will need to analyse what is meant by widely used concepts, taking into account tensions between different dimensions. A heightened awareness of relevant concepts will provide a secure platform for informed analysis and debate. It will also enable you to take a constructively critical approach to innovation.

Questions for discussion

- How can awareness of current issues enhance your own practice in the classroom?
- How can awareness of current issues enhance your capacity to relate effectively to parents and pupils?
- How can awareness of current issues enhance your capacity to relate effectively to professional colleagues?

- How important is it to continue to take an informed interest in current issues during your professional career?
- Are some current issues more important than others?

Further reading

Bartlett, S. and Burton, D. (2007) *Introduction to Education Studies*. London: Sage.
A wide-ranging book which provides a broad introduction to key areas within the field of education studies. A strength of this book is the fact that it adopts a multi-disciplinary approach.

Kassem, D., Mufti, E. and Robinson, J. (eds) (2006) *Education Studies: Issues and Critical Perspectives*. Maidenhead: Open University Press.
A book which provides a carefully focused and critical exploration of a range of important issues.

Sharpe, J., Ward, S. and Hankin, L. (eds) (2006) *Education Studies: An Issues-based Approach*. Exeter: Learning Matters.
This book is informed by a clear recognition of the key areas that feature in education studies courses. The book helps to situate themes which require discussion and analysis.

References

Anderson, J. and Ricci, M. (eds) (1994) *Society and Social Science: A Reader*. Milton Keynes: Open University Press.
Ball, S. (2007) *Education plc: Understanding Private Sector Participation in Public Sector Education*. London: Routledge.
Bartlett, S. and Burton, D. (2007) *Introduction to Education Studies*. London: Sage.
Blatchford, P. and Basset, P. (2003) *The Class Size Debate: Is Small Better?* Maidenhead: Open University Press.
Chitty, C. (1998) *The Education System Transformed*. Tisbury: Baseline Books.
Cowie, H. and Jennifer, D. (2007) *Managing Violence in Schools: A Whole-school Approach to Best Practice*. London: Paul Chapman Publishing.
DCSF (2007a) *Cyberbullying. Safe to Learn: Embedding Anti-bullying Work in Schools*. Nottingham: DCSF.
DCSF (2007b) *Guidance on the Duty to Promote Community Cohesion*. Nottingham: DCSF.

Fairbairn, G. and Winch, C. (1996) *Reading, Writing and Reasoning: A Guide for Students*. Maidenhead: Open University Press.

Foucault, M. (1977) *Discipline and Punish: The Birth of the Prison*. London: Allen Lane.

Hart, R. (2009) 'Charting Change in the Participatory Settings of Childhood', in N. Thomas (ed.) *Children, Politics and Communication*. Bristol: The Policy Press.

Hier, S. and Greenberg, J. (2007) *The Surveillance Studies Reader*. Maidenhead: Open University Press.

Jary, D. and Jary, J. (1991) *Collins Dictionary of Sociology*. London: Harper Collins.

Little, W., Fowler, H. and Coulson, J. (1959) *The Shorter Oxford Dictionary*. Oxford: Clarendon Press.

Maclure, S. (1988) *Education Re-formed*. London: Hodder and Stoughton.

Mayall, B., Bendelow, G., Barker, S., Storey, P. and Veltman, M. (1996) *Children's Health in Primary Schools*. London: Falmer Press.

Open University (1996) *Block 7: Social Science and Society*. London: Open University Press.

Parker, A., Duncan, A. and Fowler, J. (2007) *Education and Inspections Act 2006: The Essential Guide*. London: NFER.

Rawls, J. (1971) *A Theory of Justice*. Oxford: Oxford University Press.

Roland, E. and Munthe, E. (eds) (2001) *Bullying: An International Perspective*. London: David Fulton.

Smith, P. (ed.) (2003) *Violence in Schools: The Response in Europe*. London: Routledge-Falmer.

CHAPTER 15

STATUTORY PROFESSIONAL RESPONSIBILITIES

Nerina Díaz

By the end of this chapter, you should understand:

- the differences between statutory and non-statutory legislation, how they inform school policies and the implications for you as a teacher
- how statutory and non-statutory legislation is made and how it is changed
- that interpreting professional values can involve ethical dilemmas requiring discussion and reflection and examination of your personal values.

Introduction

This chapter explains what is meant by statutory responsibility. It explores the implications of statutory legislation. The examples cover employment, the curriculum, race relations, inclusion, safeguarding children's health and well-being. The chapter explores the implications of statutory legislation through scenarios and examples of events you may encounter in school. As you will by now be aware, education is integrally connected with politics and has become increasingly so. Therefore, changes in governments are frequently accompanied by changes in educational legislation, which are inevitably value-laden and controversial. As a professional educator and a citizen, it is important that you have an informed view about proposed changes and are prepared to participate in debates about them. This chapter will raise your awareness of these issues.

Legislation, statutory instruments and non-statutory guidance

Education in the United Kingdom is the responsibility of devolved national governments: the Northern Ireland government, the Scottish government and the Welsh Assembly government. Education in England is the responsibility of the UK government. Teacher's professional duties are framed by legislation, statutory instruments, and statutory and non-statutory guidance. The latest Education Act to receive Royal Assent was in 2002. It was intended to raise standards and promote innovation in schools.

Legislation

Legislation, statutory instruments (which provide the necessary detail that would be considered too complex to include in the body of an Act) and statutory guidance are all legal documents which teachers should comply with. Schools and local authorities must follow statutory guidance unless they can show they are doing something just as good or better. The Special Educational Needs Code of Practice and the Code of Practice for Schools on the Disability Discrimination Act 1995: Part 4, are examples of statutory guidance. Statutory guidance is indicated within the first few pages of a government report and is available on the government websites.

Non-statutory guidance

Non-statutory guidance does not require a legal duty for schools to have regard to it. Schools may, however, find it helpful in understanding their duties and in deciding how they should implement the statutory requirements. For example, the pamphlet, 'Religious education in English schools: guidance, January 2010', is non-statutory. However, there is a statutory requirement for a head teacher and governing body to establish a behaviour policy for a school, and there is non-statutory guidance to help in this process.

Legislative procedure

Legislative procedure consists of several stages in both the elected House of Commons and the unelected House of Lords before being enacted by royal consent and becoming an Act of Parliament. This Act is binding, even if, after a general election, the governing party does not support the policies enshrined. It requires a new Act of Parliament to supersede any existing Acts. When a general election is announced, the government needs to decide which bills to proceed with before parliament is dissolved – this is called the 'wash-up'. Some bills do not survive the 'wash-up', even though the Act has been anticipated and potential statutory information has been made available in the public domain. The incoming government may then withdraw the proposed legislation. This happened with the Rose Review of the National Curriculum for England and Wales which was published in 2009. Many schools were creating strategies for implementing the new curriculum, which was withdrawn by the Conservative/Liberal-Democrat coalition government in 2010. Consequently, the National Curriculum framed in the Education Act 2002 remained statutory until replaced with new legislation on the curriculum by the incoming government.

Statutory frameworks within which you work

Qualified teacher status

Anyone wishing to work as a qualified teacher in a maintained school or non-maintained special school in England and Wales, including a maintained nursery school or a Pupil Referral Unit, must have qualified teacher status (QTS) and have completed an induction period equivalent to three school terms. An overseas qualified teacher (OTT) can work as a temporary teacher for up to four years without QTS.

The Education (Induction Arrangements for School Teachers) (England) Regulations 2008 are effective from September 2008. A significant element of the induction regulations is that newly qualified teachers (NQTs) may only complete induction in approved institutions. Normally, these would be in the maintained sector, including some FE colleges. If you are considering applying for your first job in another setting, you are advised to check whether you are able to complete your induction year there. Note though, that while NQTs are encouraged to start their induction as soon as possible after gaining qualified teacher status (QTS), there is no requirement to complete induction within a certain time frame.

Head teachers and principals have the responsibility to ensure that a NQT has an appropriate induction programme, provided by a nominated induction tutor, and make a recommendation to the local authority (LA) on whether the NQT has met the core standards. In turn, the LA has responsibility to monitor the school's recommendation, and to communicate the decision to those involved. Overseas trained teachers can choose to be assessed against the core standards at the same time as QTS standards. If they choose not to, or do not meet these standards, they will be required to undertake induction like any other NQT.

QTS teachers are entitled to a 16-month calendar period of short-term supply work before they start induction. When the 16-month limit is reached, a teacher cannot undertake any further supply work (of any duration) in a maintained school, non-maintained special school, maintained nursery school or Pupil Referral Unit unless an extension has been granted by the appropriate body or the post is in an inductable setting and is for a minimum of one term.

Employment

Teachers' pay and conditions

This is a statutory document published by the government and refers to England and Wales. The *School Teachers' Pay and Conditions Document* (STPCD), commonly known as 'the blue book', outlines the standards and pay for the different grades of professional staff employed by the school. It is a requirement that pay scales are reviewed annually. All schools maintained by the Local Authority are legally subject to the STPCD. Schools with independent funding are not subject to the STPCD, and neither are state-funded academies. Advice concerning pay and conditions for work in academies is available from teaching unions.

In Scotland, negotiations about teachers' pay and conditions are dealt with by the Scottish Negotiating Committee for Teachers (SNCT), chaired jointly by representatives of teaching organisations, local authorities and the Scottish government. The *SNCT Handbook of Conditions of Service* gives full details of current agreements.

In Northern Ireland, the main terms and conditions are based on those in England and Wales but contextualised for Northern Ireland. A significant difference within their terms and conditions is that teachers may apply to undertake a career break of between one and five years.

However, the teachers' pay and conditions legislation is another example of changing policies. National pay agreements may be impossible to retain under the government's academy programme. The announcement that any primary or secondary school judged outstanding by Ofsted can be fast-tracked to academy status, and that there could be hundreds of new academies may destroy the unions' ability to negotiate pay and conditions centrally and, in doing so, make it virtually impossible to retain any cohesive national pay agreement.

What is an academy?

The coalition government policy signalled a key ideological change in the academies programme. Under the Labour government, academies were meant to replace 'failing' schools, predominantly in poor areas. The intention was to improve equality of opportunity for those in the more deprived sections of society. The academies were required to have sponsors who invested up to two million pounds in return for receiving state funding. Sponsors included churches, businesses, charitable trusts and private schools. The coalition government encourages all schools to become academies.

The subsequent policy on academies could lead to the handing over of education into largely private control if head teachers choose to turn their schools into academies as part of an 'educational revolution'.

Fitness to teach

Statutory regulations concerning fitness to teach are detailed in The Education (Health Standards) (England) Regulations 2003. The regulations indicate the prescribed activities that teachers should be fit for, and the procedure to be followed if a teacher is no longer considered fit for the job. However, employers also have a duty to have regard to the provisions of the Disability Discrimination Act 1995.

Teachers' conditions of service

The statutory requirements for teachers' conditions of service for maintained schools in England and Wales, which schools and Local Education Authorities must abide by, are set out in the *Conditions of Service for School Teachers in England and Wales*, commonly known as 'the burgundy book'. The burgundy book represents the national agreement between the six teacher associations and the local authorities and contains sections about:

- appointment, resignation, retirement
- sick pay scheme
- maternity scheme

- other leave
- grievance and disciplinary procedures
- miscellaneous conditions.

It also includes information concerning the following:

- premature retirement compensation
- memorandum of agreement for the release of teachers
- agreement on facilities for representatives of recognised teachers' organisations
- relations between teachers' organisations and LEAs: collective disputes procedures
- insurance and travelling allowances
- teachers and the school meals service.

However, if large numbers of schools choose to become academies, the unions (and Local Education Authorities) are unlikely to have the concerted power to agree teachers' conditions of service.

Contractual entitlements to leave

Under the burgundy book, all teachers have the following contractual rights to leave of absence:

- for examinations
- for jury and other public service
- for accredited representation of recognised teachers' organisations.

Leave for other purposes

Although there are no national agreements for leave with or without pay for other purposes, such as participation in Parliamentary elections or as a national representative in sport, an authority shall make known to their teachers any provision they may have.

Leave of absence agreements and policies

It is important to distinguish between agreements which give rise to contractual entitlements and school policies which merely assist in the interpretation of the application of the contractual provision.

Leave of absence agreements established at local authority or diocesan levels may give rise to contractual entitlements for teachers. This occurs if an agreement is expressed in such a way as to give individual entitlements to teachers rather than giving 'advice' to governing bodies and the teacher is employed by the local authority, or employed by a governing body which has accepted that such agreements are incorporated into the contracts of teachers at their school. There is no power for contractual agreements which have been established at local authority or diocesan level to be undermined at school level.

The following categories of absence are included in agreements and are usually taken as paid leave:

- hospital, GP, clinical and dental appointments
- compassionate leave for bereavement and illness of close relatives where there is a caring responsibility
- moving house
- accompanying children and close relatives to hospital or GP appointments
- domestic emergencies such as a gas leak or flood
- attendance at children's milestone celebrations, for example graduations or school performances.

There may also be provision for leave for religious observance and celebration of festivals.

Discretionary leave arrangements

There is a potential for difficulty when diocesan or local authority policies contain certain categories of leave granted at the discretion of the head teacher and/or the governing body.

Professional conduct

The Teaching and Higher Education Act 1998 established the General Teaching Council (GTC) as the independent regulatory body for teaching in England. It was tasked to contribute to improving standards of teaching and the quality of learning, maintain and improve standards of professional conduct among teachers and was the awarding body for Qualified Teacher Status (QTS). Following the election of the Conservative/Liberal-Democrat coalition government in 2010, there were plans to abolish the GTC although this can only be done through legislation. However, cases which came before the GTC are examples of what is generally regarded as unacceptable professional behaviour.

Reflective task

1 Consider the case of a teacher who accesses the internet and emails excessively during lesson times. Is this acceptable?

 Combined with knowledge of another action involving shoplifting, this teacher was given a reprimand (of 2 years).

 What are the implications of this case for teachers and trainee teachers?

2 Consider the case of a teacher having an evening out with friends and having a few drinks. The evening was cold and the teacher needed to use the toilet. As there were bushes nearby, he used those. The teacher was caught by police and cautioned for a public order offence.

 The GTCE found the teacher guilty of unacceptable professional conduct in that while a registered teacher he/she was cautioned for committing an act outraging public decency by behaving in an indecent manner.

Legislative framework guiding practice in schools

The curriculum

Prior to 1988, there was no national curriculum for England and Wales. Provision for the national curriculum is found in the 1988 Education Reform Act. Originally comprising of large detailed documents, by 1995 the national curriculum was reduced and simplified and became a manageable point of reference for teachers. What subsequent governments put in the place of The National Curriculum for England (DfEE and QCA 1999) and to what extent, if any, this will apply to academies remains to be seen.

Reflective task

What do you consider the advantages and disadvantages of the 1999 National Curriculum?

 Is a national curriculum desirable?

 What would your ideal curriculum consist of?

In 2006, the Childcare Act made provision for statutory requirements for children aged 0–5 years cared for in any setting other than the home. This is known as the Early Years Foundation Stage (EYFS). It details three elements considered necessary for learning and development and six areas to be covered.

In 2006, Sir Jim Rose published his final report of 'The Independent Review of Early Reading', which made the recommendation that the teaching of phonics incorporated into early reading should be taught using synthetic phonics. Following the acceptance of the review recommendations, the National Curriculum was amended.

The National Literacy Strategy and the National Numeracy Strategy launched in 1998, were integrated into the National Primary Strategy, named 'Excellence and Enjoyment' in 2003, followed by a renewed Primary Framework in 2006. All these documents were for guidance and did not include any statutory requirements, although reference is made to these in the QTS standards.

Head teachers are responsible for the implementation of EYFS and the National Curriculum, including assessment and reporting. (The assessment and reporting element does not apply to hospital schools.)

Assessment and Reporting Arrangements (ARA)

Assessment and reporting procedures differ for the four countries of the UK. This information concerns England. Visit the appropriate website for requirements in the other countries.

In 2010, the ARA was published, making provisions under the Education Act 2002 and the 2004 Education Assessment Arrangements order. Teacher's Assessment and Reporting Arrangements (TARA) were also published.

A wider strategy for improving children's lives

The Children Act 2004, with modifications for Wales, received Royal Assent in 2004. It detailed legislation for a wider strategy for improving children's lives. Details about the implementation of the Act were covered in the publication *Every Child Matters: Change for Children*.

The Act introduced programmes such as the Safer Schools Partnership, for which police are based in schools, working with the school in areas of crime prevention, school safety, behaviour improvement and educational achievement. It also introduced the establishment of combined working practices between schools and other education and training providers, such as the provision of lifelong learning as part of the extended schools programme, as well as in higher and further education institutions and through employers.

Collaboration both between schools and across agencies was considered essential to achieving the objectives of the Every Child Matters agenda. Partnerships across public services, including the development of good relationships with other practitioners such as social workers, nurses, GPs and educational psychologists, are considered to lead to improved outcomes in such areas as pupil behaviour, personalised learning, provision for special educational needs (SEN) and reducing the number of children missing education.

What are the benefits and potential difficulties involved in multi-agency working?

Safeguarding children

The Education Act 2002, along with Statutory Guidance issued in 2004, requires a duty of all schools, state or privately funded, and further education institutions, to safeguard and promote the welfare of pupils. They are required to create and maintain a safe learning environment for children and young people, and identify where there are child welfare concerns and take action to address them, in partnership with other organisations where appropriate.

In addition, everyone working in early years services should know how to recognise and respond to the possible abuse and neglect of a child. The Early Years Foundation Stage makes it clear that all registered providers, except childminders, must have a practitioner who is designated to take lead responsibility for safeguarding children within each early years setting and who should liaise with local statutory children's service agencies as appropriate. Early years services include children's centres, nurseries, childminders, pre-schools, playgroups and holiday and out-of-school schemes.

It is deemed the responsibility of the employers to ensure their employees are confident and competent in carrying out their responsibilities, and are aware of how to recognise and respond to safeguarding concerns.

Reflective task

Consider a situation in which a child's behaviour is causing you concern. You have, over the course of approximately six weeks, exhausted your repertoire of strategies to help the child, and the situation only appears to be getting worse. What are the next moves for an inexperienced teacher?

(a) Ask for the child to be moved to another class?
(b) Phone the parents?
(c) Discuss the situation with a trusted colleague, possibly the child's previous teacher?
(d) Discuss the situation with the pastoral team?

The ultimate answer should be d. It is unwise to phone the parents without knowledge of the child's background, and without the sanction of senior staff to support you. Option c is an intermediate step. It is important that you do not lose confidence in your abilities as a teacher, and if you feel that you are disclosing your own inadequacies as a teacher to senior staff, it may be easier to discuss the situation with another colleague initially. Nevertheless, the child's needs are the priority. Once it is established that the child is at risk, there is a hierarchical procedure which should be followed, and the potential for a number of professionals to be involved.

Health and safety

Responsibility for health and safety derives from the 1974 Health and Safety at Work etc. Act 1974. It places overall responsibility for health and safety with the employer. For maintained schools, this is the Local Education Authority; for other schools, it is usually the governing body or the proprietor. As well as the health and safety of children, staff, visitors and volunteers to the school, education employers also have duties to the health and welfare of pupils and associated adults involved with off-site visits. The employer may delegate responsibility for health and safety to an employee, but retains ultimate responsibility.

Employees also have duties. They should take reasonable care of their own and others' health and safety, informing the employer of serious risks; cooperate with their employers and carry out activities in accordance with training and instruction. Although the employer is responsible for health and safety, the employee can be implicated if they have failed to take notice of instructions and procedures.

Reflective task

When taking children on a school trip, what situations may require you to be aware of the health and safety regulations? Consider issues that may arise when:

- taking children to public toilets
- a child or accompanying adult has an accident
- an accompanying adult behaves inappropriately.

Race relations

The Race Relations (Amendment) Act (2000) places three general duties on all schools and other public bodies:

- to eliminate discrimination
- to promote equality of opportunity
- to promote good race relations.

All schools are required to:

- actively promote 'race' equality
- prepare a 'race' equality policy
- monitor attainment by ethnicity, using new, electronic data systems

- monitor exclusions by ethnicity
- monitor progress and make such information publicly available.

Schools have a legal responsibility to monitor and record any racist incidents. Inexperienced teachers may feel bound by the school's practices. The school's anti-racist or 'race' equality policy should set out suggestions for a response, but you are within your rights to point out that you think the response is inappropriate.

 Reflective task

Consider the consequences of advice to ignore a racist comment overheard in the playground with the view that the children 'don't mean anything by it'.

There are many factors which might determine your response, but consider whether ignoring the comment is dereliction of your legal duty. Overt ways of responding might include involving the senior management team to talk to the perpetrators, contacting parents/carers to discuss the school's concerns, talking to the victims of the name-calling, and ultimately, if the name-calling persisted, seeking advice from the local authority.

Pre-empting the situation could reflect a wider school ethos. How could this be achieved through the curriculum planning? Would this planning be suitable for mono-cultural schools?

Community cohesion

As a result of the Education and Inspections Act 2006, a new section 21(5) was inserted to the Education Act 2002, introducing a duty on the governing bodies of maintained schools to promote community cohesion as from September 2007. Non-statutory guidance was published in 2007, and Ofsted was required to report on schools' performance from September 2008.

Legislation relevant to community cohesion includes the Equality Act 2006, the Race Relations (Amendment) Act 2000 and the Children Act 2004.

Community cohesion is defined in the guidance as: working towards a society in which there is a common vision and sense of belonging by all communities; a society in which the diversity of people's backgrounds and circumstances is appreciated and valued; a society in which similar life opportunities are available to all; and a society in which strong and positive relationships exist and continue to be developed in the workplace, in schools and in the wider community. (DCSF 2007 p. 3)

The guidance is grouped under three headings:

- teaching, learning and curriculum
- equity and excellence
- engagement and extended services.

Reflective task

Use these headings as a guide. How could you create a learning environment that will ensure your class community is cohesive? Consider issues such as valuing diversity, the concept of citizenship, human rights, removing barriers to participation, links with other communities, and opportunities for families and the wider community to take part in activities.

Think about your physical classroom environment, yourself as a role model, your approach to the curriculum, your contact and relationship with parents and the wider community.

The guidance acknowledges that schools cannot compensate for all societal tensions. What are the potential barriers when planning activities encouraging community cohesion and how can these be mitigated?

Understanding children's rights

The UK ratified the Convention on the Rights of the Child (UNCRC) on 16 December 1991. All children, without exception, have entitlements to over 40 specific rights. (See www.unicef.org/crc/ for more information.)

The Children's Commissioner for England, responsible for promoting awareness of children's views, interests and other rights guaranteed by the Convention, must make an annual report to Parliament.

A horrific case of neglect leading to the death of Victoria Climbié, led to the passing of the Children Act 2004, providing a legislative spine for developing more effective and accessible services focused around the needs of children, young people and families. *Every Child Matters: Change for Children* (ECM) was published in November 2004, and is concerned with the well-being of children and young people from birth to age 19.

The government's aim was for every child, whatever their background or their circumstances, to have the support they need to:

- be healthy
- stay safe

- enjoy and achieve
- make a positive contribution
- achieve economic well-being.

Under the new arrangements for Ofsted inspections, schools are required to complete a self-evaluation form (SEF) which forms an integral part of the inspection process. Schools are asked to refer to how they are actively promoting the five aims of ECM.

Residential and boarding schools also have to comply with Ofsted National Minimum Standards (NMS) intended to safeguard and promote the welfare of children who live (board) at a boarding school.

Inclusion

The National Curriculum states that schools should provide relevant and challenging learning for all children. There are three principles set out in the statutory inclusion statement:

- setting suitable learning challenges
- responding to pupils' diverse learning needs
- overcoming potential barriers to learning and assessment for individuals and groups of pupils.

 Reflective task

Take each of the five aims of the ECM agenda and consider how you can ensure that you fulfil the five aims for *all* the children in the school. This could be through whole-school activities, class-based activities, out-of-school activities or individual actions. Consider how you can incorporate these into daily activities.

 Summary

This chapter has explained the legislation against which teachers' employment and professional duties are framed. It explains differences between statutory and non-statutory guidance, and the implications of legislation for changes of government policy. Teachers' conditions of employment are explored from both the employers' and employees' perspectives. Statutory professional responsibilities for the curriculum, assessment and reporting, the Every Child Matters agenda, including

(Continued)

understanding about children's rights, inclusion, safeguarding children, community cohesion, health and safety and race relations are also explained.

For current legislation and guidance, visit the relevant government websites. For commentary and explanation of legislation and guidance, visit the union websites. The largest unions for England are the NUT (www.teachers.org.uk/) and the NASUWT (www.teachersunion.org.uk/). Other teachers' unions are Voice (www.voicetheunion.org.uk/) and ATL (www.askatl.org.uk/).

Questions for discussion

These questions ask what you know about your responsibilities as an employee (guidance for answering these questions can be found in the chapter):

- Do your teaching plans, for example, medium-term planning, reflect the principles of the ECM agenda?
- Do you know how to access the school's risk assessment documents?
- Are you sure that every child in your class is treated equally, free from discrimination and any sort of bullying?
- Does every child in your class experience challenging activities suitable for their abilities?
- Do your activities involve and respect the community it serves?
- Are you aware of the school procedure if you are concerned about a child's health and well-being?
- Are you keeping records that will enable you to write a constructive and comprehensive report for the children's parents?

These questions ask what you know about your employer's responsibilities to you (guidance for answering these questions can be found in the chapter):

- Are you aware of the terms and conditions of your employment if you are not in a mainstream state school?
- Do you know the pay scales and possible progression you could make through them?
- Are you aware of what you should do if you think you require time off? Will there be tensions between family or cultural expectations and your conditions of employment? How can you resolve these?
- Are you aware of who can help you if you have a dispute with your employer?

Further reading

Children and Young People Act (2008). London: HMSO.

NSPCC (2010) *An Introduction to Child Protection Legislation in the UK*. Available at: www.nspcc.org.uk/.../child_protection_in_the_uk_pdf_48953.pdf
This is a summary of the key legislation that protects children and young people in the UK.

Reference

DfEE and QCA (1999) *The National Curriculum: Handbook for Primary Teachers in England Key Stages 1 and 2*. London: HMSO.

CHAPTER 16

MOVING INTO NEWLY QUALIFIED TEACHER STATUS AND BEYOND

Hilary Cooper

By the end of this chapter, you should:

- have reflected on what you have learned from this book

- have an understanding of what is meant by professional studies in education and that this is a fundamental, although 'fuzzy' concept

- have developed and be articulate about your personal philosophy of education and how to apply it in your teaching, within evolving statutory requirements and guidance

- be aware of the nature of a Masters level degree in education and of the ways in which you have a good foundation for studying at this level.

Introduction

This chapter will review the aims of the book and the theme which underlies it: that you should mediate changing statutory requirements and non-statutory guidance through your personal philosophy. It will consider the book as a whole and help you to reflect on what you have learned through reading and interacting with it. It will reinforce your awareness of why 'professional studies' should underpin all your teaching. It will encourage you to articulate your personal educational philosophy which, it is hoped, has developed through reading the book, and demonstrate the ways in which you are well prepared to undertake further study at Masters level.

The aims of this book

Throughout this book, you should have become increasingly aware that teachers are constantly responsible for making professional decisions related to teaching, planning and assessment, classroom organisation and behaviour management, and individual and diverse pupil needs, in order to provide equal opportunities which enable all children to reach their potential. You have been encouraged to reflect on and develop your practice and to make links between theory and practice through a raised awareness of controversial issues and by developing your ability to inform yourself about these, from relevant literature and contemporary comment. The book has aimed to promote practice informed by value judgements, promoting the educational development of the whole child: social, emotional and cognitive. It aimed to encourage innovative and creative teaching and learning.

Statutory statements about professional attributes are inevitably succinct and prescriptive and can be interpreted in simplistic ways, if students are unable to appreciate the judgements and decisions which underlie them. If you are not able to bring informed professional judgements to bear on your work, your teaching across the curriculum will be transmission of government requirements rather than informed by a unique set of personal skills and understandings. If you are not able to analyse, reflect on and take responsibility for your practice, it will remain static rather than develop. And, finally, you will be vulnerable to constant political manipulation. This book aimed to enable you to meet current and future government requirements within a broad and deep interpretation of the concept of 'professional studies'.

Were the aims achieved?

It is to be hoped that you are becoming aware of the ways, and many contexts, in which, as a primary school teacher, you need to think critically, make informed judgements and take responsibility for your own developing professional expertise. But do not worry if you feel overwhelmed by the claims that you should do so. Since you are still at the beginning of your professional journey, it could not be otherwise. The Cambridge Review (Alexander 2010) has a section on 'expertise and development: ways of thinking' (pp. 416–20). It recognises that experience shapes us differently, as people and as professionals and that by the time you retire you can expect to have a 'richly elaborated knowledge about curriculum, classroom routines and pupils that allows you to apply with despatch what you know to particular cases'. The Review is critical of the framework by which this development has been assessed by the Teaching and Development Agency (2007), saying that this is unhelpful since teachers may demonstrate their expertise in different ways. The Review suggests that teachers' development would be tracked better by evidence than government policy, which has implied that teachers use the same basic repertoire at each stage of their careers and that this depresses rather than raises standards. Development is seen by the Review as progress from novice, through competence, to expert, recognising that excellence includes such concepts as artistry, flexibility and originality, which are difficult to define precisely but instantly recognisable. So accept that you will gradually become expert by using the approaches suggested throughout this book.

Overview of the concept of professional studies

Having read this book, you should understand that 'professional studies' in education means a body of knowledge, understanding and skills, based on consideration of the values and aims which underpin the many decisions that each lesson requires. Professional studies encompass the pedagogy which brings educational aims and values to life, translates the curriculum into learning and knowing which engages, inspires and empowers learners – or not. This body of knowledge and skills involves:

- communication, collaboration and relationships with pupils, colleagues and parents
- understanding how children learn and how to progress their learning, responding in a supportive way to individual differences between children
- provision of a learning environment in which all children can reach their potential
- taking responsibility for your own professional development through reflection on and evaluation of your experience and practice, your reading and interpretation of policies.

Professional attributes

These four themes are a synopsis of the professional attributes required for achieving qualified teacher status which run throughout this book (with the exception of Q13,

Q16, Q17 and Q23 which are concerned with statistics, literacy, numeracy and information and communication technologies). You need to consider the significance of these themes in relation to your more detailed learning of how to teach each of the subjects of the curriculum.

However, it is important to remember that research (Alexander 2010 pp. 450–1) suggests that there is no single definition of teacher professionalism because the concept is fluid, plastic and dynamic and fails to recognise the 'more nuanced and dilemma-conscious private conversations of primary teachers … where feelings matter … and where subtlety and realism puncture the notions of "one-size-fits-all" and "good primary practice"'.

Reflective task

Take the plan for a lesson you have taught and the related evaluation. Highlight any of the 33 professional attributes which are stated in the lesson plan. List any of the 33 attributes which you demonstrated as an integral part of your practice but did not need to state in the plan or evaluation. Are there any which, on reflection, you could have demonstrated but did not?

Analysis of the professional attributes addressed in this book

It is clear from Table 16.1 that professional attributes are not discrete. Most of them run through several chapters of this book. Analysis of the table shows that the professional attributes which are addressed most frequently in the book are personal qualities (the ability to work collaboratively and communicate effectively and to take responsibility for your own professional development) and personal values and beliefs (particularly in relation to behaviour management and equal opportunities).

Teachers' personal responsibility for developing their practice is referred to in Chapters 2, 3, 13 and 14. The importance of constructive criticality is discussed in Chapters 1, 2, 8, 10, 12, 13 and 14 and provision of equal opportunities for children with diverse learning needs is covered in Chapters 4, 10, 11 and 12.

Personal educational philosophy

It was suggested in Chapter 2 that, while reading this book and relating it to your experience and other reading, you develop, review and adjust your personal educational philosophy statement. If you have done this, it will be helpful as a personal statement is generally required as part of an application for a teaching post.

Table 16.1   Shows professional attributes recommended for the award of Qualified Teacher Status (TDA 2007) and chapters in the book which refer to them

Attribute		Brief description	Chapters in book discussing this attribute
Q1	Relationships with Children	High expectations, achieve potential; respectful, trusting, supportive relationships with them	4, 5, 6, 10
Q2		Demonstrate positive values, attitudes and behaviour	4, 5, 6, 8, 15
Q3	Frameworks	Aware of professional and statutory duties, policies and practices of workplace	7, 15
Q4	Communicating and Working with Others	Communicate with colleagues, children, parents	5, 6, 10
Q5		Respect their contribution to raising attainment	5, 6, 7
Q6		Commitment to collaborative working	5, 10
Q7 (a) (b)	Personal Professional Development	(a) Reflect on and improve practice, take responsibility for identifying and meeting professional needs; (b) identify strengths/ areas for development	12, 13
Q8		Creative and constructively critical approach to innovation	1, 2, 12, 13, 14
Q9		Act on advice and feedback from mentors	12
Q10	Professional Knowledge and Understanding	Teaching, learning and behaviour management strategies	3, 4, 5, 8
Q11		Assessment requirements	3
Q12		Range of approaches to assessment	3, 10
Q14 Q15	Subjects and Curriculum	Secure understanding of subjects/areas and related pedagogy	4, 6, 9, 13
		Statutory and non-statutory curriculum frameworks	3, 9, 15
Q18	Achievement and Diversity	Factors influencing progress	4, 5, 11
Q19		SEN, EAL and personalised learning	4, 5, 11, 12
Q20		Role of colleagues with specific responsibilities including SEN	7

(Continued)

Table 16.1 *(Continued)*

Attribute		Brief description	Chapters in book discussing this attribute
Q21	Health and Well-being	Requirements for safeguarding the well-being of children Know how to identify and support children in difficult circumstances	7
Q22	Professional Skills	Plan for progression across age and ability range	2, 3, 6
Q24		Plan homework and out-of-class work to sustain progress	
Q25	Teaching	Range of strategies Build on prior knowledge Adapt language, explanations, questions, discussions, plenaries	2, 3, 13
Q26	Assessing, Monitoring and Giving Feedback	Range of strategies for assessment, monitoring, recording, to set challenging objectives	3
Q27		Timely, accurate, constructive feedback	13
Q28		Help learners to reflect on their learning	10, 12
Q29	Reviewing Teaching and Learning	Evaluate impact of teaching on learners and modify appropriately	
Q30	Learning Environment	Purposeful learning environment	4
Q 31		Clear framework for discipline	4, 8
Q32	Team Working and Collaboration	Work as team member to share effective practice	5
Q33		Ensure colleagues work with and understand roles in supporting learning	5

Reflective task

If you have not revised your statement of educational philosophy over time, write it now, drawing on discussions throughout this book. You might choose to use the following headings:

- My interpretation of the aims of primary education
- How I apply them in the following contexts
- Subject knowledge
- How children learn and how I support their progress

- Planning monitoring and assessment
- Inclusion, individual differences and special educational needs
- Behaviour management
- Children's personal and social development.

However you decide to structure your statement, keep it brief. There may be a hundred applicants. And do relate it to the advertisement for each particular post and school. The interviewers need to know that you are the one person they are looking for! Therefore, it is important to give a flavour of your personality and experience; what you have actually done in school in a variety of curriculum areas and with specified age groups. This will show you can make connections between theory and practice and will give the interviewers a good idea of the things to talk to you about. Be prepared to critically evaluate what you tell the interviewers about your work in schools.

Reflective task

Read 'What is Primary Education For?' (Alexander 2010 Chapter 12 pp. 180–200). Do you want to revise your statement after reading this?

Moving from qualified teacher status to a Masters Degree

Many teachers told the Cambridge Review (Alexander 2010) that they wanted more time to reflect, research and study. This echoes the need for continuing professional development and teachers who take responsibility for this. Most Masters degrees in education involve a research study, usually based on enquiry into your own practice. Throughout this book, you have been encouraged to think reflectively and critically. Part 3 focused on this process in more structured ways, through chapters on reflective practice, enquiry and critical thinking and exploring educational issues.

These chapters should have shown you how you can move from level C at level 3 to level B and beyond. Level C requires evidence of detailed knowledge and understanding of key concepts and theories including the provisional nature of knowledge, evidence of a general critical approach and evidence that you can independently identify complex problems and apply knowledge and skill to their resolution.

At level B, you demonstrate comprehensive, up-to-date knowledge and understanding of the concepts and theories and the interrelationship between them, recognising that aspects of the subject may be uncertain, contradictory or limited. You also demonstrate a critical approach using breadth of evidence, reasoning and reflection and, in identifying and defining complex problems, you can select, justify and use approaches aimed at their resolution.

At level A, your critical approach must also be 'well sustained', and show evidence of a mature and independent approach to problem solving, creating hypotheses and selecting, justifying and using imaginative and innovative approaches in your investigations.

The later chapters in this book should help you to move through this continuum of level criteria. This will put you in an ideal position for study at Masters level. This usually requires a sustained investigation of a question of your choice, based on a critical analysis of the relevant literature, theory and previous research. It will include modules on how to collect and analyse data and present and evaluate your findings.

And, finally, make a habit of reading, keeping up to date with critical professional thinking. Make it a regular habit to engage with the wide-ranging, challenging and thought-provoking papers in the *Journal of Philosophy of Education*. Recent papers deal, for example, with such debates as: What is fairness in assessment? What are educational rights? The subservience of liberal education to political ends. What does it mean to be educated? What is meant by religious education? Race, schools and the media. The relationship between research and practice and the kinds of educational research we should value. I hope this has whetted your appetite for further study! Good luck – and here's a final quotation from Alexander 2010 p. 512:

> Abandon the discourses of derision, false dichotomy and myth and strive to ensure that the education debate at last exemplifies rather than negates what education should be about.

Summary

This chapter has considered the aims of the book in developing critical and reflective practice and cautioned that, while you should understand the process, this must be seen as an area of continuing professional development. The importance of articulating your personal educational philosophy, exemplified by your experience in school, when you apply for your first teaching post was discussed. The chapter concluded by illustrating the ways in which engagement with this book and some experience as a teacher, can place you in a confident position to apply for a higher professional qualification.

Children's experience of primary school in the future is in your hands. It is an exciting prospect – and a great responsibility.

References

Alexander, R. (ed.) (2010) *Children, their World, their Education: Final Report and Recommendations of the Cambridge Primary Review*. London: Routledge.

Teaching and Development Agency (TDA) (2007) *Draft* Revised Professional Standards for Teachers in England. www.tda.gov.uk/upload/resources/pdf/draft_revised_standards_framework_jan_2007.pdf

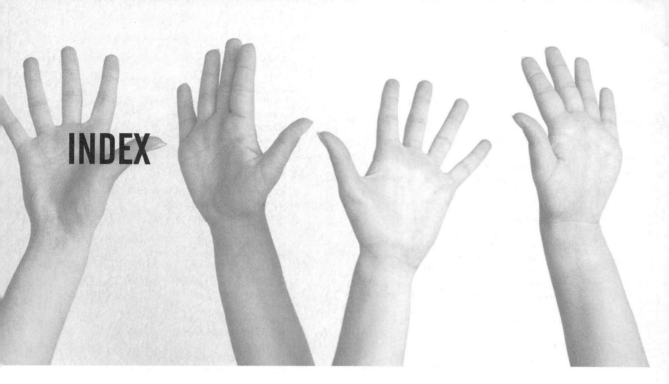

INDEX

aims, purposes, values of education 8–9, 10–11, 13, 19–22, 97, 138–9, 152–4, 157, 164, 166–70, 184, 246, web 17

behaviour of pupils 9, 66–70, 124–32
  (see also teacher professionalism)

community
  community cohesion 164–5, 236–7
  parent power 10
  school community partnerships 7, 8
  see also teacher professionalism
controversial issues
  analysing controversial issues 211–12, 216–21
clarifying contested concepts 215
  early reading 101–2, web 17
  formal and play based learning 100–101
      (see also learning)
  4-year-olds in reception classes 96–7, web 16
  identifying competing perspectives 209–10
  school starting age 98–100
critical thinking
  developing pupils'critical thinking 101, 197–8
  learning how to think critically 198–201, 247–8

critical thinking *cont.*
  teachers'critical thinking 19, web 45–6
  what is critical thinking? 196
curriculum 5, 6, 9–10, 15
  adult and child-initiated experiences 100
  Cambridge Review 36, 98, 153, 205, 247, web 5
  cross-curricular approaches 33
  curriculum in mixed age classes 97
  Foundation Stage Curriculum 95, 99
  literacy and numeracy 7, 8, 9, 12, 13–14, 37–8, 96, 97, 100
  National Curriculum 11–12, 15, 33, 96, 232
  play-based curriculum 100–1
  pupil participation in curriculum planning 154–5
  Rose Review 35–6, 98, 227, web 5
  what are curriculum basics? 19

differentiation 7, 45–6, 81

educational philosophy 20–3, web 8–10
ethos 165
  constructivist theories and the learning environment 61
  creative environment 100, 102, web 6

ethos *cont.*
    learning environment 58–61, 101
    work-centred atmosphere 67–8

faith schools 143
    history of 4, 6
    religious education 6
    personal, social, emotional and health education
        11, 58, 143

grouping of pupils 8, 46, 62, 101

inclusion 6, 46, 238 (*see also special*
    educational needs)
    gifted and talented web 18–19
    travellers web 19
independence (fostering of) 7, 58, 63–5, 83,
    128–9, 140–2, 150–9, 192
international comparisons 34, 86, 98–100, 120,
    web 16

learning
    active participation
    child-centred 8, 99–100
    creative 8
    enquiry 151–60, 203–204
    environment 8
    experiential 7
    discovery 8
    individual 8
    intrinsic motivation7
    neuroscience web 10–15
    Persona Dolls 171–5, web 39–41
    play 8
    questions about stories, web 29–38, 42–4
    thinking skills, 63–4
    transformative 82
    transmission 64
Local Education Authorities, 5, 6, 9, 10, 11, 12

Office for Standards in Education 12, 16

personal, social and emotional, moral, spiritual,
    and cultural education 6, 68–9, 136–46, 150,
    157, 168, 163
planning and assessment
    assessment 6–7, 8, 19
    assessment for learning 52, 150, 157
    assessment and reporting 13, 233
    evaluating practice 47–8
    every child matters agenda 239
    formative assessment 50–3

planning and assessment *cont.*
    levels of planning 39–47
    peer review 154
    planning 38, 202
    planning and assessment cycle 53–4
    pupil self-assessment 155
    relationship of planning to assessment
        48–9, 154–5
    Standardised Attainment Tests 13, 49–50, 96
    statutory considerations 239
    summative assessment 49, 54
    teacher assessment 11
    testing 5, 11, 14, 16,
Plowden Report 7–8

special educational needs 6–7, 10, 109–121, 238,
    web 19–20

teacher professionalism 9, web 15
    behaviour management 125–7, 130–2,
        web 21–8
    (*see also critical thinking*)
    culturally responsive approaches 163, 170
    evidence-based philosophy 19, 22, 37, 38, 55, 58,
        63, 64, 102, 24–6
    legal responsibilities 163–5, 226–7, 232–8
    modelling 85
    pay and conditions 228–32
    professional judgements
    progressing learning 84, 93
    reflection on practice 23, 155–6, 180–4
        evidence of reflection 188
        professional development through reflection
            186–91
    research 103
    statutory responsibilities 226–39, 243–4
    working with others 75
        with the community 79–80
        with governors 203
        multi-agency working 78–9, 86, 233–4
        with other teachers 78
        with parents and carers 75–7, 92–4, 115–16,
            119, 129–30, 203, 234,
        with teaching assistants 77–8
theories of learning 8, 23, 24–7
    Bruner 27
    behaviourism 23–4
    constructivism 24, 58, 61–3, 150
    hierarchies of needs 27
    scaffolding 62, 83, 84
    Piaget 24–6
    Vygotsky 26, 62

TEACHING PRIMARY ENGLISH

Jackie Brien *University of Chester*

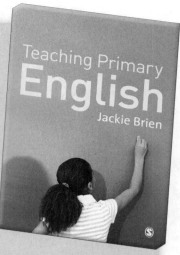

Literacy empowers learning across the whole curriculum and language is at the centre of all learning in primary education.

Aware of current curriculum developments and drawing from the latest research **Teaching Primary English** encourages teacher education students to develop a deeper understanding of the essential issues involved in teaching English in order to approach a career in the primary classroom with the confidence and knowledge required to succeed.

Taking a fresh approach to the main elements of teaching primary English, Jackie Brien strikes an engaging balance between the practical requirements of English teaching and encouraging informed reflection on key aspects of primary literacy.

Jackie Brien is Curriculum Leader for English, Communication, Language and Literacy at the University of Chester.

CONTENTS

What teachers of literacy know and do \ Speaking and listening \ Reading with and for understanding \ Teaching phonics for reading and writing \ Learning and teaching writing: the knowledge and processes of composing text \ Accuracy and presentation: the secretarial aspects of writing \ Inclusive learning and teaching of English \ Information and communication technologies in the teaching of English \ English and literacy beyond the classroom \ Planning to ensure progress in English \ Assessment and targeting in English

READERSHIP

Students studying primary English on primary initial teacher education courses including undergraduate, postgraduate and employment-based routes into teaching; also newly qualified teachers

December 2011 • 256 pages
Cloth (978-0-85702-156-4) • £60.00 / Paper (978-0-85702-157-1) • £19.99

ALSO FROM SAGE

THE PRIMARY CURRICULUM

A Creative Approach

Edited by **Patricia Driscoll** *Canterbury Christ Church University*, **Andrew Lambirth** *University of Greenwich* and **Judith Roden** *Canterbury Christ Church University*

Providing an overview of the knowledge, skills and understanding needed to teach the primary curriculum, this book offers an informed critical approach to the teaching of core and foundation subjects in primary education.

Underpinned by contemporary research and current policy **The Primary Curriculum** combines coverage of key subject-specific issues with relevant pedagogical approaches to teaching, offering a comprehensive overview of each major subject of primary education.

Particular emphasis is placed on cross-curricular and creative approaches to teaching intelligently across different subject areas within the current curriculum framework. Curriculum progression from Foundation Stage through to Key Stage 2 is also emphasised.

The Primary Curriculum is an essential companion for all students on primary initial teacher education courses.

CONTENTS

Andrew Lambirth An Introduction to Literacy \ **Gina Donaldson** An Introduction to Mathematics \ **Judith Roden** An Introduction to Science \ **James Archer** An Introduction to Design Technology \ **Rosemary Walters** An Introduction to History \ **Simon Hoult** An Introduction to Geography \ **Kristy Howells** An Introduction to Physical Education \ **Michael Green An Introduction to Information Communication Technology** \ **Vanessa Young** An Introduction to Music \ **Claire Hewlett and Claire Unsworth** An Introduction to Art and Design \ **Lynn Revell** An Introduction to Religious Education \ **Patricia Driscoll** An Introduction to Primary Languages \ **Jonathan Barnes** An Introduction to Cross-Curricular Learning

READERSHIP

All students on primary initial teacher education courses including undergraduate (BEd, BA with QTS), postgraduate (PGCE, SCITT), and employment-based routes into teaching

August 2011 • 288 pages
Cloth (978-1-84920-596-2) • £65.00 / Paper (978-1-84920-597-9) • £22.99

ALSO FROM SAGE

PRIMARY SCIENCE

A Guide to Teaching Practice

Edited by **Mick Dunne** *Bradford College*
and **Alan Peacock** *University of Exeter*

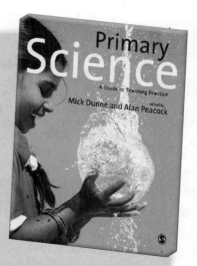

What is science? What is good science education?
How can science be intelligently linked to the wider
primary curriculum?

Becoming a confident and informed teacher of
primary science requires a strong understanding
of the key practical, conceptual and pedagogical
issues that underpin science education in the
primary school. Touching on current curriculum
concerns and the wider challenges of developing
good practice in science education **Primary Science**
provides an indispensable overview of important areas of
teaching every aspiring primary school teacher needs to understand.

Written directly for initial teacher education students this textbook supports
classroom practice and provides a broad survey of key aspects of primary science
teaching including the role of science in the curriculum, communication and
literacy in science teaching, science outside the classroom, transitional issues
and assessment.

This is essential reading for all students studying primary science on primary
initial teacher education courses, including undergraduate (BEd, BA with QTS),
postgraduate (PGCE, SCITT), and employment-based routes into teaching, and
also NQTs.

CONTENTS

Alan Peacock and Mick Dunne How Science Has Evolved \ **Alan Peacock** Lessons From
Elsewhere \ **Richard Watkins** Linking Science to the Wider Curriculum \ **Dave Howard,
Ashlee Perry, Malcolm Smith, Liz Flintoft and Robert Collins** Linking Science to Numeracy
and ICT \ **Tara Mawby** Science Literacy \ **Leigh Hoath** Learning Science Beyond the
Classroom \ **Natasha Serret and Sarah Earle** Children Communicating Science \ **Mick
Dunne and Dave Howard** Teaching Tricky Topics \ **Tara Mawby and Mick Dunne** How
Do We Know What Science Has Been Learned? \ **Leigh Hoath and Tanya Shields** Science
Across the Transitions Between Phases \ **Dave Howard and Ashlee Perry** Effective Inclusion
\ **Alan Peacock and Mick Dunne** Summing Up: The Way Forward

November 2011 • 208 pages
Cloth (978-0-85702-505-0) • £60.00 / Paper (978-0-85702-506-7) • £19.99

ALSO FROM SAGE